PATERNOSTER THEOLOGICAL MONOGRAPHS

Calvin, Barth, and Reformed Theology

PATERNOSTER THEOLOGICAL MONOGRAPHS

A full listing of all titles in this series and Paternoster Biblical Monographs appears at the close of this book

PATERNOSTER THEOLOGICAL MONOGRAPHS

Calvin, Barth, and Reformed Theology

Edited by
Neil B. MacDonald and Carl Trueman

WIPF & STOCK · Eugene, Oregon

Wipf and Stock Publishers
199 W 8th Ave, Suite 3
Eugene, OR 97401

Calvin, Barth, and Reformed Theology
Edited by MacDonald, Neil B. and Trueman, Carl R.
Copyright©2008 Paternoster
ISBN 13: 978-1-60608-017-7
Publication date 6/6/2008
Previously published by Paternoster, 2008

This Edition Published by Wipf and Stock Publishers by arrangement with Paternoster

PATERNOSTER THEOLOGICAL MONOGRAPHS

Series Preface

In the West the churches may be declining, but theology—serious, academic (mostly doctoral level) and mainstream orthodox in evaluative commitment—shows no sign of withering on the vine. This series of *Paternoster Theological Monographs* extends the expertise of the Press especially to first-time authors whose work stands broadly within the parameters created by fidelity to Scripture and has satisfied the critical scrutiny of respected assessors in the academy. Such theology may come in several distinct intellectual disciplines—historical, dogmatic, pastoral, apologetic, missional, aesthetic and no doubt others also. The series will be particularly hospitable to promising constructive theology within an evangelical frame, for it is of this that the church's need seems to be greatest. Quality writing will be published across the confessions—Anabaptist, Episcopalian, Reformed, Arminian and Orthodox—across the ages—patristic, medieval, reformation, modern and counter-modern—and across the continents. The aim of the series is theology written in the twofold conviction that the church needs theology and theology needs the church—which in reality means theology done for the glory of God.

Series Editors

† David F. Wright, Emeritus Professor of Patristic and Reformed Christianity, University of Edinburgh, Scotland, UK

Trevor A. Hart, Head of School and Principal of St Mary's College School of Divinity, University of St Andrews, Scotland, UK

Anthony N.S. Lane, Professor of Historical Theology and Director of Research, London School of Theology, UK

Anthony C. Thiselton, Emeritus Professor of Christian Theology, University of Nottingham, Research Professor in Christian Theology, University College Chester, and Canon Theologian of Leicester Cathedral and Southwell Minster, UK

Kevin J. Vanhoozer, Research Professor of Systematic Theology, Trinity Evangelical Divinity School, Deerfield, Illinois, USA

Contents

Contributors xi

Preface
Neil B. MacDonald and Carl Trueman xiii

PART ONE: HISTORICAL OVERVIEW 1

Chapter 1
Calvin, Barth, and Reformed Theology: Historical Prolegomena
Carl Trueman 3
Introduction 3
Reformed Theology in Historic Confessional Context 4
Reformed Theology and Confessional Formulation 6
Assessing Confessional Reformed Theology in Early Modern Context ... 8
The Collapse of Reformed Orthodoxy 9
Karl Barth and Reformed Orthodoxy 11
Barth and Von Harnack 11
Barth at Göttingen: Reformed Orthodoxy and the Impact of Heppe ... 14
Barth's Relationship to Reformed Orthodoxy 20

PART TWO: THE SACRAMENTS OF BAPTISM AND EUCHARIST 27

Chapter 2
Calvin and Barth on the Lord's Supper
Trevor Hart 29
Introduction 29
Some Key Issues 30
The Presence and Action of God 30
The Presence of Christ and the Elements 32
Eucharistic Modification 34
Summary 37
Calvin – Bread and Wine Trans-figured 38
Divine Sign-giving 38
Faith Alone Participates in the Sign 40
Signs and Words 41
Signification, Metonymy and the Presence of Christ 42
The Incarnation and Imaginative Trans-figuration 44
Barth – Signification, Revelation and Response 45
Signification and Analogy 46
Hypostatic and Sacramental Union 47
The Word takes Flesh 48
The Presence of Christ and the Supper 49

The Supper as a Sign of Response 51
Conclusion 54

Chapter 3
Baptism in the Theology of John Calvin and Karl Barth
Anthony R. Cross 57
Introduction 57
The Sacramental Nature of Baptism 58
The Role of the Holy Spirit 62
The Meaning of Baptism 65
Infant Baptism 73
Conclusion 79
The Sacramental Nature of Baptism 79
The Role of the Holy Spirit 82
The Meaning of Baptism 82
Infant Baptism 85
In Concluding 87

PART THREE: ATONEMENT 89

Chapter 4
Karl Barth's Narrative Doctrine of Substitutionary Atonement
Neil B. MacDonald 91
Introduction 91
YHWH, the God of Israel, who takes His own Judgement on Himself (in the
Form of His Son, Jesus of Nazareth) 93
Barth: 'Front-Wheel Drive' or 'Back-Wheel Drive' Theologian? 96
Step One: The Locus of Barth's Doctrine in the Synoptic Narratives 97
*Step Two: The Literary Shape of the Synoptic Narrative
– the Three Essential Parts* 99
*Step Three: The First Two Parts are to be Understood in Terms of
a Judicial Framework* 100
Step Four: The Resurrection and the Identity of Jesus of Nazareth 103
Barth's Theological Move: The Judicial Framework as
Substitutionary Atonement 104
The Theological Identity of Pilate's Judgement: YHWH's Judgement
on Jesus 105
The Two Narrative Conditions of Substitutionary Atonement 108
Jesus takes His own Eschatological Judgement on Himself 110
The 'Directorial Eye' of the Evangelist 112
The 'Eye of Faith': The 'Directorial Eye' that becomes Your 'Eye' 114
Conclusion 115

Chapter 5
Calvin, Barth, and the Subject of Atonement
Myron B. Penner 118
Introduction 118

Calvin on Atonement 119
Christ our Redeemer 120
For whom did Christ die? 128
The Calvinist Barth? 135
Barth for/against Calvin 136
Christ, Election, and Atonement 136
Calvin or Barth? 141
Conclusion 144

PART FOUR: SCRIPTURE 147

Chapter 6
Calvin on Scripture
Stephen R. Holmes 149
Introduction 149
Calvin's Fundamental Beliefs about Scripture 151
The Unity of Scripture: The Person and Work of Jesus Christ 153
Factual Error in the Claims of the Bible? 156
Natural Theology and Accommodation 157

Chapter 7
Calvin, Barth, and Theological Interpretation
Craig G. Bartholomew 163
Introduction 163
Common Ground 165
The Bible as the Word of God 169
Biblical Interpretation and Theology 171
Critical Scholarship and Exegesis 173
The Role of Historical Criticism 174
The Role of Philosophy and General Hermeneutics in Biblical Interpretation 175
Calvin, Barth, and Postmodern Interpretation 176

Author Index 179

Contributors

Craig G. Bartholomew is H. Evan Runner Professor of Philosophy, and Professor of Theology and Religion at Redeemer University College, Ancaster, Canada, and Visiting Professor in Biblical Hermeneutics at the University of Chester, UK

Anthony R. Cross is a Fellow of the Centre for Baptist History and Heritage, Regent's Park College, University of Oxford, UK

Trevor Hart is Professor of Divinity and Dean of the Faculty of Divinity, St Mary's College, University of St Andrews, UK

Stephen R. Holmes is Lecturer in Theology, University of St Andrews, Scotland, UK

Neil B. MacDonald is a member of the Center of Theological Inquiry in Princeton, USA, and Reader in Theological Studies, Roehampton University, London, UK

Myron B. Penner is Professor of Philosophy and Theology, Prairie College, Canada

Carl Trueman is Professor of Historical Theology and Church History at Westminster Theological Seminary, Philadelphia, USA

Preface

There can be little doubt that John Calvin (1509-1564) and Karl Barth (1886-1968) belong to the first rank of great theologians of the Church, and both continue to exert profound influence on friend and foe alike. Both were, of course, theologians whose writings have particularly helped to shape the world of Reformed theology. Historically, there can be little doubt that Calvin's influence on Reformed doctrine has been much greater than that of Barth, and this continues to be so in the present day. In contrast, Barth's Reformed credentials have at times been questioned – not least because of his distinctive reformulation of the doctrines of election and atonement. This raises a number of questions pertinent to the question of the future direction of the Reformed faith and its continuing relevance to the age in which we live and in which the Church witnesses to Jesus of Nazareth. Can there be a fruitful dialogue or engagement between those who seek to maintain the traditional, Calvin-orientated stance of the Reformed faith and those who are persuaded of the value of Barth's reconstruction of Reformed theology? What is the contribution of each to the Reformed Church as regards its mission to the world? Do we find in their respective theologies a persuasive interpretation of the witness of the Bible?

In this book, scholars from both camps seek to engage in an informed and open manner with some of the central preoccupations of the Reformed faith in order to point the way forward for the church in the twenty-first century as she seeks to be faithful to the Bible, to her own theological heritage, and to the needs of the present day. Though pedagogical in the best sense, the chapters you will encounter in this book – on the sacraments of eucharist and baptism, on the atonement, and on scripture – are written in terms accessible to interested lay-people of the Church faithful and beyond. Ultimately, the book offers readers an opportunity to assess how Calvin and Barth might help to carry the mantle of Reformed theology into the future.

Neil B. MacDonald and Carl Trueman

PART ONE

HISTORICAL OVERVIEW

CHAPTER 1

Calvin, Barth, and Reformed Theology: Historical Prolegomena

Carl Trueman

Introduction

In writing the opening essay in this volume, I am acutely conscious that my own task is specifically historical and contextual. The rest of the essays are written by theologians and thus address directly the issue of whether the Reformed theology of Calvin and his contemporaries and immediate successors, or that of Barth is a better guide to Reformed theology in the present day; and, indirectly, the issue of how modern, ecclesiastical theology can and should relate to the formulations of the past, whether of 45 or 450 years ago. My task, by contrast, is to provide a broad background to Reformed theology in both its original early modern context and in its appropriation in the writings of Karl Barth, and to do this as a way of setting the scene for the theological work of my more theologically acute colleagues. Such is not an easy task, especially given the significant lapse of time between the work of the Reformers and that of Barth himself; yet it is nonetheless necessary, if for no other reason than to highlight the complexity of undertaking any contemporary theological synthesis.

In a famous essay, 'Travelling Theory', Edward Said, the distinguished literary critic, commented on the problems of the transmission of theories over time. This he saw as involving four broad phases: the set of initial circumstances in which the idea came into being; a transmission of the idea through time and space to a new set of circumstances in which it takes on a new prominence; a set of conditions of acceptance and resistance which confront the transplanted idea in its new context and which make possible its acceptance; and, finally, the idea is accommodated or incorporated in its new context and is transformed by its new uses, position etc.[1] In other words, the particular circumstances in which ideas are formulated and in which they are appropriated is of critical importance in understanding how they are shaped and modified over time. This is a useful model for thinking about the relationship between historic confessional Reformed theology and the interaction with this

---

[1] Edward Said, 'Traveling Theory,' *The Edward Said Reader* (ed. Moustafa Bayoumi and Andrew Rubin; New York: Vintage, 2000), 195-217, 196.

exhibited in the works of Barth.[2] What I intend therefore in this chapter is to outline the origins and development of Reformed theology up to and including its confessional codification, and then to describe how and why this theology was then mediated to, and appropriated by, Barth in a very different context.

Reformed Theology in Historic Confessional Context

Within the context of the sixteenth century, Reformed theology represented one of the two major intellectual streams of the so-called Magisterial Reformation, which sought to tie Protestantism and the state together in a fruitful social alliance. Unlike Lutheranism, however, Reformed theology cannot be traced to the overarching genius of a single individual.[3] Instead, it developed in a variety of contexts in the sixteenth century at the hands of a number of gifted theological leaders. The eclectic origins of the movement are reflected in the fact that there is no *central dogma*, no single organizing doctrinal principle, which defines Reformed theology in the way that, say, justification by faith both defines and structures the nature of Lutheranism.[4]

Having said this, there are a number of issues upon which there was substantial agreement with Luther and Lutheranism on certain precise points, if not on issues of overall structure and emphasis. Against the background of a perceived overweening authority of the institutional church, Protestant theologians revised their understanding of authority, arguing for the supreme authority of scripture as the norm of theological reflection. This was part and parcel of the breaking down of the power of the institutional Church of Rome, and had the collateral effect of generating significant interest in textual and interpretative matters. In this context, both Reformed and Lutheran moved to accent the so-called literal sense of scripture as foundational for biblical exegesis, a point which stands in continuity with exegetical developments from the twelfth century onwards.

---

[2] I specifically talk here about 'confessional Reformed theology' rather than 'the theology of Calvin' precisely because Calvin's theology in itself has had no normative ecclesiastical status within the Reformed churches either then or now. That position has been reserved for official church confessions. On Reformed Orthodoxy in general, see the following collections of essays: Carl R. Trueman and R. Scott Clark (eds), *Protestant Scholasticism: Essays in Reassessment* (Carlisle: Paternoster, 1998); Willem J. Van Asselt and Eef Dekker (eds), *Reformation and Scholasticism: An Ecumenical Enterprise* (Grand Rapids: Baker, 2001).

[3] Of course, Lutheran theology is a more eclectic construction than this characterization would suggest; yet it is true that Luther was the single most significant architect of Lutheran theology in a manner which has no parallel in Reformed thinking; further, Luther's writings are specifically included in the confessional documents of the church and thus possess an ecclesiastical status beyond that of any Reformed theologian. The best English edition of the standard Lutheran confessional documents is Robert Kolb and Timothy J. Wengert (eds), *The Book of Concord* (Minneapolis: Fortress, 2000).

[4] On the shape of Lutheranism, see Werner Elert, *The Structure of Lutheranism* (trans. W Hansen; St Louis: Concordia, 1962).

Closely connected to this development was the Reformers' attitude to church tradition. Often characterized in popular Protestantism as rejecting the notion of traditions wholesale, the actual position of the mainstream Protestants was more subtle than such a picture allows. In fact, the magisterial Reformers maintained a high respect for those theological traditions that were closely tied to the text of scripture and to the exegesis of the same; what they rejected was the independent and definitive authority of the institutional church as providing a second, parallel line of authoritative teaching.[5] The notion of *sola scriptura*, scripture alone, was something which accented scripture as the ultimate normative authority by which all theological formulations were to be judged; it was not something which meant that Christianity had to be reinvented every Sunday, or which claimed that scripture could ever be read in a vacuum. On these points, there was no formal difference with the Lutherans. In addition, on the point of justification by imputation and the instrumentality of faith, the major Reformed confessions speak with one voice, although some variation can be found amongst individual Reformed theologians.[6]

One could characterize these points of agreement by regarding them as examples of the Reformation emphasis upon the priority of divine action God's dealings with human beings. Indeed, the Reformation can be seen from one perspective as an intensification of the ongoing anti-Pelagian tradition that had always existed within Western Christianity from the time of Augustine onwards. What the Reformers did with their understanding of authority and justification as to accent this in a way that undercut the sacramental authority of the institutional church. On this, both streams of magisterial Reformation were in substantial agreement.[7]

Where the major difference with Lutheranism lies, and the point upon which the two confessional identities of the respective groups were formalized, is that of Christology. This became clear at the Marburg Colloquy in 1529, where Luther and Zwingli failed to reach agreement on the nature of Christ's presence in the Lord's Supper and thus laid the foundation for the basic confessional breach that exists to this day. While the formal point of disagreement was over whether Christ's humanity was present in any real sense in the elements of bread and wine, the real

---

[5] Heiko Oberman coined the helpful terminology of T1 and T2 to refer to these two phenomena, a move which helps nuance discussion of the Reformers' attitude to tradition and authority: see his *The Harvest of Medieval Theology: Gabriel Biel and Late Medieval Nominalism* (Durham: Labyrinth, 1983), 365-93.

[6] The single best collection of Reformed confessions is that by E.F. Karl Müller, *Die Bekenntnisschriften der reformierten Kirche* (Leipzig: Deichert, 1903). The seventeenth century saw a certain diversity among Reformed theologians on the issue of justification, particularly in England. A good primary text, involving a discussion between an antinomian, a legalist, and an evangelical, is Edward Fisher, *The Marrow of Modern Divinity* (London, 1645); see also Hans Boersma, *A Hot Peppercorn: Richard Baxter's Doctrine of Justification in Its Seventeenth-Century Context of Controversy* (Zoetermeer: Boekencentrum, 1993).

[7] See the essays in Heiko A. Oberman, *The Dawn of the Reformation* (Edinburgh: T&T Clark, 1986).

issue underlying this was that of the communication of properties between the divine and human natures in the hypostatic union.[8] Luther (and later Lutheranism) maintained a direct communication between the natures, which then allowed the human nature to participate in the properties of the divine (and thus, for example, perform certain actions, such as being present in the bread on the altar, which would not normally be possible for human bodies). The Reformed, however, argued for an indirect communication of properties in the person, which maintained the integrity of each nature. Thus, Christ was present in the eucharist *but only according to his divine nature*. Lutherans accused the Reformed of Nestorianism and rationalism; the Reformed responded with accusations of monophysitism and Apollinarianism.[9]

Underlying the difference was another basic principle: the Reformed held as axiomatic that the finite was not capable of comprehending the infinite (*finitum non capax infiniti*). Dubbed the *extra Calvinisticum* by Lutheran opponents in an attempt to impute novelty, and thus obvious heresy, to the Reformed, it is actually a concept with an impeccable historical pedigree, finding precedent in the work of Athanasius and Thomas Aquinas among others. This axiom had implications primarily for incarnation, as noted above, but also for epistemology and scripture: knowledge of God as he is in himself, was, literally, unbearable for finite creatures and thus needed to be accommodated to their finite capacity. Thus, in Christ God manifested and revealed himself to human beings in a way that was true and absolutely reliable but not exhaustive. The same applied to scripture: scripture was a true revelation of God, but was accommodated to human capacity and thus could not be regarded as exhaustive. Both of these principles, the christological and the scriptural, are evident in the work of John Calvin and had significant impact on his understanding of, among other things, Christ's presence in the eucharist.[10]

Reformed Theology and Confessional Formulation

The question of how Reformed theology 'travels' from the early sixteenth century to Karl Barth in the twentieth is intimately connected to the development of the Reformed churches as confessional institutions. Unlike much of modern evangelicalism, the Reformed had a high view of the church and a high view of the doctrinal documents produced by the church. While the Reformers emphasised scripture as the sole cognitive ground for theology, they also acknowledged the need for creedal documents to identify orthodoxy over against heresy for, as the old Dutch

---

[8] See W.P. Stephens, *The Theology of Huldrych Zwingli* (Oxford: Clarendon Press, 1986), 218-59; Bernhard Lohse, *Martin Luther's Theology: Its Historical and Systematic Development* (Edinburgh: T&T Clark, 1999), 306-13.

[9] For standard orthodox statements of this, see J.T. Mueller, *Christian Dogmatics* (St Louis: Concordia, 1934), 263-86 (Lutheran); Louis Berkhof, *Systematic Theology* (Edinburgh: Banner of Truth, 1958), 321-30 (Reformed).

[10] The best study of this remains that of E.D. Willis, *Calvin's Catholic Christology: The Function of the So-called Extra Calvinisticum in Calvin's Theology* (Leiden: Brill, 1966).

proverb has it, 'Every heretic has his text.' These documents were not simply private matters, produced by individuals, but confessions and catechisms which were approved by various churches at official synods and assemblies.

The need for such documents was not simply theological. There was, of course, the obvious pedagogical need for confessions and catechisms as a means of cultivating theological identity among the ordinary people, and this had perceived social benefits, given the nature of religion as one key instrument of social control in the early modern period. Further, the territorial nature of religion in the sixteenth and seventeenth centuries meant that political leaders needed clear theological identities for the churches under their jurisdiction both to demarcate spheres of influence and provide the tools for political negotiations with other powers. Thus, the Lutherans produced the Augsburg Confession in 1530 in an attempt to promote political ecumenism between the Lutheran and Catholic territories within the Holy Roman Empire. Then, with the Council of Trent producing clear Catholic definitions on all of the major points at issue between Protestants and Rome by the early 1560s, an equally massive concern for confessionalised theology was exhibited among the Lutheran and the Reformed.

While the Lutheran church came to a consensus on the documents contained in (or given the imprimatur of) the Book of Concord in 1580, the Reformed churches never adopted a single set of documents as authoritative for all Reformed Christians everywhere. The late 1550s and 1560s saw the production of a series of confessions which enjoyed some influence, including the French (1559), Scots (1560), Second Helvetic (1561), the Erlauthal (1562), the Hungarian (1562), and the Belgic (written 1561; adapted and adopted 1566). As will be noted below, the confessional documents of the Reformed churches, precisely because they were *church* documents and not simply the private musings of individuals, were significant as a source of Barth's knowledge of the development of Reformed orthodoxy.

The polemical situation in Europe continued to become more complex, however, with the development of new schools of theological thought, most notably that of the Remonstrants in the Netherlands and of the Socinians in Poland. The former offered a modified form of Reformed theology which allowed the human will a decisive role in salvation; the latter group were more radical still, offering a radically anti-metaphysical and literal biblical hermeneutic which dispatched doctrines such as the Trinity = the Incarnation, and their corollaries to the theological dustbin. Given these new challenges from within the Reformed Protestant fold, the confessionalising of the Reformed faith could not terminate in the 1560s but continued in light of the constant need to respond to new developments. Thus, the Synod of Dordt in 1618–1619, a gathering of Reformed theologians from across Europe charged with dealing with specific theological and political issues arising in the Netherlands, gave its imprimatur to the Belgic Confession and the Heidelberg Catechism as the standards of the Reformed churches in the Netherlands; however, it did not stop there but also went on to formulate the famous 'five points of Calvinism' over against the five articles which had been proposed by the Remonstrant theologians.

This process of elaborating confessional identity under the pressure of polemical controversy is evidence in the documents of the Westminster Assembly of the 1640s, a specifically British gathering designed to further the cause of Reformation within the Church of England against the background of the struggles between King Charles I and Parliament. The Westminster Confession of Faith (1647) represents a full elaboration of the Reformed theology of the early seventeenth century, engaging polemically with Rome, Remonstrants, Socinians and Anabaptists while at the same time standing in positive connection to the Assembly's two catechisms (Larger and Shorter) and the Directory of Public Worship. Indeed, the Assembly itself produced what can appropriately be described as the most thorough manifesto of Reformed faith and practice hitherto seen. To this day, most Reformed denominations either look to the Westminster Standards (usually the Confession and two Catechisms) or to the Three Forms of Unity (Belgic Confession, Heidelberg Catechism, Canons of Dordt) as providing their basic confessional identity.[11]

Assessing Confessional Reformed Theology in Early Modern Context

Before moving to Barth, it is important to make some general comments about the theology of these confessions. This has proved an area of remarkable controversy over the past century, and there is a sense in which the question of Barth's relationship to Calvin and the Reformed faith has itself shaped much of this discussion.[12] That relationship is, of course, a central part of the agenda of the essays in the rest of this volume. Our task here is to note some of the ways in which Reformed theology travelled from the era of Calvin to that of Barth. The principal means by which this was done was via the confessions of the Reformed churches. Thus, a few general observations on these confessions would seem to be in order.

The first thing to note about the confessions is that they are ecclesiastical consensus documents. As such, they are broad in their scope and designed to set the bounds of orthodoxy as wide as possible given the constituency which they were designed to encompass and define. The modern age is one which is averse to creeds and confessions, partly because of a basic suspicion in tradition that is endemic in Western society, and also, no doubt, because of the ways such creeds have been used in the past in an abusive and manipulative manner. It must be remembered, however, that the Reformed creeds and confessions were developed in an era when tradition was considered, even (as noted above) by Protestants, to carry significant weight. Further, we should not allow modern pejorative conceptions of creeds to trick us into thinking that confessions were always designed to make the bounds of orthodoxy as narrow as possible. In fact, such confessions were designed initially to exclude only those who were absolutely beyond the bounds of theological acceptability.

---

[11] These documents are available in Müller, *Die Bekenntnisschriften*.

[12] See the essays in Richard A. Muller (ed.), *After Calvin: Studies in the Development of a Theological Tradition* (Oxford: Oxford University Press, 2003).

The second thing to note is that, although the Reformed churches did not have one uniform confessional standard akin to the Lutheran Book of Concord, yet they did not consider the creeds they produced to be discrete entities but rather considered them to reflect a single, broad tradition of Reformed theology. Thus, the different documents exhibit different structures: the Heidelberg Catechism focuses (most beautifully, in this writer's opinion) on the assurance of the believer's faith, reflecting the typical concern of Protestantism and reflecting a topical order which is clearly pastoral in orientation; the Westminster Catechisms, however, focus much more clearly on how human beings have knowledge of God (primarily through scripture) and are thus structured in a way which reflects a more directly epistemological ordering. The significance of the varieties of topical ordering, however, does not lie in major theological differences but in the pedagogical agenda of the respective documents. Both the Westminster Standards and the Three Forms of Unity stand as representative of the Reformed orthodox tradition and should not be set over against each other in any fundamental way.

Following on from this, it is worth noting, thirdly, that the basic contours of Reformed theology remain fairly constant from the days of Calvin to the collapse of orthodoxy under the impact of Cartesianism, Wolffianism and, in Britain, empiricism at the beginning of the eighteenth century. The commitment to essentially Augustinian notions of sin, grace, and predestination is clear from the time of Zwingli onwards. This has a significant epistemological impact in the way that it radically delimits the possibility for natural theology in any meaningful sense. Certainly, there is general revelation; but outside of grace, this serves primarily to render human beings without excuse before God, not as the foundation of a sound theological structure. There are indeed variations within the confessional tradition between, say, the single predestinarianism of Bullinger and the Second Helvetic Confession and the double predestination of Calvin and Dordt and Westminster, but these are not seen as fundamentally disruptive of the basic unity of Reformed thought. In addition, this basic position stands in line with the typical Augustinian teaching on the relationship between the revealed God and the hidden God. Further, the basic Anselmic structure of doctrines of the incarnation is to be found in Calvin and in the confessions, establishing a profound connection between the logical priority of sin and the response of God in the incarnation.

The Collapse of Reformed Orthodoxy

A number of factors served to bring an end to the era of Reformed Orthodoxy, and the whole transition to a more liberal theological trajectory cannot be reduced simply to intellectual factors. Nevertheless, for the sake of brevity, I will focus here on two issues which bring about major theological transformation. First, there is the rise of biblical text criticism. Ironically, this was driven in large part by the high premium which the Orthodox placed upon the actual text of scripture, as given in the Hebrew and Greek, as the Word of God. This generated an obvious concern for learning the original languages, and also a correlative interest in original manuscripts and text traditions, something which played very well in Catholic circles where variant readings could be used a basis for undermining the Protestant emphases on the sufficiency and perspicuity of scripture, and for bolstering Catholic insistence on the necessity of the Church as the locus of interpretative authority. That this is the case is indeed demonstrated by the changing attitude of the Reformed Orthodox on the antiquity of the Masoretic vowel points, from indifference in the sixteenth century to insistence in the seventeenth, under pressure from Catholic polemicists and the impact of Protestant critical studies in this area.[13] Indeed, in the Helvetic Formula Consensus, this is one of the points of complaint addressed to the Amyraldians and the School of Saumur.[14] Yet given the axiomatic role that scripture as an authoritative text plays in classic Reformed theology, the inroads made by the text criticism which Protestantism's own scripture principle ultimately fostered, those who were prepared to concede on the text of scripture were inevitably faced with the task of restructuring Reformed theology accordingly.[15]

As the classic understanding of scriptural authority was slowly abandoned at the end of the seventeenth century, Reformed theology was also undergoing epistemological; shifts. This is the second major intellectual factor in the collapse of orthodoxy. While Reformed Orthodoxy had always placed a high premium on rationality, the belief that Reformed theology was coherent and capable of internal logical investigation on its own terms, the impact of Cartesianism, Wolffianism, and empiricism led to further alterations in epistemology. For understanding Barth's response to and appropriation of Reformed theology, the key figure is undoubtedly Friedrich Schleiermacher, or at least the way in which Schleiermacher is presented as heir of Reformed Orthodoxy by Heinrich Heppe. We will look at Heppe later, but it is important to note at this point that he presents Schleiermacher very much as the heir of Calvin on the grounds that the latter emphasized *pietas*, somewhat inadequately expressed by the modern English word, 'piety,' with all its quaint Victorian associations, which points forward to the former's emphasis on theology as human psychology shaped by the feeling of absolute dependence upon God. This connection undoubtedly combined with Barth's dislike of pietism to influence his understanding of how Reformed theology, from Calvin onwards, contained certain seeds that would lead to its own destruction.[16]

---

[13] For detailed discussion of the importance of the vowel-points debate to Reformed understanding of scripture in the seventeenth century, see Muller, 'The Debate over the Vowel Points and the Crisis in Orthodox Hermeneutics', in Muller (ed.), *After Calvin*, 146-55.

[14] See Müller, *Die Bekenntnisschriften*, 861-870.

[15] See Richard A. Muller, *Post-Reformation Reformed Dogmatics* (4 vols; Grand Rapids: Baker, 2003). (Hereafter Muller, *PRRD*.)

[16] On the erosion of Reformed Orthodoxy, see Muller, *PRRD* II; Martin Klauber, *Between Reformed Scholasticism and Pan-Protestantism* (London: Associated University Presses, 1994); Theo Verbeek, *Descartes and the Dutch: Early Reactions to Cartesianism (1637–1650)* (Carbondale: Southern Illinois University Press, 1992); also the essays in R. Popkin and A. Vanderjagt (eds), *Scepticism and Irreligion in the Seventeenth and*

Karl Barth and Reformed Orthodoxy

While it is, of course, Karl Barth's work as systematician which has ensured his importance to subsequent generations, the manner in which he pursued that task means that anyone seriously interested in wrestling with Barth's thought and its possible relevance to the grand narrative of Christian theology must at some point address the issue of his own approach to church history. In this context, the anecdote of the visit of Barth's old teacher, Adolf von Harnack, to his former pupil during the latter's time at Münster is perhaps instructive. The meeting is mentioned in Eberhard Busch's biography:

> When Barth's old teacher came to see him, to his surprise his former pupil was interested in a commentary on the Gospel of John by Cocceius. The two then had a long conversation about the task of a Protestant dogmatics...[17]

Busch's description is significant: that the young theologian was found reading Cocceius, a seventeenth-century theologian, and that the conversation that followed from this encounter focused on the task of Protestant dogmatics, speaks eloquently about how Barth perceived – and how he was to pursue – his role as systematician. For him, positive theological construction in the present was not simply a matter of biblical exegesis; nor was it only a question of interrogating the biblical text in the light of questions thrown up by modern culture; it also involved a dialogue with the tradition of the church down through the centuries. Thus, church history, particularly the history of dogma so-called, was a crucial part of the overall systematic task.

Barth and Von Harnack

Barth's first major exposure to academic church history occurred during his time at the University of Berlin. Here, he attended the lectures on the history of dogma of von Harnack.[18] Von Harnack's approach to the history of dogma represented a development and application of the anti-metaphysical trajectory of German liberal

---

Eighteenth Centuries (Leiden: Brill, 1993); Jonathan I. Israel, *Radical Enlightenment: Philosophy and the Making of Modernity, 1650–1750* (Oxford: Oxford University Press, 2001).

[17] Eberhard Busch, *Karl Barth: His Life from Letters and Autobiographical Texts* (trans. John Bowden; Grand Rapids: Eerdmans, 1994), 165.

[18] The best study of the relationship between Barth and von Harnack is by H. Martin Rumscheidt, *Revelation and Theology: An Analysis of the Barth-Harnack Correspondence of 1923* (Cambridge: Cambridge University Press, 1972). A good summary of, and brief commentary upon, the famous correspondence between the two men is provided by George Hunsinger, 'The Harnack/Barth Correspondence: A Paraphrase with Comments', in George Hunsinger, *Disruptive Grace: Studies in the Theology of Karl Barth* (Grand Rapids: Eerdmans, 2000), 319-37. For details of Barth's intellectual biography at this time, in addition to Busch, see Bruce L. McCormack, *Karl Barth's Critically Realistic Dialectical Theology: Its Genesis and Development 1909–1936* (Oxford: Clarendon Press, 1995).

theology after Kant to the realm of historical inquiry.[19] Thus, the history ly church dogma was essentially the history of the corruption of the simple ethical gospel, focused upon the Christian community, by the intrusion of inappropriate Hellenistic metaphysics. According to Von Harnack, this corruption developed rapidly after 130, but was even present in certain elements of the canonical writings of Luke, John and Paul.[20] At this early stage in his life, Barth became a great admirer of the elder statesman, neglecting the usual cultural experiences of student life so that he might devote himself more thoroughly to learning at the feet of the master:

> I said to myself, "This is the great moment: here you are with *the* theologian of the day, why should you be bothered with museums, theatres and concert halls" So I saw little of Berlin – I did not even hear the great speech by the Kaiser from the balcony of the Schloss against the center and against social democracy.[21]

Indeed, such was Barth's admiration for *the* theologian that he obtained permission to become a regular member of the seminars offered by von Harnack, and the fact that he was the youngest ever student to do so must surely tell us something about the manner in which he must have impressed the senior scholar.[22] Of course, the long-term impact of von Harnack's approach to church history on Barth is inseparable from Barth's relationship to the wider contemporary liberal theology of which his teacher was a – perhaps even *the* – classic representative. Even in the above quotation we see dark hints of Barth's later awareness of how his intellectual infatuation with von Harnack had blinded him to some of the less savoury political developments which were taking place in Germany at this time; and, indeed, Barth's devotion to von Harnack was to be irrevocably shaken by the event which played a pivotal role in shattering his confidence in the liberal theological agenda as a whole: the political support of the liberal theological establishment for the political establishment and the coming carnage of the First World War. In a famous passage, Barth describes his disillusionment in dramatic terms:

> One day in early August 1914 stands out in my personal memory as a black day. Ninety-three German intellectuals impressed public opinion by their proclamation in support of the war policy of Wilhelm II and his counselors. Among these

---

[19] For a provocative interpretation of the relationship between Barth and nineteenth century German liberalism, see Richard A. Muller, 'Karl Barth and the Path of Theology into the Twentieth Century: Historical Observations', *Westminster Theological Journal* 51 (1989), 25-50.

[20] 'Dogma in its conception and development is a work of the Greek spirit on the soil of the Gospel': Adolph Harnack, *History of Dogma*. Vol. 1 (trans. Neil Buchanan; London: Williams and Norgate, 1896), 17; also Adolph Harnack, *What is Christianity?* (trans. by Thomas Bailey Saunders with an introduction by Rudolf Bultmann; Gloucester: Peter Smith), esp. 199ff.

[21] Quoted in Busch, *Karl Barth*, 39.

[22] Rumscheidt, *Revelation and Theology*, p. 4.

intellectuals I discovered to my horror almost all of my theological teachers whom I had greatly venerated. In despair over what this indicated about the signs of the time I suddenly realized that I could not any longer follow either their ethics and dogmatics or their understanding of the Bible and of history. For me at least, 19th-century theology no longer held any future.[23]

The inability of nineteenth century liberal Protestantism to offer any critical perspective on the pressing politics of the day – indeed, its co-option into precisely these corrupt politics – drove Barth decisively away from the liberal theological program – including its approach to church history. His political disillusionment at this point, exacerbated by his perception of liberalism's further failure to give him anything to say to the downtrodden miners and the poor in his parish of Safenwil was soon to be reflected in his positive theological convictions, and these had profound implications for his theological rejection of the basic narrative of dogmatic history as proposed by von Harnack. In a famous essay on Protestant theology in the nineteenth-century, Barth summed up the problem of nineteenth century theological reflection – from the dogmatic to the church historical – as focusing too much upon the Christian faith and not enough upon the Christian message.[24] For him, this was the fatal flaw in the approach to theology advocated by Schleiermacher and developed under men such as Ritschl and von Harnack: theology as reflection upon the religious psychology of the Christian community rather than upon the revelation of God which was always going to be vulnerable to the devastating critique of a Feuerbach who declared that all theology was therefore merely anthropology.[25] He expressed such misgivings in the following fashion:

> Was Jesus Christ really nothing more than the original phenomenon of Christian faith? Was he not to be comprehended as its ground, content, and object on the basis of the first records – the New Testament – as well as of the later accounts – those of the Church – varied and conditioned by their time as they were? Was therefore Christ's historical existence at all accessible to a research which reached beyond the texts of the New Testament? What if the structure of these texts disqualified them as a proper "source" for use by neutral historical science?[26]

Underlying this statement is a wealth of theology with implications for Barth's approach to church history, and we cannot understand the relationship between Barth and von Harnack with regard to church history without taking proper account of the

---

[23] This declaration occurs in a fascinating essay on the state of Protestant theology in the nineteenth century from Barth's later perspective: 'Evangelical Theology in the 19th Century', in Karl Barth, *The Humanity of God* (trans. John Newton Thomas; Richmond: John Knox Press, 1960), 11-33; the quotation can be found on pp. 12-13.

[24] Barth, 'Evangelical Theology in the 19th Century,' 23.

[25] Barth makes it clear in his essay on nineteenth century theology that its fatal flaw was the assumption that theology need to be pursued according to criteria of rationality which were external to itself: Barth, 'Evangelical Theology in the 19th Century', 19.

[26] Barth, 'Evangelical Theology in the 19th Century', 11-33, 30.

theological breach which opened up between them. Basic to this was Barth's rejection of the central historicist premises of his teacher's work. Von Harnack was concerned to relate faith to a proper, critical account of the history of the church and of dogma, eschewing the kind of fundamentalisms and idealisms that lifted the Christian gospel above the flow of history itself. Only careful and, above all, disinterested study of the Bible and of church history, could the gospel be repristinated in terms of its original simplicity. For Barth, however, the history of dogma is to be no disinterested exercise; it is to involve the construction of a narrative which views the history of dogma as the history of the church's reflection upon the basic content of her message: Jesus Christ. As Harnack's theological presuppositions drove his reading of history, so we will find that Barth's drive his; and the story of Reformed theology in particular is, for Barth, the story of the Reformed church's varying fidelity to the dogmatic Christ principle as he chose to formulate it.

In this sense, we can perhaps conclude the section on von Harnack by noting that, for all that there is a decisive break between the two men on many points, there is still a certain similarity between them: both are committed to a theology which presupposes that the intrusion of metaphysics (for Barth, in the form of a natural theology, according to his definition; for von Harnack in the form of Greek patterns of thought) into theology represents a corruption of the Christian gospel; and, consequently, both construct historical narratives of doctrinal development which sees this history in terms of decline and fall in relation to the presence or absence of such metaphysical content. In this manner, both are bound together by the kind of concerns bequeathed to German thought by the anti-metaphysical philosophical trajectory of post-Kantian thought.

Barth at Göttingen: Reformed Orthodoxy and the Impact of Heppe

Barth's break with the liberalism of his mentors has been variously charted by scholars, but it would seem to be relatively safe to say that the initial impulses for this break did not come from a close reading of the sources of Reformed Orthodoxy but rather an eclectic engagement with the works of thinkers as disparate as Kierkegaard, Nietzsche, and Overbeck. Reformation theologians came to prominence in his thinking not so much in the heady years surrounding the publication of the two editions of the Romans commentary but rather during his tenure as Honorary Professor of Reformed Theology at the University of Göttingen between 1921 and 1924.[27] Barth found the appointment challenging for a number of reasons. First, he saw the move as changing him from a basic critic of the contemporary theological world, one charged with merely tearing down what was wrong or inadequate, into

---

[27] On Barth's theological development during this time, see McCormack, *Karl Barth's Critically Realistic Dialectical Theology*, 291-323; also Daniel L. Migliore, 'Karl Barth's First Lectures in Dogmatics: *Instruction in the Christian Religion*', in Karl Barth, *The Göttingen Dogmatics: Volume 1. Instruction in the Christian Religion* (trans G.W. Bromiley; Grand Rapids: Eerdmans, 1991), xv-lxii.

someone on the frontline who was now responsible for positive theological leadership. The rebellious critic and iconoclast was now responsible not so much for tearing down the idols of modern liberalism as with building a theology which would equip pastors and build up the church. The task of dogmatics proper clearly beckoned[28]

Second, the Faculty was Lutheran, and Barth, being Reformed, now faced directly the problem of communicating Reformed dogmatics in a context which was at best alien to him, at worst somewhat hostile to what he had to say, something which would drive him back on the sources as a means of developing and defending his position coherently in a highly political pedagogical situation. The situation was soon made more difficult by the fact that, at the start of the second semester, Lutheran students were voting with their feet and attending the lectures of Barth in preference to the lectures of one of the senior liberal Lutheran theologians on Faculty, Carl Stange.[29]

The net result of these pressures was that Barth was now faced with problem of teaching Reformed theology in this apologetic setting in a manner which really required him to come to grips with the historic materials of the Reformed tradition in a manner which he had previously been spared. In education, as in car design, there is little point in reinventing the wheel: when Protestantism became and established force in the sixteenth century and moved into the university, so its teachers looked to the paradigms and approaches of the medieval past to steer a course for the future; so, when Barth arrived at Göttingen, he was to find himself driven unexpectedly back in time to find the resources for the articulation of his theology in the present.

The courses Barth was to teach during his eight semesters at Göttingen included the following of direct relevance to his relationship to the history of Reformed theology: Exposition of the Heidelberg Catechism (Winter 1921/22); The Theology of Calvin (Summer 1922); The Theology of Zwingli (Winter 1922/23); The Theology of the Reformed Confessions (Summer 1923); and three courses on dogmatics, including prolegomena (Summer 1924-Summer 1925). Much of this has recently been edited and translated into English and it provides perhaps the most important material for understanding Barth's approach to the history of the Reformed tradition.[30] While each of these courses exposed him to significant areas of Reformed heritage, by Barth's own account it was another event which proved to be most

---

[28] 'Now it was no longer a question of attacking all kinds of errors and abuses. All at once we were in the front rank. We had to take on responsibilities which we had not known about while we were simply in opposition. Suddenly we had been given an opportunity to say what we really thought in theology, and to show the church our real intention and ability.' Quoted in Busch, *Karl Barth*, 126.

[29] See McCormack, *Karl Barth's Critically Realistic Dialectical Theology*, 297. McCormack quotes Stange as declaring that 'The Reformed Church in Hanover has no more significance than a millennial sect!'

[30] E.g., Karl Barth, *The Theology of John Calvin* (trans. G.W. Bromiley; Grand Rapids: Eerdmans, 1995); *The Theology of the Reformed Confessions* (trans. Darrell L. Guder and Judith J. Guder; Louisville: Westminster John Knox Press, 2002).

significant for his teaching and thinking at this time. Indeed, it is crucial that we note the importance of his discovery of a particular text-book at Göttingen upon which he was to draw for much of his understanding of the shape and content of Reformed Orthodoxy. The discovery took place during anxious preparations for his first cycle of dogmatics lectures. Barth himself provides us with the following account (somewhat reminiscent of Luther's account of his Tower-Experience) of how he was ultimately able to find a way to approach the task. The central problem was that, faced with the need to construct lectures which took the Bible seriously as book which was unlike any other, and whose message was unlike any other, he found the paradigms provided by modern theology to be wholly inadequate. Yet help was at hand in a most unexpected quarter:

> It was then that Heppe's *Dogmatics* fell into my hands, along with the parallel Lutheran work by H. Schmid. It was out-of-date, dusty, unattractive, almost like a logarithm table, dreary to read, rigid and incredible on almost every page that I opened: in form and content very much like so many of the other writers on 'the old orthodoxy' on which I had heard lectures for years. Fortunately I did not dismiss it too lightly. I read, I studied, I pondered and found myself rewarded by the discovery that here at any rate I was in an atmosphere in which the way through the Refo   s to holy scripture was more meaningful and more natural then in the atmos   e which was all too familiar to me from the theological literature dominated by Schleiermacher and Ritschl.[31]

Barth goes on to emphasize that, in Heppe's book, he found a dogmatics with both form and content, and, more than that, a union of church and academic concerns – precisely what he felt should be found in a dogmatics. Significantly, however, he also learned from this initial encounter with Heppe that the theology articulated was no longer in itself adequate, for 'the "bane of Israel" which hitherto I had met in its neo-Protestant form, was already in evidence and was making itself felt.' Barth's reference here is to the incursions of philosophy and rationalism into the content of Reformed theology, something which the Reformers failed to purge entirely in their break with medieval thought and which came to fruition in the pietistic rationalism of the eighteenth century.[32]

What kind of a book is Heppe? Heppe first published *Die Dogmatik der evangelisch-reformierten Kirche* in 1861 while he was professor of Church History at the University of Marburg. Ostensibly, he was attempting to provide a basic overview and summary content of the Reformed faith through extracting quotations

---

[31] The text is drawn from the translation of Barth's foreword to the 1935 edition of Heppe reprinted in Heinrich Heppe, *Reformed Dogmatics* (trans. G.T. Thomson; Grand Rapids: Baker, 1978), v-vii. The German original can be found in H. Heppe, *Die Dogmatik der evangelisch-reformierten Kirche* (ed. Ernst Bizer; Neukirchener Verlag: Neukirchen, 1958), vii-x. The equivalent Lutheran work to which he refers is that of Heinrich Schmid, *Doctrinal Theology of the Evangelical Lutheran Church* (trans. Charles E. Hay and Henry Jacobs; Minneapolis: Augsburg, n.d.).

[32] Heppe, *Reformed Dogmatics*, vi-vii.

from original Reformed sources and then arranging them under topical headings in a manner not dissimilar to that of Peter Lombard's *Four Books of Sentences*. As with the work of Lombard in relation to Augustine and the theology of Lombard's predecessors, the result was not simply a re-presentation of classic theology of the past; Heppe's ordering of topics, arrangement of quotations, and running commentary on the whole served to make the result something of a synthesis of Reformed Orthodoxy and the views of Heppe himself.

One obvious example of the way in which Heppe offers a distinctive interpretation of doctrinal development which clearly indicates his own theological roots in liberal pietism occurs early in the volume under the topic of 'Natural and Revealed Religion'. Here, he explicitly presents Schleiermacher as the man who was the first to gather together and give clear conceptual expression to the thinking about religion which is found in earlier dogmaticians – specifically, in this case, Wyttenbach, Calvin, Cocceius and Olevianus. The positing of continuity between these men and Schleiermacher on the issue of the very nature of religion as experience represents a significant historical and dogmatic move. This ties in closely with his overall historiographical approach to Reformed theology, where Heppe in fact sees two streams emerging, the more influential (and the one with which he is himself more comfortable) being that which finds its origin in the thought of Melanchthon and which offers a framework for a coherent understanding of humanity as possessing significant freedom.[33] Heppe's sympathetic leaning towards experientialism and pietism are obvious. Barth makes it clear in his introduction to the *Reformed Dogmatics* that he is aware of the author's tendencies in this regard, but also indicates that he considers his approach to be less reductionist with regard to Schleiermacher and to predestination than his close contemporary, Alexander Schweitzer; yet the embryonic connection between Reformed Orthodoxy and the later liberal, anthropocentric piety of the trajectory of Schleiermacher, is something that will continue to form a key element in Barth's own interpretation of orthodoxy, as we have already hinted.[34] For example, the connection between, say, Cocceius and later liberalism is one which Barth was happy to adopt and which has only died a

---

[33] The overall structure of his historiography is laid out in Heinrich Heppe, 'Der Charakter der deutschen-reformirtent Kirche und das Verhältnis derselben zum Lutherthum und zum Calvinismus', *Theologische Studien und Kritiken* (1850), 669–706.

[34] Alexander Schweizer's major work, *Die Glaubenslehre der evangelisch-reformirten Kirche* (2 vols; Zurich: Orell, 1844–47), represents an attempt to read the history of doctrinal development in the Reformed churches from the perspective of an Hegelian view of history combined with a Schleiermacherian understanding of theology. In this scheme, predestination becomes the synthetic central dogma which finds its purest articulation in Schleiermacher's feeling of absolute dependence upon God. Unlike later attempts to cast the development of Reformed doctrine in terms of a central dogma (e.g., that offered by Ernst Bizer), the predestinarian synthesis is regarded as a positive phenomenon, not an example of rationalism.

slow and painful death in the secondary literature.[35] Where Barth (and much of the subsequent historical-theological scholarship which took its cue from him) differs from Heppe is in seeing this tendency as, generally speaking, a development in the generations after Calvin, not in Calvin himself.[36]

Given Barth's awareness of the synthetic nature of Heppe, what exactly was the benefit of the book to him? McCormack sees the impact as lying in two significant areas: first, Barth found that the book placed him squarely within an ecclesial setting. By this, McCormack means that it exposed Barth to the ongoing conceptual and linguistic tradition of the Reformed *church* which, while having a distinctive Protestant face, was yet not isolated from its patristic and medieval roots.[37] It was distinctive theology done within a larger stream of catholic theological endeavour. This was to have immense theological significance for Barth as he proceeded to develop his own distinctive theology in a manner which was always sensitive to the teaching of the church in the past, peculiarly concerned with the trajectories of reflection embodied in the Reformed confessions, and developed in constant critical dialogue with this confessional heritage.

We should of course acknowledge that Barth was of course already somewhat familiar with historic confessional theology by the time he discovered Heppe: his lectures on the Heidelberg Catechism of 1921/22 and those on Reformed Confessions more generally in 1923 would no doubt have prepared him for the positive reception of the work of Heppe. Thus, while there is no compelling reason not to take Barth's account of the significance of Heppe seriously, the intellectual ground had clearly been under preparation since his arrival in Göttingen. Indeed, even the most cursory reading of the lectures on the confessions reveals a man who is already familiar with the major theological and historical contours of the Reformed tradition and concerned to pursue theology in a confessional manner in the sense that theology was a discipline inseparably connected to the teaching office of the church and thus to the history of the doctrinal actions of the church as embodied in creedal documents.[38] Heppe, however, undoubtedly *deepened* Barth's understanding of the wider theological world which had produced the confessions, not least in the way it introduced him to a technical vocabulary and to a range of approaches to crucial

---

[35] See the criticism of this position by Willem J. Van Asselt in his two monographs on Cocceius: *Johannes Cocceius: Portret van een zeventiende-eeuws theoloog op oude en nieuwe wegen* (Heerenveen: J.J. Groen en Zoon, 1997); and *The Federal Theology of Johannes Cocceius (1603–1669)* (Leiden: E J Brill, 2001).

[36] This is part and parcel of the 'Calvin against the Calvinists' thesis, articulate most notably from a broadly Barthian perspective by Ernst Bizer, *Frühorthodoxie und Rationalismus* (Zurich: EVZ, 1963).

[37] McCormack, *Karl Barth's Critically Realistic Dialectical Theology*, 335.

[38] Barth's source for confessional documents of the Reformed churches was Müller, *Die Bekenntnisschriften*, although he was also familiar with the similar, though far less complete, work of Philip Schaff, *The Creeds of Christendom* (New York, 1878).

biblical themes such as Christology and predestination which were to prove invaluable later.[39]

The second benefit which McCormack sees Heppe as giving Barth is that it provided a pedagogical framework for his own dogmatic lectures which were a fusion of the '"scholastic" and the "*loci*" approaches' to theology and which were, in effect, a sentence commentary upon Heppe.[40] We might summarize by saying that Heppe therefore shaped Barth's theology at the level of vocabulary, concepts, structure and approach. Indeed, the basic nature of Heppe to Barth's theological work is reflected in the fact that this book is one of the key sources recommended to students who wish to keep pace with his lectures.[41]

Barth's debt to Heppe, and to the Reformed tradition as mediated through his collection of Reformed sources, was to continue at a formal level into his mature theological work. The very idea of a systematic theology built upon a doctrine of God and of revelation, while not distinctively Reformed Orthodox, is nevertheless communicated to Barth via this dusty, logarithmic nineteenth century book. On this formal point, Barth's work stands closer to his seventeenth century precursors that to the theological world of today. The Reformed Orthodoxy upon which Heppe drew rested upon a series of basic distinctions and presuppositions which, while not determining the topical order of dogmatics, yet exerted a profound influence upon the way the dogmatic task was itself pursued.[42] Even in the realm of theological prolegomena, Reformed Orthodox systems were by and large dogmatic, not predogmatic in their conception, as recent scholarship has clearly indicated: in

---

[39] It is perhaps worth noting that central to McCormack's (re)interpretation of Barth's theological development is his argument that the decisive move away from the theology expressed in the second edition of the Romans commentary takes place in 1924, under the impact of Heppe's *Reformed Dogmatics* and not the 1931 book on Anselm, *Fides Quaerens Intellectum*. Barth himself identified the latter as the crucial book and has been followed in this by earlier influential Barth interpreters, such as Hans Urs von Balthasar, *The Theology of Karl Barth* (New York: Holt, Rinehart and Wilson, 1971). See also the exchange between Bruce McCormack and Colin Gunton in *Scottish Journal of Theology* 49 (1996), 483-98.

[40] McCormack, *Karl Barth's Critically Realistic Dialectical Theology*, 349.

[41] Barth, *Göttingen Dogmatics*, 324. Barth mentions Heppe here along with related works by Seeberg, Lüdemann, Rade, Girgensohn, Elert and Schmid.

[42] It is sometimes forgotten that Heppe's work, while containing a large number of extensive quotations from original sources, has a number of obvious limitations. First, the ordering of topics, while not exceptional in itself, is still an imposed order which does not necessarily reflect the topical order in the individual sources. Heppe's order represents only one possible arrangement; and order itself is imposed from without and not the result of internal doctrinal factors. Second, and an obvious implication of the first, questions of context (genre, intention etc) are precluded by the book's very nature as a catena of quotations. Given that Barth's knowledge of Reformed Orthodoxy is, initially at least, largely mediated via Heppe, the question of Barth's relationship to Reformed Orthodoxy rests itself upon the prior question of Heppe's relationship to the same Orthodoxy.

theory, at least, God was not the object of theology so much as its subject; and theology was therefore shaped by God and not primarily by the human.[43]

Barth's Relationship to Reformed Orthodoxy

It is quite clear that, by the mid 1920s, Barth had emerged from his background in the theological worlds of Ritschl and Harnack and that, while this move was triggered by a variety of social and intellectual influences, it was at least in part consolidated by the dialogue in which he was subsequently able to engage with Reformed Orthodoxy via his discovery of both the confessional literature of the Reformed churches and of the textbook of Heppe. This, of course, raises all kinds of interesting questions about the details of Barth's relationship to the old orthodoxy. These certainly deserve detailed treatment in a monograph, but it is nonetheless possible to trace out a basic map of the territory.

It is certainly worth reiterating and expanding upon the fact that Barth's primary contact with Reformed Orthodoxy in the early phase of his career, which established many of the trajectories of interpretation which remained in his later work, was mediated via Heppe (and, in terms of the parallel movement, Lutheran Orthodoxy, Schmid). Thus, Barth as theologian did not in his initial encounter with Reformed Orthodoxy grapple with primary texts as one might have expected an historian of dogma to do. Given the often tendentious nature of the presentation of sources in Heppe's work (Cocceius being the example cited above), it is indeed questionable whether a reading and appropriation of Heppe can in fact be regarded as a reading and appropriation of Reformed Orthodoxy *as intended and understood in the sixteenth and seventeenth centuries* at all. The approach of Heppe and Schmid has much to do with the Repristination Theology of the nineteenth century, which focused on eclectic use of sources as a means of building confessional consensus in the nineteenth century in response to the various challenges faced by the churches at that particular time. Thus, for example, Barth's belief that the reformed Orthodox had little time for prolegomenal and methodological discussion is, from the vantage point provided by more recent scholarship on the primary sources, rather a sign of his dependence on Heppe and on Heppe's failure to emphasize this than on Reformed Orthodoxy as it was; indeed, the movement was marked from the latter part of the sixteenth century by the presence of highly elaborate examples of such, a characteristic shared with the writers of Lutheran Orthodoxy.[44]

From the outset, it is clear that Barth in no way considered the old confessional orthodoxy as a fully valid option for modern theology. It is true that in a letter to Thurneysen, he declared that he agreed 'with orthodoxy on almost all points' but this

---

[43] See Muller, *PRRD*, I: *Prolegomena to Theology*.

[44] See, for example, Francis Turretin, *Institutio Theologiae Elencticae*, I-II; on the development of Reformed theological prolegomena, see Muller, *PRRD*, I; on related developments in Lutheranism, see Robert D. Preus, *The Theology of Post Reformation Lutheranism I: A Study of Theological Prolegomena* (St Louis: Concordia, 1970).

comment should not be taken completely at face value.[45] We have noted above that Barth's reading of Heppe led him to regard natural theology as already making incursions into the theology of the Reformed Orthodox in a manner that would pave the way for Schleiermacher and the rise of full-blooded liberalism. The respective work of Susan Schreiner and of Richard Muller has indicated that the relationship between Reformed theology and 'natural theology' is, from its earliest phase, a somewhat complex one, and the imposition of later understandings of nature and grace, of natural and special revelation, upon pre-Enlightenment Reformed sources is neither unproblematic nor particularly helpful, on the grounds that the epistemological problems with which later theologians such as Schleiermacher were grappling were really significantly different from that of pre-Kantian thinkers such as Calvin, Wollebius, Voetius and company.[46] As any reader of both Barth and Reformed Orthodoxy knows, there are a significant number of points at which Barth's theology diverges from that of Reformed Orthodoxy, even as he draws upon it for his theological vocabulary. Nevertheless, detailed doctrinal content was only part of the problem. At a deeper level, he considered the very nature of confessions and of theology itself prevented any direct appropriation of Reformed Orthodoxy in its original form for the present day.[47]

To take confessions, Barth faced early on the issue of the normativity of confessional documents in relation to an ecclesiastical confession of the sole and unique authority of scripture. Thus, in an early lecture at Göttingen, he declared:

> The significance of the confession in the Reformed church consists in its essential *non*significance, its obvious relativity, humanity, multiplicity, mutability, and transitoriness... The Reformed confession points *beyond* itself. Its center of gravity, if not in fact its very content, is not in itself but rather *beyond* itself.[48]

For Barth, this means that formal confessions – indeed, any dogmatic formulation – will always be more or less inadequate. With confessions in particular, the historical, geographical and political particularity of the circumstances of their composition render them radically limited and, not to put too fine a point on it, fundamentally flawed, though Barth does not see this so much as a problem as a means of clearly

---

[45] Barth-Thurneysen, *Briefwechsel*, II, 328-29, as cited by Migliore, 'Karl Barth's First Lectures in Dogmatics', xv-lxii, xx.

[46] See Muller, *PRRD I*; Susan Schreiner, *The Theatre of His Glory: Nature and the Natural Order in the Thought of John Calvin* (Durham: Labyrinth, 1991).

[47] Migliore provides a helpful list of points at which Barth considered himself to diverge in significant ways from Reformed Orthodoxy: the order of topics; the lack of prolegomena; the importance ascribed to the distinction between natural and supernatural revelation; the reduction of doctrine to a formula, or system of formulas; the doctrine of election; the naivete of the dialectic; the attributes of God; the covenant scheme as elaborated by Cocceius et al; legalism; and the isolation and spiritualization of eschatology. See Migliore, 'Karl Barth's First Lectures in Dogmatics', xxxv-xxxviii.

[48] Barth, *Theology of the Reformed Confessions*, 38.

distinguishing the unique nature of revelation (Christ) from any linguistic form or composition of mere human origin and authority.[49]

On the surface, many of the Reformed Orthodox would have agreed with Barth concerning the provisionality and particularity of Reformed creeds; but they would, I suspect, have located such in the context and form of the creeds rather than in the content. The confessions were, after all, seen by the churches that framed them as referential and as apprehensive of a larger reality, and not simply as unstable symbols, liable to evaporate as times and circumstances changed. In a very real sense, they defined and delimited theological discussion and did not simply provide theologians with a taxonomy for their work. Confessional formulation in the late sixteenth and seventeenth centuries was a Europe-wide phenomenon, with churches in different areas formulating or adopting those confessions which were seen by the particular church concerned to embody the truths of the faith. This did not, however, undermine a strong cultural conviction across Europe that the various documents embodied a basic commonality of mutually agreeable theological substance. Underlying this was theological commitment to the idea that true doctrine could be expressed truly in words. Now, obviously, one criticism which could be lodged at this point would be that based upon the radical discontinuity that exists between the infinite nature of God and the finite nature of doctrinal formulation. Barth overcomes this by focusing on revelation as Christ, and on scripture as witness to that revelation, thus pressing the non-identity of human statements about God and God's own revelation of himself. The Reformed, on the other hand, including Calvin, refused the exclusive identification of God's Word, of revelation, with Christ; instead they operated with a broader understanding which included scripture as revelation, not merely as witness to revelation. They were able to do this because their epistemological presuppositions were closely connected to the kind of theological formulations relating to the doctrine of God which had been developed in the high Middle Ages and which provided a means of understanding how the finite could reliably reveal the infinite, a privilege which was extended to language as well as to the Incarnation.

Underlying much of this was the Reformed acceptance of the medieval Scotist distinctions in the knowledge of God, for example, between the *theologia viatorum*, the theology of the pilgrims, those 'on the way' (*in via*), and the *theologia beatorum*, the theology of the blessed, underlined the difference between the knowledge of God possessed by those Christians on earth and those in heaven who possessed the beatific vision. More important, the Reformed cast the difference between God's infinite knowledge of himself and humanity's finite yet reliable knowledge of God in terms of a distinction between *archetypal theology* and *ectypal*

---

[49] Barth, *Theology of the Reformed Confessions*, 1-37, 39; see also his exploration of these issues in relations to the problem of composing a Reformed creed that is both contemporary and universal in his 1925 lecture 'The Desirability and Possibility of a Universal Reformed Creed', in Karl Barth, *Theology and Church: Shorter Writings 1920–1928* (ed. T.F. Torrance; New York: Harper and Row, 1962), 112-35.

theology.⁵⁰ What this distinction did was to allow a referentiality to language which yet made no complains to comprehension or to 'putting God in a box.' Ectypal theology was always dependent upon the archetype, and was always an act of God's sovereignty in his revelation. This is surely related to one of the key points of divergence between Barth and the Reformed Orthodox (or at least Barth's understanding of the Reformed Orthodox) as highlighted by Daniel Migliore: the reduction of doctrine to a set or system of formulae, and its close corollary, the reduction of scripture to a set of true propositions.⁵¹ The issue of scripture in both Barth and Reformed Orthodoxy is a highly complex one and, in the case of Barth, is scarcely a point of scholarly consensus.⁵² Yet the impact of Scotism on Reformed Orthodoxy is relevant to how close Barth can be said to stand to the Reformed Orthodox tradition, or at least to how legitimate criticisms of that tradition are from within the Barth camp. For a start, the notion that theological language is apprehensive, not comprehensive, of theological reality, and that it derives it power to apprehend from an act of God, not a power resident in the language itself, points up the contingent nature of revelation within the Reformed Orthodox tradition and means that any criticism of Reformed Orthodoxy as 'rationalist' requires both careful parsing of the term 'rationalist' and an acknowledgement of the nuanced Reformed orthodox position.⁵³

---

⁵⁰ The specific terminology is introduced into Reformed thought by Francis Junius in his *De Theologia* Vera (1594). The best study of the epistemological impact of this Scotist idea on Reformed epistemology is Willem J. Van Asselt, 'The Fundamental Meaning of Theology: Archetypal and Ectypal Theology in Seventeenth-Century Thought', *Westminster Theological Journal* 64 (2002), 319-35. On the importance of Scotism in general to Reformed theology, particularly on the issue of contingency and reality, see Andreas J. Beck, 'Gisbert Voetius (1589-1676): Basic Features of His Doctrine of God', in Van Asselt and Dekker (eds), *Reformation and Scholasticism*, 205-26.

⁵¹ Migliore, 'Karl Barth's First Lectures in Dogmatics', xxxvi.

⁵² The issue of Scripture in Barth and the Reformed tradition is addressed later in this volume so need not detain us here. Barth's mature discussion can be found in *CD* I/2, § 19-21, although these sections should not be abstracted from their context in Barth's wider discussion of revelation; scholarly interpretations can be found in Klaas Runia, *Karl Barth's Doctrine of Holy Scripture* (Grand Rapids: Eerdmans, 1962); Neil B. MacDonald, *Karl Barth and the Strange New World within the Bible: Barth, Wittgenstein, and the Metadilemmas of the Enlightenment* (Carlisle: Paternoster, rev. edn, 2001). On Scripture in Reformed Orthodoxy, the best study is that by Muller, PRRD, II); on Scripture in Lutheran Orthodoxy, see Preus, *Theology of Post-Reformation Lutheranism*, I, pp. 254-403.

⁵³ A failure to understand this basic point underlies some of the more wrong-headed criticisms of Reformed Orthodox views of Scripture: see John R. Franke, 'Reforming Theology: Toward a Postmodern Reformed Dogmatics', *Westminster Theological Journal* 65 (2003), 1-26, which, while claiming to offer a Reformed response to contemporary philosophical challenges, demonstrates no real knowledge of the orthodox Reformed position as rooted in the archetypal/ectypal distinction.

Of course, the task of evaluating Barth's relationship to Reformed Orthodoxy is further complicated both by the fierce church politics which rage about his name, both pro and con, in the contemporary Reformed world and, more precisely, by the fact that his respect for Reformed Orthodoxy as a phenomenon is not reflected in his positive appropriation and repristination of it in his doctrinal system as a whole. To put the point another way, Reformed Orthodoxy is one of those theological sources the direct influence of which appears far more clearly in the dialogical small print sections of the *Church Dogmatics* than the main text. So how do we answer the question of the relationship between Barth and Reformed Orthodoxy?

The question is more complex than might first appear to be the case. Given Barth's rejection of standard confessional positions on revelation, covenant, *extra calvinisticum* and election, the straightforward answer would seem to be that his theology is clearly discontinuous with the orthodox tradition as embodied in the great confessions. Such an assessment is certainly valid on the doctrinal level, and any who might be tempted to make Barth's work into simply another more or less traditional contribution to a kind of conservative Reformed evangelicalism demonstrate little more than their own ignorance of the orthodox tradition or of Barth's theology, or of both. Doctrinally, on many key issues, Barth's theology represents a radical break with the trajectories of Reformed Orthodoxy.

Nevertheless, the answer to the question is at times more subtle than a simple point-by-point comparison of dogmatic conclusions will yield. After all, Reformed Orthodoxy is more than the simple repetition of a narrow range of equally narrow dogmatic conclusions. Even a basic understanding of the confessional documents which embody much of its doctrinal content reveals that these things were consensus documents, designed to produce broad agreement on essentials while allowing considerable flexibility in many of the details. After all, Reformed Orthodoxy was – and is – a *traditionary* exercise: although Reformed theologians take as their starting point the basic canonical text of the Bible, they read and interpret this Bible using a vast array of linguistic, methodological and conceptual tools which have been developed over the centuries for precisely this task, a task which by its very nature is ongoing and never finally completed this side of the eschaton. Thus, at the level of ecclesiastical documents, Reformed theologians have the great creeds of the early church and the confessions and catechisms of the sixteenth and seventeenth centuries; in addition to this, they have the exegetical and doctrinal traditions provided by the great commentators and theologians of the church; further, as basic pedagogical tools, they have the formal divisions of theology and the technical vocabulary established over the centuries in the theological halls of universities. All of these factors are part and parcel of what constitutes Reformed Orthodoxy and are influential in shaping the theological horizons of Reformed theologians in their engagement with the horizon of the biblical text itself. Framed in these terms, the question of Barth's relationship to Reformed Orthodoxy is one that is obviously more subtle. Clearly, he draws heavily upon the language and concepts of the tradition; his dogmatics in terms of the doctrinal divisions around which it is organized is shaped by his reading of the Reformed Orthodox writers of the seventeenth century; and he is also in constant dialogue with the theology of Reformed Orthodoxy, albeit initially mediated through, and obviously shaped by, the selective presentation of Heppe. Given all this, we might allow that a very good case can be made for saying that Barth's theology stands in some *formal* continuity with the Reformed Orthodox tradition at the level of sources, language, and pedagogical organization, providing we are careful to point out the fundamental material changes.

This brings us to the heart of the traditionary question: given not only that the doctrinal content of Barth's theology is significantly different to that of Reformed Orthodoxy on central points, but also that he constructs it in part through dialogue with the tradition, can we say that the changes he introduces represent a legitimate development in continuity with the tradition, and one with which the other contributors to this volume will wrestle in greater depth? It is a far more problematic question than that of the existence of mere influence, on the grounds that the difference between a legitimate development or continuity and one which is deemed illegitimate is not infrequently simply a matter of whether the particular development is one based upon presuppositional criteria with respect to what is being developed or modified. Legitimacy of development, if you like, is a gift all-too-frequently bestowed by the reader on those positions which confirm cherished personal convictions, while illegitimacy is often used as a cheap means of marginalizing those things of which the reader disapproves. This is reflected, for example, in the legal world where schools of approach to law are broadly divided into those who focus on the original intention of the lawmakers in close correlation to the language actually used, and those who opt for more broadly intentional models which allow for an evolutionary approach to the law's meaning and application. Such choices of approach are not infrequently determined by the prior social, class and political commitments of the interpreter, with the criteria of what qualifies as original intention or legitimate evolution (as opposed to perversion) of meaning, being shaped by ideological considerations and not some purported value-neutral interpretative technique.

With Barth and Reformed Orthodoxy this problem is somewhat acute. Reformed confessionalism is both committed to a definite doctrinal system, albeit one that is somewhat broader than many friends and foes try to argue, while at the same time also committed to the supreme authority of scripture in doctrinal matters. Thus, the Reformed system both embodies definite doctrinal commitments and a principle whereby those definite doctrinal commitments are themselves continually corrigible in the light of the teaching of scripture. Yet, on the whole, the Reformed Orthodox have tended to conceive of this relationship of one whereby scripture will be used to ensure increasing precision of doctrinal formulation, driven by theological reflection in relation to the exigencies of polemical and pastoral contexts, and that what should be expected in doctrinal development is not so much the emergence of dramatic new formulations or paradigms but modifications and refinements of well-established patterns of thought. This is the approach most ably summarized by the Princeton theologian, B.B. Warfield:

> It is utter folly to suppose that progress [in theology] can be made, otherwise than by placing ourselves in the line of progress; and if the temple of God's truth is ever to be completely built, we must not spend our efforts in digging at the foundations which have been securely laid in the distant past, but must rather give our best efforts to rounding the arches, carving the capitals, and fitting in the fretted roof.[54]

By Warfield's criteria, Barth deviates from Reformed Orthodoxy not only in its letter or content but also in its spirit, on the grounds that he really does not offer gentle revisions and refinements of the past, nor modifications of details, but rather wholesale reconstructions of major Christian doctrines, albeit in the light of a serious engagement with the Reformed Orthodox tradition. Indeed, Migliore's specific comments about Barth's work in the *Göttingen Dogmatics* can be applied to his relationship to reformed Orthodoxy as a whole:

> Barth's attitude to the old Reformed tradition is deferential yet critical. He approaches the old theologians respectfully and encourages his students to do the same: 'I see no reason why we should not listen to them. Let us try to think with and after them'... Yet his appropriation of the tradition is critical and reconstructive. He thinks *with* and *after* but not infrequently also *against* old Reformed orthodoxy.[55]

Migliore's points – that Barth is neither an evangelical, with a knee-jerk contempt for church confessions is clear, nor is he Reformed Orthodox in terms of his theological content – is well-made. Indeed, to return to Said, in Barth it would appear that Reformed confessional orthodoxy has traveled very far – theologically, philosophically, exegetically, and in terms of its general context. The language is familiar to those steeped in the old orthodoxy; but that which it describes has a strange, alien feel to those who see the Reformed confessions as marking not so much the original point of departure but as in some very real sense, mapping out the journey as well.

The remaining essays in this volume will address these issues of theological content more directly. What I have hoped to do here is merely to give some context to the whole, to allow the reader some understanding of how and when Barth approached the old orthodoxy, and to focus the reader's mind on certain key issues and questions. Is Barth an example of orthodox Reformed theology? Certainly, in his concern for confessions and for dialogue with the church's tradition, he captures something of the Reformed Orthodox spirit; but, as one committed to the old confessional trajectories, my own verdict on Barth must ultimately be a negative one. Yet the essence of the Reformation was that each must take responsibility for his or her own beliefs: so do not take my word for it; read the following essays and, like the Bereans, may every reader examine the scriptures themselves and see if these things be so!

---

[54] B.B. Warfield, 'The Idea of Systematic Theology,' in B.B. Warfield (ed), *Studies in Theology* (Oxford: Oxford University Press, 1932), 49-87, 77.

[55] Migliore, 'Karl Barth's First Lectures in Dogmatics', xxxviii-xxxix.

PART TWO

THE SACRAMENTS OF BAPTISM AND EUCHARIST

CHAPTER 2

Calvin and Barth on the Lord's Supper

Trevor Hart

Introduction

There are many reasons to regret the fact that Karl Barth did not live to complete the fourth or the projected fifth volume of the *Church Dogmatics*.[1] Barth himself (with tongue in cheek?) likened the truncated nature of his life's work to certain medieval cathedrals, and to well-known compositions by Mozart and Schubert. Certainly, there are some very important parts of the pattern still missing, and a sense in which it cries out for completion. Yet, even the most modest attempts to extrapolate the probable lines and angles of the absent architecture must remain tentative, not least because Barth manifested some significant changes of mind in the few years before his death in 1968. This presents a problem for this chapter, since the theology of the Lord's Supper was one of those other topics of which Barth had delayed his full discussion until too late, but his attitude to the 'so-called sacraments' was chief among those where a radical new trajectory could already be identified. Barth recognised the problem, but in the preface to the published 'fragment' of *CD* 4/4 (in its extant form on baptism, but his treatment of the Lord's Supper was to have formed 'a conclusion and a crown' to this chapter) surmises that – on the basis of what the fragment actually contains – 'intelligent readers may deduce … how I would finally have presented the doctrine of the Lord's Supper' (*CD* 4/4, ix).

The task is less simple, though, than this might suggest, and the results of such reconstruction must inevitably be tentative. There are, to be sure, scattered and suggestive references to the Supper[2] be attended to in earlier volumes, and a handful in the posthumously published 'lecture fragments' on the Christian life[3] (which would have found their way eventually into the text of *CD* 4/4 had Barth survived). But of Barth's developed view there is no substantial version available. To ascertain its contours we shall be forced precisely to rely on 'deductions' from the late direction of his wider thinking about the sacraments, and his decision to situate his

---

[1] Karl Barth, *Church Dogmatics* (Edinburgh: T.&T. Clark, 1936–69), hereafter referred to in references as *CD*.

[2] In this chapter I shall refer variously to the 'Lord's Supper' and the 'Eucharist', partly to conform to the use of the writers being studied. I shall, though, use Eucharist and its cognates as my default, not to indicate any specific theological agenda or liturgical preference, but simply in order to benefit from its possession of an adjectival form!

[3] Karl Barth, *The Christian Life* (Grand Rapids: Eerdmans, 1981).

discussion of them within a part-volume on Christian ethics as 'the free and answer of man to the divine work and word of grace' (*CD* 4/4, ix). First, though, I shall set a theological context by reflecting on some of the key issues at stake in Eucharistic theology, and then turn to Calvin's account of the Supper in *Institutes* Book IV. This will hopefully provide a coherent framework in relation to which to situate things which Barth actually says on the subject, and in terms of which duly to evaluate his contribution (actual and reconstructed).

Some Key Issues

The Presence and Action of God

Rowan Williams observes that the Eucharist is fundamentally an event of meaning-making which involves both God and human beings in activity of one sort or another.[4] There is nothing contentious about such a claim. Whatever else we may wish to say about the nature of what happens here, it is clear enough that it involves the use of symbolic objects and actions. This is acknowledged in the ancient description of the bread and the wine as 'signs'. But very different things have been made of and intended by this, not least since the Reformation when talk of the Supper as essentially 'symbolic' came to be associated in particular with a reductionist account of its significance. The most basic question in Eucharistic theology, therefore, concerns whether, where and how in this event God himself is held to be present and active under, with and through empirically observable human activities.

At one level these activities lend themselves perfectly well to analysis in terms proper to what today we number among the 'human sciences' (especially semiotics, ritual theory, dramaturgy and the sociology of knowledge). Considered thus, the Eucharist is a ritual performed with specific material objects – bread and wine – in which those same objects are symbolically re-ordered through a distinctive act of human meaning-making. The precise actions performed in this ritual may vary (sometimes significantly) in their particulars and they are interpreted in a variety of ways; but the actions and the understandings of them conform broadly to an identifiable template modelled on the words and actions of Jesus at the supper he shared with his disciples on the night before his death. 'In these acts', writes Williams, 'the Church "makes sense" of itself, as other groups may do, and as individuals do'.[5] The question which remains to be answered, though, is whether there are other levels at which an account of the Eucharist's reality must be given in order to appreciate its proper significance? Is there, that is to say, something more than a human act of meaning making occurring in its midst, something which transcends the reach of empirical description and demands a properly theological vocabulary? In short, is God involved here, and if so how?

---

[4] See his essay 'The Nature of a Sacrament', in Rowan Williams, *On Christian Theology* (Oxford: Blackwell, 2000), 197-208.

[5] Williams, *On Christian Theology*, 205.

Perhaps, though, we need to reformulate and sharpen our question further still, and ask instead about the *peculiar mode* of God's presence and activity in the Eucharist.[6] Few theologians are likely to concede that God is absent or inactive altogether from any human context or activity in the world he has made. Thus Williams insists that 'the meaning of our acts and relations rests, moment by moment, on God's creative grace'.[7] There is at least a general presence of God to be reckoned with in all times and places, holding the created cosmos in being and drawing it towards its creaturely goal. If the psalmist found God present even in the depths of Sheol (Ps. 139:8), then it is surely unlikely that we shall discover him to be absent from Eucharistic worship. Furthermore, Williams continues, 'the sacraments are performed, in obedience to Christ, by those already caught up in God's work, those who have received and live by God's promise'.[8] The meaning of the Eucharist, in other words, whatever theological view of it is entertained, could never be *ex opere operato* in the strictest of senses. On the contrary, the significance of what is done *here* is essentially contingent and 'kenotic', referring us away from itself to that which it *signifies*; namely, the prior and promised redemptive work of God in Christ and the Spirit. Apart from this wider pattern of divine presence and action in the world, then, what is done makes no sense – or at best *arbitrary* sense which is no longer really Eucharist at all. Clearly, then, in numerous ways Eucharistic theology necessarily affirms that God's presence and activity are basic to the meaning of the rite.

But we must press the matter further and more precisely. Is there, we must ask, a peculiar and distinctive mode of God's presence and activity to be identified within the Eucharist? Does God promise to do something *special* as and when bread and wine are taken within the Church and certain things done with them (as for example, it might be supposed that he does when Scripture is read and the Word is preached)? And, if so, what is this special something, and where does it occur? It is at this stage of the discussion that some views of the Supper have parted company with the mainstream.

Some theologians have been eager to draw the line after an affirmation of God's wider presence and activity, preferring to construe the Eucharist itself as constituted by a series of distinctly human actions and dispositions. Acknowledging that God is present and active as Creator here as everywhere, and that the meaning of what happens here is utterly contingent upon God's prior and promised work in which we are caught up (so the Supper cannot be seen as an autonomous act), such a view nonetheless understands the Supper as such as something which we do rather than something that God does (albeit something that we do *in response* to God or as an expression of *faith in* God). So, for example, the Swiss reformer Zwingli, in his *Commentary Concerning True and False Religion* (1525), interpreted the Lord's Supper precisely as an activity of human meaning-making, in which bread and wine

---

[6] See on this, helpfully, D.M. Baillie, *The Theology of the Sacraments and Other Papers* (London: Faber, 1957), 97-98.
[7] Williams, *On Christian Theology*, 205.
[8] Williams, *On Christian Theology*, 205.

(following Jesus' lead at the Last Supper) are invested by faith with symbolic value as 'signifying' Jesus' body and blood, and the wider Eucharistic action signifies or expresses the faith of the believing community in Jesus' redeeming sacrifice on the cross. The essential meaning of the Supper, therefore, lies in its nature as a symbolic response of *eucharistia* (thanksgiving) for what God has done in Christ, an act of human faith and obedience.

Most traditions, though, have understood things differently. Something happens here, they have held, which cannot finally be accounted for in human terms alone. To make sense of it, talk of human symbolising requires to be supplemented by recognition of an accompanying divine sign-giving and –making. This alone grants the Eucharistic objects and actions the significance which they have but could never otherwise acquire, as the symbolic means of our sharing more fully and more deeply in Christ, in his offering of himself to God in his life and his death on the cross. Beyond this baseline of agreement, particular interpretations of how all this should be thought of or expressed again part company and travel in radically different directions. But there is concurrence at least that the 'all this' to be made sense of involves a special, and not just a general, presence and action of God, and that this special presence and action is in some way focused upon the physical elements of bread and wine, and what is done with these – taking, breaking, eating, drinking, and so on.

It is important to keep this talk of divine action central, since discussions of 'sacramentality' sometimes proceed as if their proper concern were with the intrinsic capacity of certain material things to put us in touch with 'spiritual' realities, or 'the divine', or 'the transcendent', or God. Quite apart from the problems involved in presuming easy identification between any of these indefinite terms, there is already a problem (for Christians at least) in thinking and speaking as though material realities could have any capacity in and of themselves to be the bearers of divine meaning. That they may themselves be *granted* such a capacity by God's acting upon and through them (and upon and through *us* in our corresponding activity) is, of course, another matter. Indeed, this is the only basis upon which faith and theology could be possible at all. Such capacity, though, is not bestowed upon these objects in isolation or permanently but within the particular actions into which they are assimilated. We must be very careful how we speak of such things, and loose talk about 'sacramental' this, that and the other (or about the 'sacramental principle' in Christian theology) often appears not to be.

The Presence of Christ and the Elements

Discussions of 'Eucharistic presence' have in fact generally spoken not so much about *God's* presence, but about the presence of *Christ* in relation to the bread and wine. We may note several things about this. (1) The two names are not simply synonymous in the Eucharistic context, since it is the risen and ascended *humanity* of Christ that is in view here; (2) despite this, the pattern of orthodox Christology does permit the substitution of the name 'Christ' for the name 'God' (since in Christ it is God with whom we have to do), and talk about the presence of Christ may therefore legitimately perform more than one function in this context; (3) Christ's humanity is, therefore, the humanity of God and a further mode of God's own presence in the world; (4) For the humanity of Christ to be 'really' present in the eucharist, a special presence and activity of God as such must be presupposed; (5) Christians also believe that Christ is 'really' present in other contexts[9] – in the preaching of the Word for example, indeed 'wherever two or more are gathered' in his name – but while these various modes of his presence are clearly analogous to one another, it has generally been considered important to differentiate them, thereby recognizing the peculiar modes of presence and activity of God proper to different contexts; (6) different ways of thinking about the relationship between God's mode of presence 'in' or 'to' the humanity of Christ in the incarnation and 'in' the Eucharistic elements and actions[10] result in quite different accounts of what is effected through the sign.

In the above I have made a particular point of twinning the terms 'presence' and 'activity' whenever speaking of God's involvement in the Eucharist (or anywhere else). This seems to be important for a number of reasons. First, it reflects a fundamental biblical concentration upon God's activity as the way in which God's character (the Bible does not really pay much attention to the later philosophical categories of 'being' or 'nature') is apprehended. Second, it encourages us to recognise that when God is active, he is also 'present' in the midst of his own action, and not functioning via remote control from some distant 'place' (and therefore, in effect, absent); and correspondingly whenever God is present he is active and not to be thought of as a static 'substance' exposure or proximity to which alone is in some sense transformative of human existence. Thus, if we suppose that the Eucharist is a context in which we are granted 'communion with' or (as some traditions have expressed it) 'participation in' God, then this is not by virtue of God simply 'being' in the same place as us (or 'in' the physical elements which we ingest), but because God is himself *doing* something distinctive to bring such communion about, acting upon us, and with us and through us. As Schillebeeckx notes[11], the ancient church adhered to a model of God's relationship to this-worldly realities which was inherently dynamic and made sense of the Eucharist in these terms; but this tended to be obscured later by the borrowing of philosophical terms concentrating attention upon the abstract and the inert.

Whatever terms we choose, though, it may help us to think of what occurs in the Eucharist (unless we opt for a purely human account of its meaning) as a dynamic *appropriation* by God of the elements of bread and wine and the actions which we perform with them, lifting them up beyond the level of their own intrinsic

---

[9] See, helpfully, E. Schillebeeckx, *The Eucharist* (London: Sheed and Ward, 1968), 43.

[10] For a helpful discussion of the problems associated with the preposition 'in', and its association with an Aristotelian 'container' notion of space, see T.F. Torrance, *Space, Time and Incarnation* (London: Oxford University Press, 1969).

[11] Schillebeeckx, *The Eucharist*, 67-68.

capacities. Thinking about the Eucharistic presence of God in this dynamic way evokes obvious parallels with his appropriation of human flesh in the incarnation itself and his appropriation of human language in preaching and other contexts in which Scripture is read and interpreted. It may thus offer a more congenial model for Protestant sensibilities than is suggested by the language of bare 'presence' alone. Another benefit of insisting upon a dynamic conception of presence is that it reminds us that it is precisely in *actions* (God's and ours) that the bread and wine are symbolically re-ordered. To think and speak of God's presence in the 'elements' as if they remained inert on the table throughout, therefore, is to misplace the centre of symbolic gravity. At its best, Eucharistic theology has always insisted that it is the bread and wine *as they are set apart, taken, broken, poured out, received and consumed* which are the focus of what God does here. Again, a suggestive parallel lies in the sort of bibliolatry which treats the Bible almost as an object to be venerated, forgetting that its meaning for faith is tied to the human activity in which it is read and made sense of. Eucharist, like proclamation, is a dynamic event on God's part and on ours.

Eucharistic Modification

A further question to be faced concerns the implications of all this for the creaturely realities involved. After all, many Eucharistic liturgies refer unashamedly to the bread 'becoming' Christ's body, and the wine his blood, so that, in some sense, in receiving the creaturely elements we are at the same time 'receiving' Christ and him crucified. Does this mean that the bread and wine are somehow changed, that the reality which confronts us in them is different in the midst of the Eucharistic celebration than it was before it? From very early in the church's history, it seems that theologians have felt compelled to insist that some such change must be recognised. Schillebeeckx cites the fifth century bishop Theodore of Mopsuestia (c.350-428) who, on the basis of Christ's words of institution, insists: 'Christ did not say "This is the *symbolum* of my blood," but "This *is* my blood," a *change* of the wine takes place'.[12] Many have followed in this basic insistence, and for essentially similar reasons. Hence debates about the Eucharist over the centuries have tended to centre on analysis of the words Jesus used in referring to the bread and the wine, and the precise implications of those words.

While, though, consideration of a 'change' in the bread and wine may begin here, it cannot end here, as if only on the basis of a crudely 'literal' and pedantic interpretation of Jesus' words can the notion of change be taken seriously and made sense of. If we ask whether, in the context of the Eucharistic celebration, what confronts us in the bread we take and eat and the wine we drink is 'merely' bread and wine any longer, then any who subscribe to some notion of God's presence and activity here are bound to resist this suggestion, and to admit at least that there is now, and for the moment, 'something different' or 'more' to be said of the bread and

---

[12] Cited in Schillebeeckx, *The Eucharist*, 67.

wine than this. They may well wish to insist that there is nothing *less* than bread and wine here, but they will accept that there is something more. For, they will recognise, when something is appropriated by God and taken up into his activity and purposes in a manner that was not true of it before, we can and must say that its 'reality' (that which is true of it) has in some way been modified and enlarged. Again, we may note that directly parallel issues have arisen in discussion about the humanity which the Son of God assumed in the incarnation. This humanity, it has traditionally been insisted, is certainly not *less* than fully human by virtue of its assumption, but its 'reality' is unique by virtue of its unique relationship to God, and if we overlook this difference and insist that it is 'mere' humanity like any other, then we miss all that matters most about it. Analogously, human words (written and spoken) are, in being laid hold of by God when Scripture is read and the gospel preached, no less human than they were before; yet we attend to them expecting to hear the Word of God in and through them. So, whether or not we get hung up on particular terminology, the recognition of a particular and peculiar presence and action of God in relation to the Eucharistic elements does seem to compel an acknowledgment that there is now something other and more to be said about them, and hence that something about them has indeed changed.

As the western Church sought to underwrite this acknowledgment in the Middle Ages it did so by borrowing terms from Aristotelian philosophy. We can see how its application of these terms was intended to safeguard both the profundity of the change that occurs to mere bread and wine and the fact that these things remain (perceptually at least) the same as they were before in the midst of the divine action. The medievals expressed all this, though, by saying that the 'substance' (the underlying essence of the thing) of the elements had changed, while the 'species' or 'accidents' (the particular qualities manifest to our senses) remained the same. Since, in terms of the philosophy upon which they were drawing, a given thing could only *be one sort of thing* (possess one substance or nature) at once, theologians were driven to suggest that that which had once been bread *was actually now bread no longer*, but had been changed into the substance of the body of Christ, and the 'substance' which had been wine was correspondingly now the blood of Christ[13]. As well as focusing attention unhelpfully on the physical elements as such (rather than

---

[13] Cf, e.g., Aquinas' insistence: 'Now, what is changed into something else is no longer there after the change. The reality of Christ's body in this sacrament demands, then, that the substance of the bread be no longer there after the consecration' (Aquinas, *Summa Theologiae*, 3a., Q.75, Art.2 – Vol. 58, p.59). The same point is reaffirmed in an anathema approved by the Council of Trent on 11 October 1551: 'Should anyone maintain that, in the most holy sacrament of the Eucharist, the substance of bread and wine remains (in existence) together with the body and blood of our Lord Jesus Christ and should deny this wonderful and unique changing of the whole substance of bread into the body and of the whole substance of wine into the blood, while the species of bread and wine nonetheless remain, which change the Catholic Church very suitably calls transubstantiation, let him be excommunicated' (cited in Schillebeeckx, *The Eucharist*, 38).

their situation within a symbolic *action*) these technical claims travelled far beyond the simple profession of faith that the Eucharistic bread and wine are transfigured by their assimilation into God's purposes. Rather than their creaturely 'reality' being *enhanced*, the medieval doctrine effectively displaces that reality altogether, transmogrifying it into something else which now confronts us in its place.

The intentions of this notion of 'transubstantiation' (which was adopted by the Fourth Lateran Council in 1215, endorsed and clarified by major medieval theologians such as Thomas Aquinas, and duly reaffirmed in the sixteenth century by the Council of Trent and again in the 1960s by Vatican Council II[14]) may have been commendable, but its way of articulating things was clearly highly problematic. In particular, its language, inevitably suggesting to the theologically unsophisticated that Christ's actual flesh was now physically present on the altar, and about to be bitten by human teeth and swallowed, reinforced all manner of popular misperceptions and superstitions concerning what was taking place.[15]

If, though, we return to the theological concerns lying behind the doctrinal formulation, Schillebeeckx is surely correct to claim that the gap between Catholic and mainstream Protestant understanding is less wide than first appearances suggest? Most traditions, following such clues as exist in the New Testament, have wanted to insist that when God appropriates bread and wine in the Eucharist what he does with it (and with us as we take and bless and share it) involves 'uniting us to Christ' in some redemptive way.[16] This being so, it seems reasonable to say – along the lines indicated above – that to the 'reality' of the bread and wine is added now a new determination in relation to Christ's body and blood (effective metonymy for his

---

[14] See Austin Flannery (ed), *Vatican Council II: The Conciliar and Post Conciliar Documents* (Grand Rapids: Eerdmans, 1992), 104.

[15] The doctrine was not responsible for introducing this crude realism. It was already extant in the eleventh century as the case of Berangarius of Tours shows. Forced to recant his original adherence to a careful distinction between the physical 'signs' of bread and wine and the 'spiritual' reality of sharing in the body and blood of Christ, in 1059 Berangarius signed a statement including the words 'the true body and blood of our Lord Jesus Christ ... are sensibly ... handled by the hands of the priests and broken and crushed by the teeth of the faithful'. See on this, Alasdair Heron, *Table and Tradition: Towards an Ecumenical Understanding of the Eucharist* (Edinburgh: Handsel Press, 1983), 94-95. While his own view of the matter was anything but crude, even Aquinas endorsed the rejection of Berangarius' original distinction as heretical (*Summa Theologiae* 3a., Q.75, Art. 1) and the doctrine of transubstantiation did nothing to qualify more unfortunate and macabre interpretations among the masses of the 'physical' handling and chewing of Christ's actual body in the sacrament.

[16] The New Testament does not contain a developed theology of the Eucharist, but it is clear that both Paul and John understand the eating and drinking which occurs there within the context of a theology of the union of the believer with Christ. Each understands union with Christ's humanity as central to human salvation, and sees the eucharist as a vital (if not absolutely necessary) means whereby our active sharing in Christ is sustained and deepened. See, for example, 1 Cor. 10-11 and Jn 6:47-58, and Heron's commentary on these passages in *Table and Tradition*, 34-53.

'humanity' in its entirety[17]), even though this is not visible and leaves their physical reality unscathed. Were we to set the specific terms of Aristotelian metaphysics aside, and take the word 'substance' simply in its more ancient, non-technical sense of 'the underlying reality' (*sub-stantia* = 'that which stands beneath') which confronts us in a thing, then as Schillebeeckx indicates, talk of a 'change of substance' is no more or less problematic as such than our talk of a 'change of reality' or, if preferred, an enhancement or enlargement of it.[18] But 'substance' talk is probably too heavily stained by its history of use to be helpful in constructive Eucharistic theology today. It is, in any case, the language of another era, and it generally makes sense for theologians to seek contemporary ways of articulating the basic issues at stake. When we turn, shortly, to consider Calvin we shall see that he recasts the terms of the discussion, setting substance largely aside and accounting for what occurs in the Supper instead in terms of the alternative category of figuration.

Summary

To recapitulate, then, we have seen in this section that central to historic discussions about the Eucharist are questions (1) about God's dynamic presence in the midst of the event, (2) about the outcomes of this divine activity (uniting participants with Christ), (3) about Christ's own 'presence' by virtue of this union and (4) about the nature of the reality which confronts us in the bread and the wine as they are appropriated by God's action. These are by no means the only issues, and we shall see that Calvin and Barth attend to others also; but these are the chief issues which have preoccupied the Church's discussion, and our rehearsal and clarification of them should furnish a helpful background against which now to set the their particular accounts.

---

[17] Heron, following Betz, notes a tension in the New Testament's emphasis, observing Luke's and Paul's form of the 'words of institution': 'This is my body ... This cup .. is the new covenant in my blood' (see Luke 22:19-20; 1 Cor. 11 24-25). This formulation, Heron suggests, points to the whole humanity of Christ in its history from birth to resurrection as the content of that 'new covenant' with which faith is effectively united in the sacrament. The versions in Matthew and Mark, with their disentangling of body and blood, draw attention rather to the death of Jesus on the cross as such. Both emphases, Heron notes, should be permitted to resonate through our liturgies and our theology, and it is important to remember that 'body and blood' do indeed refer not just to the sacrificial death of Jesus, but to his whole life offered in obedience to his Father for our sakes. See Heron, *Table and Tradition*, 13.

[18] See Schillebeeckx, *The Eucharist*, 73-4.

Calvin – Bread and Wine Trans-figured

Calvin follows Augustine and Aquinas in linking the sacraments to our propensity, as embodied creatures, for sign-making.[19] This, he recognises, is central to our attempts to make sense of and to represent for ourselves the reality confronting us in the world, and in particular those aspects of it which transcend the limits of sense perception as such. Hence Aquinas writes, 'it is connatural to man to arrive at a knowledge of intelligible realities through sensible ones, and a sign is something through which a person arrives at knowledge of some further thing beyond itself. Moreover', he continues, 'the sacred realities signified by the sacraments are certain spiritual and intelligible goods by which man is sanctified'.[20] If, then, we are to 'know' or engage with these same realities, it will inevitably be through the mediation of physical signs such as the water of baptism and the bread and wine of the Eucharist. Calvin concurs, drawing attention to the fact that the 'signs' in question are not just the material objects themselves, but the wider 'ceremonies' or actions in which these objects are taken up (*Inst.* IV.xiv.19). 'Here', he writes, 'our merciful Lord, according to his infinite kindness, so tempers himself to our capacity that, since we are creatures who always creep on the ground, cleave to the flesh, and, do not think about or even conceive of anything spiritual, he condescends to lead us to himself even by these earthly elements, and to set before us in the flesh a mirror of spiritual blessings ... because we have souls engrafted in bodies, he imparts spiritual things under visible ones. Not that the gifts set before us in the sacraments are bestowed with the natures of the things, but that they have been marked with this signification by God' (*Inst.* IV.xiv.3)

Divine Sign-giving

From this, though, it emerges at once that while the sacraments may be understood at one level in terms of a wider semiotics, the fundamental thing about this particular sign-giving or -making is that it is a matter of God's own gracious action in accommodating himself to our condition. Calvin insists that the relation of signification, through which in the handling of material things 'spiritual realities' are genuinely bestowed and received, is in an important sense arbitrary rather than natural: the bread and the wine have no intrinsic relationship to that which, in this context alone, is offered and received through them. It is a matter of convention peculiar to their use within the Christian community.[21] But this is, as it were, a

---

[19] J. Calvin, *Institutes of the Christian Religion* (ed. John T. McNeill; Philadelphia: Westminster Press, 1960) is the version used in this chapter; thereafter it will be referred to in the references as *Inst.*

[20] Aquinas, *Summa Theologiae*, 3a., Q. 60, Art. 4.

[21] It is true, of course, that bread and wine as such do have a certain natural correspondence to 'flesh' and 'blood' in their simple physical properties, and Calvin acknowledges that it is through 'a sort of analogy' that we are led from the physical to the 'spiritual' things involved in the Eucharistic action. See *Inst.* IV.xvii.3 (McNeill, 1363). So the association between these 'signifiers' and that which they signify is not

divine rather than a merely human convention, resting firmly upon God's determination of the signs rather than the 'symbolific'[22] activity of the Church. The signs, we might say, are more securely spoken of in this particular context as 'given' and 'received' rather than 'made';[23] 'given' by God, not just once in the dominical 'institution' of the Supper, but again and again wherever it is celebrated, the efficacy of the signs being contingent on the 'miracle' of God's repeated renewal of the signifying relation. What happens in the Supper, therefore, is no mere sociological phenomenon, but the gracious approach of a holy God to sinful creatures, condescending to furnish the symbolic means of their reciprocal approach to him.

Calvin does not deny the importance of human activity in the ceremony, but he does set it decisively within the context of a logically prior divine action which under-girds ours and makes it meaningful. Thus, a sacrament may helpfully be defined as 'an outward sign by which the Lord seals on our consciences the promises of his good will toward us in order to sustain the weakness of our faith; and we in turn attest our piety towards him' (*Inst*. IV.xiv.1) 'In one place Chrysostom therefore has appropriately called (the sacraments) "covenants", by which God leagues himself with us, and we pledge ourselves to purity and holiness of life, since there is interposed here a mutual agreement between God and ourselves' (*Inst*. IV.xiv.19). There is a dual dynamic of activity in the 'sign' (which, therefore, is complex, signifying more than one thing), but God is finally responsible for all that happens, and the preponderance of 'doing' is in any case located by Calvin in the God-humanward direction rather than the reciprocal response elicited from the human side. Thus God manifests himself through the signs (*Inst*. IV.xiv.6), draws us to himself (*Inst*. IV.xiv.13), increases, nourishes and deepens faith (*Inst*. IV.xiv.7), grants assurance (*Inst*. IV.xiv.1), and confirms or seals the content of his promise pertaining to our redemption (*Inst*. IV.xiv.1). There are other, more specific things which Calvin holds are 'shown' and 'executed' in the sign of the Supper, and we shall consider these duly. But this list is sufficient to indicate already the nature of the event as one in which God is definitely and pre-eminently involved from first to

---

'arbitrary' in quite the sense ascribed in modern semiotics by Saussure to the linguistic sign (see Ferdinand De Saussure, *Course in General Linguistics* [London: Peter Owen, 1958], 68). But the relationship of these everyday realities to the *particular* body and blood of *Christ* (and therefore their further analogical correspondence as 'food for the body' under which 'food for the soul' is actually given and received in the Supper) is 'arbitrary' inasmuch as it rests wholly on the decision and action of God.

[22] The term coined by Susanne Langer to refer to the peculiarly human mode of meaning making through symbols of one sort or another. See her *Philosophy in a New Key* (Cambridge: Harvard University Press, 3rd edn, 1957).

[23] This is not to deny that, in an important sense, human 'making' of meaning is essential to what occurs. It is simply a way of insisting, as Calvin does, that the priority of action lies with God, into whose activity humans are duly drawn as responsible participants, but apart from whose activity no sense can be made of the Eucharistic sign and what it effects.

last, and any 'power' attaching to the Eucharistic signs is God's own power through his presence and activity in the Spirit, appropriating the bread and wine as his 'instruments' (*Inst.* IV.xiv.17; *Inst.* IV.xiv.12). Indeed, 'the sacraments properly fulfil their office only when the Spirit, that inward teacher, comes to them, by whose power alone hearts are penetrated and affections moved and our souls opened for the sacraments to enter in. If the Spirit be lacking, the sacraments can accomplish nothing more in our minds than the splendour of the sun shining upon blind eyes, or a voice sounding in deaf ears' (*Inst.* IV.xiv.9).

Faith Alone Participates in the Sign

The appropriate mode of apprehension of and correspondence to the Spirit's work, here as elsewhere for Calvin, is faith. Thus, he insists, only those who eat and drink in faith truly receive what is offered to them. While the offer is indiscriminate and the table open, unbelief stops short at the level of a merely physical participation, the bread and the wine being for it 'cold and empty figures' (*Inst.* IV.xiv.7), opaque rather than transparent, and devoid of that divine signification which, for faith, renders sharing in them an actual sharing in the body and blood of Christ. Where faith is lacking, therefore, bread and wine remain merely bread and wine, and Calvin is emphatic that a careful distinction be drawn at every point between the physical signs and that which, under God's appropriation, they signify for faith. In a manner directly parallel to orthodox prescriptions concerning talk about the incarnation, he insists that while there is indeed a real union between sign and signified (or the 'matter') whereby the latter is genuinely shown and genuinely 'present' to be received in faith, nonetheless, 'they are not so linked that they cannot be separated; and ... even in the union itself the matter must always be distinguished from the sign, that we may not transfer to the one what belongs to the other' (*Inst.* IV.xiv.15).

There are twin errors to be avoided here Calvin urges, following Augustine (*Inst.* IV.xvii.5). First, we may confuse what is proper only to the matter with what is proper to the physical sign, and thereby ascribe to the signs in and of themselves some beneficial power to be availed in the mere act of physical eating and drinking. This extols the signs immoderately, and obscures the 'mysteries' to which they properly refer us, missing what is really important. The other danger, though, is that we shall separate the sign from the matter, breaking the relation of signification, and failing to appreciate that 'by the showing of the symbol the thing itself is also shown' and received (*Inst.* IV.xvii.10). One is, as it were, a form of Eucharistic Eutychianism, and the other its Nestorian equivalent.[24] Both result in a damaging of the proper relation of 'union in distinction' and 'distinction in union' between sign and matter, and both end up in a fascination with the signs as such, prohibiting them from performing their essential figurative function of lifting our hearts up to heaven

---

[24] Calvin does not draw out these Christological analogies, but he can hardly have been unaware of them.

(*Inst.* IV.xiv.5; *Inst.* IV.xvii.36) to apprehend Christ who is, nonetheless, truly exhibited in them, truly 'present', and truly given and received when we eat and drink in faith. Accordingly, Calvin rejects the theology of transubstantiation and the associated practices of venerating and reserving the sacramental elements.[25] This robs the bread of its integrity as bread, confuses the two realities within the signifying relation with one another, and effectively denies the need for faith (since Christ is de facto present *as* the bread and wine which are physically consumed) (*Inst.* IV.xvii.33). He is equally concerned, though, to reject accounts of the Supper which turn the bread and wine into the stage props of a merely human symbolising of faith in Christ.[26] Of course what is said and done in the Supper *is* a profession of faith, but this aspect must be acknowledged as secondary to faith's place as the mode in which we receive from the hand of God all that he offers to us through the mediation of the bread and wine; that is, Christ and all his benefits (*Inst.* IV.xvii.5). For it is indeed Christ (and not our faith), Calvin insists, who is the true 'matter' or 'substance' signified in the Supper, and while figuration is necessarily involved in the ceremony, we should not suppose that Christ is offered or received 'only' figuratively. Thus 'the godly ought by all means to keep this rule: whenever they see symbols appointed by the Lord, to think and be persuaded that the truth of the thing signified is surely present there' (*Inst.* IV.xvii.10). Otherwise, we accuse God of being a deceiver, offering to us only 'empty symbols'.

Signs and Words

Before exploring further Calvin's understanding of the presence of Christ in the Supper, we should note again the importance which he ascribes to the event of *the Supper as a whole* (and not just the bread and the wine) in this regard. It is the 'ceremony' as such which constitutes the wider 'sign' within which the particular signifying power of bread and wine is located. And the ceremony is, of course, a synthesis in which objects, actions and words are juxtaposed and related to one another. So, while Calvin insists that the material signs are vital, he also refuses to detach their meaning from the accompanying immaterial symbolics of narrative.[27] The bread and wine are 'seals' and 'confirmations' of a promise already given, and make sense only when faith apprehends them as such. There must therefore always be some preaching or form of words which interprets the 'bare signs' and enables us to make sense of them, and the 'faith' which apprehends them, while not mere intellectual assent, has nonetheless a vital cognitive dimension (*Inst.* IV.xvii.39). 'Augustine calls a sacrament "a visible word" for the reason that it represents God's promises as painted in a picture and sets them before our sight, portrayed graphically and in the manner of images' (*Inst.* IV.xiv.6). This does not, it should be noted, reduce the elements to dispensable visual aids, as if the essential meaning of the

---

[25] See *Inst.* IV.xvii.13-15.
[26] See *Inst.* IV.xiv.13.
[27] See *Inst.* IV.xiv.3-4. Cf. on this Aquinas, *Summa Theologiae*, 3a. Q.60. Art. 6-8.

Supper could be conveyed equally well in their absence. Calvin's choice of similes is helpful here. Certain sorts of images (in our day we might cite photographic as well as painted images) may well require some verbal context before we can make appropriate sense of them,[28] yet when viewed in this context they undoubtedly possess a power or force of their own which transcends the limits of meaning to which words alone may take us. So, too, Calvin insists, (exchanging images!) 'as a building stands and rests upon its own foundation but is more surely established by columns placed underneath, so faith rests upon the Word of God as a foundation; but when the sacraments are added, it rests more firmly upon them as upon columns' (*Inst.* IV.xiv.6). Faith, then, is more surely established, more firmly founded through God's appropriation of tangible things as bearers of his meaning, and by them he 'attests his good will and love toward us more expressly than by word' (*Inst.* IV.xiv.6). Again, this seems to be due not just to a certain 'dullness' on our part, but to our very nature as embodied beings in a world where meaning is finally bound up with physicality. 'Because we are of flesh' these things 'are shown us under things of flesh' (*Inst.* IV.xiv.6), there being a 'surplus' of meaning which supervenes upon the narrative and is available only through these accompanying physical signs. Calvin, like most other commentators, terminates his consideration here, stopping short of potentially fruitful reflection on the further dimension of the 'drama' of the Supper, that is, the equally symbolic *actions* in the performance into which the bread and the wine are taken up.[29]

Signification, Metonymy and the Presence of Christ

As we have been seeing, at the heart of Calvin's understanding of the sacrament of the Supper there lies a careful account of the working of signs, and it is these same terms that he develops his theology of Eucharistic presence. There are, he tells us, three factors to be taken into consideration in the Supper: 'the signification, the matter that depends upon it, and the power or effect that follows from both' (*Inst.* IV.xvii.11). The 'signification' is the physical sign, together with its narrative context ('the promises, which are, so to speak, implicit in' it). The 'effect' is redemption, the continuing transformation of our lives through the communication to them of Christ's own life lived before his Father. The 'matter' is that which the signs signify, that beyond themselves to which they refer and 'unite' us as we follow or indwell the signifying relation. And the matter of these particular signs is Christ's own humanity together with all its 'benefits'. Here it becomes apparent that Calvin's understanding of the Supper in Book IV of the *Institutes* is founded firmly on the Christology and soteriology already expounded in Books II and III, especially his echoing of the biblical and patristic insistence that incarnation and atonement are organically united, and Christ's whole incarnate history from conception to

---

[28] See on this Susan Sontag, *On Photography* (London: Penguin, 1979), 23: 'Only that which narrates can make us understand'.

[29] See *Inst.* IV.xvii.43.

ascension part of that which he offered for us once for all and now offers to us as the 'substance' of our salvation.[30] It is clear that Calvin understands the 'body and blood' of Eucharistic symbolism in this way as metonymic reference to the whole Christ, and while he certainly follows the western tradition in placing due weight on the death of Jesus he does not limit the significance of what is signified to this. What is set before us in the Eucharistic signs is the truth of the union of our own humanity with Christ's whereby all that he has and is becomes the root and source of our redemption. 'This', Calvin writes, 'is the wonderful exchange which , out of his measureless benevolence, he has made with us; that, becoming Son of man with us, he has made us sons of God with him; that, by his descent to earth, he has prepared an ascent to heaven for us; that, by taking on our mortality, he has conferred his immortality upon us; that, accepting our weakness, he has strengthened us by his power; that, receiving our poverty unto himself, he has transferred his wealth to us; that, taking the weight of our iniquity upon himself (which oppressed us), he has clothed us with his righteousness' (*Inst.* IV.xvii.2).

For Calvin, then, the Eucharistic signs refer us away from themselves to Christ. Our participation in their symbolic meaning, though, is no mere 'calling to mind' of Christ's saving significance. By virtue of the Spirit's action and of our response in faith, it is itself a mode of sharing in that significance and being transformed by it. As we eat and drink, so, under the symbols, Christ 'really' offers his 'body' and 'blood' to us and we receive and are 'fed' by them (*Inst.* IV.xvii.10; *Inst.* IV.xvii.32). In other words, the mysterious organic union of believers with the humanity of Christ is actually realised and deepened through this ritual performance, and the sanctification of our sinful and weak humanity duly furthered. This 'flesh and blood' communion with Christ in the present moment presupposes that Christ is himself 'present' to us in some sense, and Calvin insists that it will not suffice to suggest that this presence is of the same sort as his wider presence in the Spirit (*Inst.* IV.xvii.7). Something more and specific is going on here which compels us to speak of a distinctive Eucharistic mode of Christ's presence to us and ours to him. Calvin is emphatic, though, in his rejection of various medieval attempts to account for this in terms of a local physical presence in the elements of bread and wine.[31] This is not because he thinks such an account too incredible to take seriously, but because it compromises a proper understanding of the incarnation and the nature of Christ's risen and ascended humanity. Christ's body, he argues, remains in its risen and ascended state finite and subject to 'the laws of common nature' (*Inst.* IV.xvii.29); to predicate of it some capacity for Eucharistic ubiquity contradicts this truth, and effectively loses sight of the difference between Christ's deity and his humanity, resulting in a form of post-resurrection docetism (*Inst.* IV.xvii.29). If we take Scripture seriously, we find that Christ's humanity is 'in heaven' at the right hand of the Father, from where we are to await his return in glory and for judgment (*Inst.*

---

[30] See on this Trevor Hart, 'Humankind in Christ and Christ in Humankind: Salvation as Participation in Our Substitute in the Theology of John Calvin', *Scottish Journal of Theology* 42.1 (May, 1989), 67-84.

[31] See *Inst.* IV.xvii.12-13 (McNeill, 1372-73.)

IV.xvii.26-9). It cannot, therefore, also be physically present in the bread and wine of the Supper. This being so, we must make sense of the 'presence' of Christ in such a way that it acknowledges his simultaneous 'absence' (located spatially in heaven). This, Calvin admits, is in its way no less remarkable a claim than that entailed in the doctrine of transubstantiation, and entertains a 'miracle' no less challenging to the bounds of day-to-day common sense. The difference, he suggests, is that it is a miracle consonant with and even required by the witness of Scripture concerning what occurs in the Supper.

The Eucharistic union of believers with the humanity of Christ is, Calvin insists, a mystery which the mind cannot comprehend (*Inst.* IV.xvii.7), something to be experienced rather than understood or analysed (*Inst.* IV.xvii.32). It is for this very reason that God accommodates himself to the limits of our reasoning, and furnishes an essentially imaginative mode in which we may approach and partake of it, showing the 'figure and image' of a mystery 'by nature incomprehensible' in visible signs (*Inst.* IV.xvii.1). The signs function to assure us of the reality of Christ's body and blood once offered for us and now offered afresh to us, 'as if we had seen it with our own eyes' (*Inst.* IV.xvii.1). This, though is no mere token of something in reality absent, like a tattered photograph of a loved one kept in a wallet. For, Calvin insists, the signs are themselves the mode of Christ's actual presence to us, the 'truth' or reality of what is signified being 'inseparable from the sign' (*Inst.* IV.xvii.16). The symbols 'represent' Christ to us (*Inst.* IV.xvii.1), but they do so because they are, as it were, the form of Christ's own presence in absence, so that as we share in the sign we actually share in Christ himself. Thus Calvin expounds the meaning of Jesus' words at the Supper, 'This *is* my body', precisely through an appeal to linguistic trope. It is, he argues, metonymy, the substitution of a part to represent a larger whole (as 'the White House' is used in news bulletins to refer to the machinery of American government) to which the part properly belongs (*Inst.* IV.xvii.21). In the Supper, the bread (and wine) 'not only symbolises the thing that it has been consecrated to represent as a bare and empty token, but also truly exhibits it' by virtue of a divine determination uniting it, and us through it, to Christ's humanity. The appropriateness of the metonymy lies, therefore, not in any natural relation between bread and the humanity of Jesus, but in a miracle by which the Spirit 'truly unites things separated in space' and 'Christ's flesh, separated from us by such great distance, penetrates to us' as we take and eat and drink (*Inst.* IV.xvii.10).

The Incarnation and Imaginative Trans-figuration

It is vitally important to note, though, that Calvin does *not* understand the believer's union with Christ is *established* by the Supper. On the contrary, this union (the 'fraternal alliance of the flesh' as Calvin calls it) rests on the sharing of the Son in our humanity by virtue of the incarnation, and it is on this basis that he is 'truly' for us the 'bread of life' and we partakers of his 'flesh'.[32] But his objective 'once for all' healing of this same 'flesh' through obedience and sacrifice remains to be applied to us in the course of our Christian living, and the Supper is a central mode (though by no means the only mode) of this existential participation. 'Therefore, the sacrament does not cause Christ to begin to be the bread of life; but when it reminds us that he was made the bread of life, which we continually eat, and which gives us a relish and savour of that bread, it causes us to feel the power of that bread' (*Inst.* IV.xvii.5). The other thing to note here is that for Calvin the union established between the Eucharistic signs (and thereby believers who partake in the wider 'sign' of the ceremony) is precisely with the *humanity* of Christ. For Calvin this is vitally important, for to deny it, and to posit some direct rather than indirect relation between the signs and God, would effectively be to short-circuit Christ's role as mediator. Instead, his understanding reinforces this theology of Christ's continuing priesthood, since the Supper is precisely a means of its being realised in practice, uniting us to his 'flesh' through which alone we may approach the Father with confidence. While, therefore, there is a clear analogy between the 'materiality' of God's dealing with us in the Supper and in the incarnation, the analogy needs to be handled very carefully indeed. The mode of God's presence in the bread and wine is different, more indirect, than his presence in Christ, and the sacrament, therefore, should not (for Calvin at least) be thought of as 'extending' the incarnation in any way. It does not 'extend' it (as if the bread now performed the same role as Christ's flesh once did) but is a symbolic form whereby the incarnate Christ himself, risen and ascended at the right hand of the Father, makes himself present to us and grants us a participation in his own redeemed humanity.[33] The 'presence' of Christ, therefore, is realised through an appropriation by God's Spirit of the sign's capacity to trespass beyond the boundaries of actual physical presence, and while Calvin is careful to avoid any suggestion that faith partakes of Christ 'only by ... imagination' (*Inst.* IV.xvii.11) (we might better render this 'in a merely imaginary way'), it is clear that his understanding of what occurs in the Supper is, from first to last, articulated in terms of 'poetic' logic and God's active appeal to our nature as imaginative creatures.

Barth – Signification, Revelation and Response

As James Buckley has noted, during the 1930s when Karl Barth was writing his *Protestant Theology in the Nineteenth Century*, he expressed profound disquiet about the tendency in modern theology to found theological description upon general, non-theological discourses, seeking the meaning of the church and its practices (for instance) in some accidental modification of normative human community, its

---

[32] See *Inst.* IV.xvii.4.
[33] On the Eucharist as an extension of the hypostatic union see Schillebeeckx, *The Eucharist*, 68.

rituals and symbols.[34] The key phrase here, though, is *'found* theological description upon'. For in this same period Barth was working on the first volume of his *Church Dogmatics*, and here he was entirely happy to cast his fleeting account of the Lord's Supper in the terms of a wider model of signification. In doing so, though, he did not permit secular discourse to lay down the rules for or determine the limits of his description, let alone appeal to it for external intellectual warrant. Instead, he borrowed such aspects of it as lay usefully to hand in order to articulate something about the structure of God's engagement with humankind, an engagement which, Barth asserted unashamedly, begins and ends unambiguously with God himself. The Lord's Supper, he insisted, is one example of the wider pattern of that *divine sign-giving* in which the dynamic of *revelation* consists (*CD* 1/2, 229).

Signification and Analogy

Like Calvin before him, therefore, in his writings prior to the late 1950s Barth appeals to the logic of signification as a way of thinking about what occurs in the Lord's Supper. More explicitly than Calvin, though, Barth employs this same scheme in order to make sense of the wider pattern of God's revelatory dealings with the world, of which the sacraments are a part. When the God who is wholly other than the world gives himself to be known in the world, Barth argues, it is through the appropriation of this-worldly objects, events, relations and orders, all of which are wholly other than himself, but all of which are duly drawn into a new relationship with him whereby they are granted the capacity to 'mean' something radically new and unexpected. These creaturely phenomena are granted a 'special determination' whereby 'along with what they are and mean within this world ... they also have another nature and meaning from the side of the objective reality of revelation' (*CD* 1/2, 223). The physical entities are in and of themselves incapable of such signification, but are laid hold of by the Word of God in his speaking to the world. The essential *arbitrariness* of the signs is thus a vital correlate of Barth's denial of any *analogia entis* between God and his creatures.[35] For their part, the 'signifiers' (the things appropriated) must be set in a new, transcendent relation in order to function as 'signs'; and in order to apprehend and follow their new meaning we, too, must be lifted up beyond our natural capacity as knowers to behold them now 'from the standpoint ... of transcendence' (*CD* 1/2, 223). Furthermore, neither of these occurrences (which are not once for all, but, in God's faithfulness, repeated and renewed) grants either the signifiers or us any enduring capacity apart from God's gracious appropriation and activity. Revelation is always, for Barth, an event, a happening. Thus 'the activity of the sign is, directly, the activity of God Himself'

---

[34] J. Buckley, 'Community, baptism and Lord's Supper', in J. Webster (ed.), *The Cambridge Companion to Karl Barth* (Cambridge: Cambridge University Press, 2000), 197.

[35] On the relationship between Barth's account of the Supper and his doctrine of analogy see Paul D. Molnar, *Karl Barth and the Theology of the Lord's Supper* (New York: Peter Lang, 1996).

(CD 1/2, 224). 'The given-ness of these signs does not mean that God manifest has Himself as it were become a bit of the world' or placed himself at general human disposal (*CD* 1/2, 227). The Church is bound by these signs, called to return again and again to these particular words, events and things as she seeks an encounter with the living God who has met her in them before. But God, Barth insists, is not bound by them (*CD* 1/2, 224). They are no magic lamps which we have only to rub in order to conjure up his presence. God remains free in his Lordship. Yet he has graciously committed himself to these signs and promised to renew his communion with us as we seek him here in faith and obedience.

Hypostatic and Sacramental Union

At the very heart of this economy of divine sign-giving, of course, lies the history of the man Jesus Christ whose humanity is in its entirety 'taken up' by God as the ultimate 'sign' of his own reality. Here, most obviously and most vitally, God lays hold of creaturely reality and makes it his own, establishing it in a new and unprecedented relationship whereby it serves as a marker of God's own presence with us, Immanuel. The structure of the incarnation as it were parallels the structure of signification: that which is 'not God' is reordered within the scheme of things and becomes for us a sign (for those with eyes to see and ears to hear) of God present in our midst. Thus, Barth admits, 'the humanity of Jesus Christ as such is the first sacrament' (*CD* 2/1, 54). But Barth already knows that he is on dangerous ground here, lest the nature of the relationship between God and the humanity of Christ in the incarnation be *confused* with other divine 'appropriations' of worldly phenomena.[36] There is a radical difference which renders the incarnation unique, and relegates all other divine sign-giving in comparison to a secondary and derivative status. For here, as nowhere else in human history, God relates to creaturely reality by *becoming* it, establishing an absolute identification between himself and the creature. Jesus' humanity functions as a sign (in the strictest sense *the* sign) of God in the world because Jesus himself *is* the form which God takes humanly in history, the Word who has 'become flesh' for our sakes. But this relationship of 'hypostatic union' is unique, and does not pertain to any other God-given sign. 'It happened only once. It is not therefore the starting-point for a general concept of incarnation' (*CD* 2/1, 54). Yet this act of 'primary objectification' on God's part is itself the basis and meaning of all other divine signifying (acts of 'secondary objectification' as Barth refers to them). The content of this particular and unique sign, we might say, becomes the substance or 'matter' (to use Calvin's term) of all the other signs through which revelation occurs. As such, it both calls into question any assumption that other creaturely realities are in themselves capable of directly bearing 'divine meaning' (and thus contradicts rather than offers warrant for general

---

[36] See, e.g., his discussion in 1955 of the 'temptation' of drawing this comparison; *CD* 4/2, 54-55. By the end of the decade the cautious and almost grudging acknowledgment that the parallel may nonetheless be an illuminating one for understanding the Supper had given way to an abandonment of it.

'principles' of sacramentality in Christian theology) and nonetheless offers hope that, in God's gracious accommodation of himself to our capacities, they might come to serve as secondary and indirect signs. 'He and no other creature is taken up into unity with God. Here we have something which cannot be repeated. But the existence of this creature in his unity with God does mean the promise that other creatures may attest in their objectivity what is real only in this creature, that is to say, God's own objectivity – so that to that extent they are the temple, instrument and sign of God as He is' (*CD* 2/1, 54).

When, twenty five years or so after writing these words, Barth began to espouse a very different notion of Baptism and Lord's Supper, the change in his thinking may in part have been due to a deepening conviction that this (for him vital) distinction was too easily and too often overlooked and these 'so-called sacraments' mistakenly vested with attributes and propensities proper only to the humanity of Jesus. That the *unio hypostatica* and the *unio sacramentalis* must be carefully differentiated was something he insisted upon from the outset (the man Jesus Christ, he notes bluntly, is identical with God whereas the bread and wine of the Supper are not) (*CD* 1/2, 162), but he came eventually, as we shall see, to deny the *unio sacramentalis* altogether. For the later Barth the Lord's Supper was no longer to be identified as a place where God appropriates creaturely realities to serve extraordinarily as bearers of divine meaning, lifting us up to know him more fully through our participation in the signifying relation. It is certainly an event of signification, and a divinely 'given' one since Jesus himself instituted it. But the signification requires no peculiar divine action to establish or sustain it, and its 'matter' (that which is signified by it) is to be identified elsewhere than in Christ as such. Before shifting our attention to this late version of things, though, we must first trace more of the pattern of Barth's earlier thought about the Lord's Supper. The evidence for this is patchy and fragmented, and will involve us in making occasional inferences on the basis of things he has to say about 'the sacraments' more generally.

The Word takes Flesh

As we have seen, for Barth the Lord's Supper is to be understood in terms of a wider pattern of divine sign-giving whereby God grants us knowledge of and communion with himself. Chief among the phenomena appropriated by God to serve as signs is human language in both its written and spoken forms, but in the Supper and in Baptism we are confronted with *elementa*, 'elements of a spatially extended, corporeal nature' which duly become the bearers of divine significance (*CD* 1/2, 230). Barth plays down any suggestion that we are dealing with an essentially different mode of divine engagement here though, insisting upon the parallels between the various sorts of signs[37] and avoiding the notion that the bread and wine in the Supper are significant in their inert physicality. That they are tangible signs is certainly important, but Barth reminds us that 'the spiritual, historical and moral

---

[37] See, e.g., *CD* IV/3/2, 737-38.

being of man is also steeped in the elemental sphere, in the cosmos of corporeality, in an ultimately inextricable unity with his natural being, of which it is the counterpart' (*CD* 1/2, 230). Furthermore, the signifying force of these *elementa* resides not in their physical manifestation as such, but in their deployment within the context of an *actio sacra*, an action in which body, soul, spirit, mind and will are all engaged. So, while Barth does not make the point explicitly, we cannot doubt that he sees the accompanying words of the Supper (which are, he reminds us, themselves part of an action, and though not tangible nonetheless sensible signs, *audible* in nature, [*CD* 1/2, 229-30]) as inseparable from the physical elements as part of the wider liturgical drama in which meaning is realized. Following Heinrich Vogel, though, he acknowledges that the supra-linguistic dimensions of this dramatic sign do have their own irreplaceable force, asserting clearly, 'and with relatively greater eloquence than the word in the narrower sense can ever do, that the *iustificatio* or *sanctificatio hominis*, which is the meaning of all divine sign-giving, does not rest upon an idea but upon reality, upon an event' (*CD* 1/2, 230). The physical and active dimensions of the Supper, therefore, are not incidental but vital, for they go further than words can in driving home the truth which lies at the centre of the Christian gospel – *Et incarnatus est*.

In the Lord's Supper, just as in preaching, Barth maintains, mundane realities are laid hold of by God in such a way that while at one level they are 'simply and visibly there', at another they receive a new 'form' from the Word of God, and can no longer be regarded as 'mere' bread and wine. In the Eucharistic context they acquire a new designation as *nota a verbo Dei insculpta* (a sign inscribed by the Word of God) (*CD* 1/1, 88-9), a designation accompanied by a new capacity alien to their nature as such, but leaving it intact. This new capacity has to do with their role as instruments of God's purpose to justify and sanctify human beings, applying what was done once for all in Christ to believers in the here and now. This much they have in common with all divinely ordained signs (*CD* 1/2, 230), but the four-dimensionality of the Supper does this in its own way. 'It is ... a question of (believers') nourishment by Him. It takes place in the fact that, as often as they here eat and drink together, He proffers and gives Himself to them as the One He is, as the One who is absolutely theirs; and conversely, that He continually makes them what they are, absolutely His' (*CD* 4/2, 703). Of course one might also speak analogously of Christ 'offering' himself to us whenever the Gospel is proclaimed; but again, the 'eating and drinking' of the bread and wine do this in their own peculiar way which outstrips the reach that words alone possess.

The Presence of Christ and the Supper

This brings us to the question of 'presence'. While he rejects the Roman Catholic doctrine of transubstantiation and variations upon it, Barth insists that the 'becoming' in which bread and wine are appropriated as signs is no less 'realistic' than what was intended by that doctrine (*CD* 1/1, 89). The action of the Supper is therefore no merely human action, but one over which Christ himself presides, to which he invites us, and in which he 'proffers and gives Himself' to us anew for our conscious reception (*CD* 4/2, 703). Indeed, the Supper makes no sense, Barth suggests, apart from the presupposition that 'the One whom we remember is Himself in action now, to-day and here' (*CD* 4/2, 112). Whereas for Calvin the Spirit mysteriously transgresses the boundaries of space, uniting the Eucharistic sign to the humanity of Christ which is in heaven, Barth indicates rather that the Christ who is present and active is the Christ of the gospel accounts, the one who 'overcomes the barrier of his own time and therefore historical distance'; and the 'action' in which he is present is 'His then action' which, though historically particular, transcends the limits of its own time and breaks into our present (*CD* 4/2, 112). Barth too, though, appeals to spatial metaphor in his theology of presence, not in relation to the Eucharistic event specifically, but in his account of the wider Pauline claim that Christians are 'in Christ' and Christ reciprocally 'in' them. This language, he suggests, while having an extended metaphorical range (Christians live their lives after the pattern of Christ's humanity, and that pattern is duly formed in them) has a logically prior and determinative 'local' sense in which 'the spatial distance between Christ and Christians disappears', 'Christ is spatially present where Christians are, and ... Christians are spatially present where Christ is ... not merely alongside but in exactly the same spot' (*CD* 4/3/2, 547). Such talk, Barth insists, suggestive as it is of a perichoretic transgression not just of the boundaries of time and space but also the boundaries separating Christ's particular humanity from ours (without breaching the integrity of that particularity) must not be demythologised.

This strong, 'realistic' notion of Christ's wider presence in the Church helps us to make sense of Barth's passing observation about the Supper that in it Christ is in some sense 'present without needing to be made present' (*CD* 4/2, 113). This acknowledgment sets the Supper in a wider context and relativizes the emphasis laid upon it as such (the union of Christ with the believer is certainly not dependent upon Eucharistic participation). But Barth traces a link between the two, and seems content to admit that there is nonetheless a special or peculiar moment to be identified in this God-given sign in which the wider 'presence of' or 'union with' Christ is, by virtue of a distinctive divine activity perceptible only to faith, realised and reinforced in particular lives and in the Christian community. Here, 'In the work of the Holy Spirit there takes place ... in a way which typifies all that may happen in the life of this people, that which is indicated by the great *touto estin*, namely, that unity with its heavenly Lord, and the imparting and receiving of His body and blood, are enacted in and with their human fellowship as realised in the common distribution and reception of bread and wine' (*CD* 4/3/2, 761). This realisation of the believer's union with Christ through the sign of the Supper is 'impossible' from the human side, but 'on God's side it is not only possible but actual', taking place 'in the gracious act of the gracious power of the Holy Spirit which co-ordinates the different elements and constitutes and guarantees their unity' (*CD* 4/3/2, 762). While, therefore, Christ's union with and indwelling of the believer is a wider phenomenon pertaining to the whole Christian life, Barth indicates here that the

Supper plays a distinctive and central role in realising it,[38] and that what occurs has to do with the Spirit's 'co-ordinating' or 'uniting' of the earthly and the heavenly, so that the one may serve appropriately as a sign and mediator of the other.

The Supper as a Sign of Response

In the last two decades of his life Barth's views on Baptism and the Lord's Supper underwent a profound shift. The roots of this shift lay primarily in considerations of exegesis, most notably the influence of a book on Baptism published by Barth's own son, Markus.[39] Barth was persuaded by the argument of this work that the notion of 'sacrament' as it had arisen in the early centuries of Christian history was lacking in adequate biblical basis. Linking the New Testament's occasional use of *mysterion* in an unwarranted manner to the events of Baptism and the Supper, it resulted in a decisive relocation of the centre of gravity in the Church's understanding of them. *Mysterion* (*sacramentum*), Barth tells us in his own eventual account of the matter, in the New Testament 'denotes an event in the world of time and space which is directly initiated and brought to pass by God alone, so that in distinction from all other events it is basically a mystery to human cognition in respect of its origin and possibility' (*CD* 4/4, 109). In the sub-apostolic church an understanding developed of Baptism and the Lord's Supper in these terms, as ritual participations in an activity of God which in themselves afford a share in salvation to participants. 'Baptism and the Lord's Supper now (for the first time) began to be regarded as cultic re-presentations of the act and revelation of God in the history of Jesus Christ, and consequently as the granting of a share in His grace' (*CD* 4/4, 109). This idea, Barth argues, was borrowed from parallel rituals in the religions of Asia Minor and, more importantly, obscures rather than illuminates the Bible's teaching about the Christian rites, a case which he then argues at length in relation to Baptism.

As we have already noted, no parallel argument was ever developed concerning the Lord's Supper, and very few positive statements indicating the shape of Barth's revised view of it are extant. Those that are, though, indicate clearly enough that the same basic concerns that mark his account of Baptism pertain here too, and it is therefore legitimate to extrapolate from them the broad shape his developed account would likely have taken had he survived to produce it. The things that are not true of Baptism, he indicates clearly enough, are not true of the Supper either. Thus, he writes, 'Baptism and the Lord's Supper are not events, institutions, mediations or revelations of salvation. They are not representations and actualizations, emanations, repetitions, or extensions, nor indeed guarantees and seals of the work and word of God; nor are they instruments, vehicles, channels, or means of God's reconciling

---

[38] See, e.g., *CD* 4/3/2, 901 where he refers to it as a 'repeated and conscious' appropriation by the church of that which is offered.
[39] Markus Barth, *Die Taufe ein Sakrament?* (Zollikon, Zurich: Evangelischer Verlag, 1951).

grace. They are not what they have been called since the second century, namely, mysteries or sacraments'.[40]

Central to Barth's theological concern about wider sacramental understanding and practice (concern which the new exegesis enabled him now to resolve in relation to Baptism) was an unhealthy emphasis upon the rites themselves as if human performance of and participation in them was essential to and guarantee of the benefits of salvation.[41] This both detaches the signs from their proper relation to what God has done for us in Christ and neglects the need for a wider and radical discipleship as the form of the outworking of that same redemption. As we have seen above, his earlier appeal to the category of the sign sought precisely to avoid the former error. The Supper refers the believer beyond itself, empties itself out in the interests of directing faith to Christ, the real and only source of salvation. To collapse the structure of the sign, thereby confusing the signifiers of the rite with that which they signify, is effectively a form of idolatry. But if the Supper is nonetheless spoken and thought of as a time and place where God himself is active in applying to us the benefits of what he has done objectively and once for all in Christ, and if the signifying force or 'meaning' of the event (the 'matter of the sign' in Calvin's phrase) lies in our being united to Christ, then there is always the danger of such misunderstanding occurring. If God 'does something redemptive' here, then an *ex opere operato* view of the rite will no doubt always be lurking in the shadows waiting for an opportunity to emerge.

What Barth's rejection of the category of 'sacrament' did was effectively to liberate his understanding of the Supper from any such danger. For now he bluntly denied that God was at work in this event mediating or applying the benefits of salvation. Furthermore, the meaning of the Supper, while certainly related to the objective fashioning of salvation for us in the humanity of Christ and its day-to-day application to us through our mysterious 'union' with him, did not lie in divine action as such, but elsewhere. 'With all that the community of Jesus Christ and its members are and say and do, (Baptism and the Lord's Supper) belong to something that God has permitted and entrusted and commanded to Christians, namely, the answering, attesting, and proclaiming of the one act and revelation of salvation that has taken place in the one Mediator between God and man ... they are actions of human obedience for which Jesus Christ makes his people free and responsible. They refer themselves to God's own work and word, and they correspond to his grace and commands'.[42] In other words, there is not a dual dynamic in the sign of the Supper, as Calvin had insisted, and as Barth had himself earlier accepted, but only a single movement. The meaning of the sign lies not in God's movement towards us in his Son, but in our reciprocal and corresponding movement towards God in faith and obedience. Instead of being secondary, this human movement now becomes primary and, indeed, the sole meaning of the rite. Of course it presumes the prior and

---

[40] Barth, *The Christian Life*, 46.
[41] See, on Baptism in this regard, *CD* 4/4, 71.
[42] Barth, *The Christian Life*, 46.

subsequent activity of God, without which it would not be possible or meaningful, since here faith looks both backward and forward and offers thanks for God's grace and faithfulness, centred upon the death of Christ to which the bread and wine testify.[43] But their role is precisely to serve as *signs of our testimony and response* to this self-offering, and not as divinely given signs of the offering in which faith is laid hold of by God, united to the offering and thereby nourished. Such 'union' occurs, but it occurs elsewhere, in the wider pattern of Christian living and the communication of Christ to the believer by the Holy Spirit. While there is a 'strict correlation' between this divine action and the human action of the Supper, there is also a 'no less strict distinction' to be observed which locates the meaning of the Supper decisively in the latter rather than the former. The Lord's Supper is a 'distinctly human action',[44] an ethical event, and not a mystery in which God gives himself to be known. It is, as Barth tells us in one of the few positive statements on the subject dating from this period, 'the thanksgiving which responds to the presence of Jesus Christ in His self-sacrifice and which looks forward to His future' (*CD* 4/4, ix).

Of course Barth does not deny the presence and activity of God in the Supper in any absolute way. But he limits it to that general presence and activity which undergirds all human action and which alone sets faith free to make a responsible response of thanksgiving.[45] Here his second concern about sacramental practice, its tendency to encourage an antinomian reliance upon mechanistic ritualism detached from a life of faith and obedience, comes to the fore. The human action of the Supper is not merely the outward form of some secret, mysterious thing that God does, but a fully responsible moral act, corresponding to God's prior and promised activity in Christ and the Spirit. Indeed, Barth suggests that if the Supper is 'basically a divine action' then it becomes difficult for us to take it seriously as a human action at all.[46] This does not seem to follow at all, not least given some of Barth's own earlier statements about the Spirit's work in co-ordinating divine and human activities.[47] What he is seeking to avoid, though, is any notion of Eucharistic action as a *merely* mechanistic human performance by and under the guise of which God is compelled to do something for our benefit. That wholly misses the significance of its ethical dimension. Again, this danger too is circumvented if, on other grounds, the claim that God is present and active in some special Eucharistic manner is set aside, and the Supper seen instead as *essentially* and *distinctively* a human action, significant of human response and only indirectly of the divine initiative which calls it forth and renders it possible. This view, of course, risks falling prey to a different danger – that of Pelagianism and perfectionism. But, Barth observed, perfectionism was not the problem confronting the church in the

---

[43] See, on Baptism in this regard, *CD* 4/4, 134.
[44] See, on Baptism in this regard, *CD* 4/4, 143.
[45] See, on Baptism in this regard, *CD* 4/4, 105-6.
[46] See, on Baptism in this regard, *CD* 4/4, 106.
[47] See, e.g., *CD* 4/3/2, 762.

context in which he wrote, an acknowledgment that it was not exegesis alone which lay behind his ready and relieved embrace of a new view of the 'so-called sacraments'.

Indeed, the main issue attaching to Barth's late view of the Lord's Supper is that he did not yet appear to have engaged in the sort of careful exegetical work that would enable him to sustain it. The impression one gains is that, under the influence of Markus Barth's exegesis he arrived at a new understanding of the nature of Baptism and the way God works in and through it. This duly led him to reject its status as a 'sacrament' in the traditional sense, and to revise his understanding of (effectively to abandon) the category of sacraments. On the basis of this revised understanding, he posited (but never developed) a parallel revised understanding of the Lord's Supper, as yet lacking the sustained exegetical base which would grant it support.

Conclusion

There would seem, though, to be in principle no reason to make such a lateral move from Baptism to the Supper. In his reflection on the subject Alasdair Heron advises that 'the sacraments' ought never to become an independent subject of theological interest. Otherwise we may proceed from some generic definition of what a 'sacrament' is (about which the New Testament knows nothing whatever) and then proceed to 'squeeze the Eucharist, baptism, and perhaps other things as well into that framework'.[48] Barth's suggestion that one might deduce 'the sorts of things' he would have wanted to say about the Eucharist from the things he actually said about baptism (and understand both in terms of his rejection of a presumed notion of 'sacraments') suggests that he fell into this very trap. There seems to be no reason why one might not in theory hold quite radically differing views of the nature of God's involvement in Baptism and the Lord's Supper respectively, especially if one were to begin, as Heron insists we must, not with an *a priori* notion of what a sacrament is, but with the New Testament's account of each. The only satisfactory basis for a revised account of the nature of the Lord's Supper, that is to say, will be precisely an *exegetical* one, akin to that which led Barth to a new view of Baptism. A theology of 'the sacraments' ought not to be permitted the sort of *a priori* role which he appears to have granted it.

In due course, but long after his father's death, Markus Barth published another work which offered just such an exegetical basis. The focus of his consideration was John 6, and Jesus' discourse on the 'bread of life'. This passage does, indeed, seem to lie close to the exegetical heart of the matter, and to be central, therefore, to any attempt to weigh the relative merits of Calvin's and Barth's (later) view of the Supper.

To go back to where we began this chapter, the central question at issue in Eucharistic theology concerns whether, and if so where and how, God is peculiarly present and active in the Supper's midst. Historic debates have centred (perhaps

---

[48] Heron, *Table and Tradition*, 56.

unhelpfully) around Jesus' words at the last supper with his disciples. Taken in themselves, though, these words hardly bear the weight that has traditionally been placed upon them. Only one of the three synoptic accounts of the supper indicates that this was a practice which Jesus expected his disciples to repeat, and 'do this in remembrance of me' (Luke 22:19) might suggest that what was intended was simply a symbolic way for the community regularly to call to mind Jesus and the significance of his death for others. Nothing in the passage (or its parallels in Matthew and Mark) warrants an insistence that this is to be a locus of peculiar divine activity, let alone some of the things claimed over the centuries concerning what happens to the bread and the wine. The earliest New Testament testimony to the supper is 1 Cor. 11:23-24, which supports Luke's account of Jesus instituting a normative practice for the community, but describes its purpose in a way which initially seems to support to Barth's rather than Calvin's account. 'For as often as you eat this bread and drink the cup, you proclaim the Lord's death until he comes'. The emphasis here is ostensibly upon human rather than divine action, and more specifically faith's testimony, keeping the cross-centred identity of the community clearly in its own view and that of the world.

In the wider context of chapters 10 and 11 though, Paul introduces notes of caution about the Supper which at the very least indicate that the early church took its approach to it very seriously indeed.[49] There is a certain sense of 'sacrality' about it which means that one may approach it 'unworthily' (11:27), and by doing so 'provoke the Lord to jealousy' (see 10:22). Such sentiments are not incompatible with an interpretation of the Supper as an occasion on which the church symbolically represents and reflects upon its identity as a community rooted in its unity with Christ. They are perhaps more likely, though, if this same unity is understood as being somehow at stake in the event itself. The latter suggestion is reinforced by Paul's specific claim that 'whoever ... eats the bread or drinks the cup of the Lord in an unworthy manner *will be answerable for* the body and the blood of the Lord' (11:27, my italics), a statement which duly urges a more rather than less 'realistic' reading of 10:16, 'The cup of blessing that we bless, is it not a sharing in the blood of Christ? The bread which we break is it not a sharing in the body of Christ?' Such words, like Jesus' own in the synoptic accounts, *can* be read as 'merely' poetic, indicating a purely human act of signification; but the wider context raises questions about the adequacy of reading them in this way.

It is John 6, however, that arguably furnishes the most awkward material for the sort of 'neo-Zwinglian' view advocated by Barth. If one subscribes to an interpretation of the chapter which sees no deliberate Eucharistic allusion, then the awkwardness dissolves. But if one accepts that Jesus' words here constitute a Johannine reflection on the Supper, then what emerges is a more solid biblical base for a view of it as a place where God is active in nourishing and deepening believers' union with Christ, *as well as* believers being active in receiving Christ in faith and obedience. 'Unless you eat of my flesh and drink my blood, you have no life in you.

---

[49] I am indebted to my colleague Richard Bauckham for this point.

Those who eat my flesh and drink my blood have eternal life, and I will raise them up on the last day; for my flesh is true food and my blood is true drink. Those who eat my flesh and drink my blood abide in me, and I in them' (6:53-57). When read as commentary upon the Supper these words situate our understanding of it firmly within John's wider theology of union with Christ, and appear to indicate that it is of peculiar significance for the believer's day to day 'remaining' in that union. Faith itself has no control over this; the bread from heaven is given by the Father (6:32), and it is Jesus himself, the divine Word who has been 'made flesh' (1:14), who now offers (as he once offered) his flesh and blood for our participation via the symbolism of eating and drinking (6:51-52).

Approaching Scripture as canon, such a reading encourages a more 'realistic' interpretation of Jesus' words at the last supper and Paul's statement that our eating and drinking *are* a participation in the body and blood of Christ. If we adopt this reading, then we shall understand the Eucharist as a divine, and not merely a human, act of meaning-making, and be inclined towards Calvin's rather than Barth's final account of the matter.

CHAPTER 3

Baptism in the Theology of John Calvin and Karl Barth

Anthony R. Cross

Introduction

While much that Calvin says on baptism is not original and had already been said, he nevertheless, as Geoffrey Bromiley sates, 'elaborates certain points, achieves a notable comprehensiveness, and adds the touch of elegance which distinguishes all his work. With some truth, then, he may be said to have made the definitive Reformation statement.'[1] For this and its enduring influence his baptismal theology needs to be seriously studied. Karl Barth, however, does not occupy a similar position in the history of the doctrine of baptism, though his influence in modern theology in general and Reformed theology in particular is so great that it is important to take it into account.

The present study of Calvin is based predominantly on the definitive edition of his *Institutes of the Christian Religion* (1559).[2] The reason for this is the comparative ease with which his *Institutes* can be consulted in comparison with the less accessible and multiple volumes of his commentaries, but, more importantly, because Calvin intended the *Institutes* and his commentaries to inform each other: the former giving the larger picture, dealing with doctrinal treatises (Latin *loci communes*) in which he went into greater detail[3] than in his commentaries.[4]

---

[1] G.W. Bromiley, *Historical Theology: An Introduction* (Edinburgh: T&T Clark, 1978), 279.

[2] J. Calvin, *Institutes of the Christian Religion* (trans. H. Beveridge; 2 vols; London: James Clarke, 1949) is the version used in this study.

[3] J. Haroutunian and L.P. Smith (eds), *Calvin: Commentaries* (Library of Christian Classics, 23; Philadelphia: Westminster Press, 1958), 24, note that in his commentaries 'every salient point of Calvin's theology is discussed, and is often more briefly and clearly and persuasively presented...than in the sustained and usually technical arguments of the *Institutes*'.

[4] The opposite approach is adopted by R.S. Wallace, *Calvin's Doctrine of the Word and Sacrament* (Edinburgh: Oliver and Boyd, 1953), who focuses primarily on Calvin's commentaries.

Unlike Calvin whose theology develops but does not substantially change from the first edition of the *Institutes*[5] to the last, Barth's theology underwent a major shift between his earlier writings[6] and his final work on baptism published shortly before his death.[7] The primary focus of the present study is on Barth's later work.

Given the confines of this study it is not possible, or necessary, to discuss every aspect of Calvin's and Barth's theologies of baptism or related doctrines. Rather, it will focus on four key issues—the sacramental nature of baptism, the role of the Holy Spirit, the meaning of baptism, and infant baptism—and in the process other important themes will also be examined. It should be noted that in following this outline some of the progression of their thought, particularly Barth's, is obscured, and also that it is not our purpose to compare and contrast the two writers on every issue, rather it is to highlight the main thrust of their thought on these four and related issues and, as far as possible, allow them to speak for themselves.

The Sacramental Nature of Baptism

From the outset of his discussion of the sacraments Calvin connects them to the gospel. In fact his opening words declare that they are 'Akin to the preaching of the gospel' and are 'another help to our faith'. He then offers two definitions: 'an external sign, by which the Lord seals on our consciences his promises of good-will toward us, in order to sustain the weakness of our faith, and we in turn testify our piety towards him, both before himself, and before angels as well as men'; and 'a testimony of the divine favour toward us, confirmed by an external sign, with a corresponding attestation of our faith towards Him'. Calvin then admits that neither definition differs from that offered by Augustine of 'a visible sign of a sacred thing, or a visible form of an invisible grace' (*Inst.* 4.14.1).

For Calvin the sacraments are secondary to the word,[8] in fact they derive their significance from it: 'there never is a sacrament without an antecedent promise, the sacrament being added as a kind of appendix, with the view of confirming and sealing

---

[5] To make a comparison, see J. Calvin, *Institutes of the Christian Religion: 1536 Edition* (trans. F.L. Battles; Grand Rapids: Eerdmans, rev. edn, 1986), esp. 87-123. For the development in his thought, see the discussion in J.W. Riggs, *Baptism in the Reformed Tradition* (Louisville: Westminster John Knox Press, 2002), 39-70, who also discusses Calvin's indebtedness to Luther, Zwingli and Bucer. Calvin's work is set within the broader context of developments in Reformed baptismal liturgy by H.O. Old, *The Shaping of the Reformed Baptismal Rite in the Sixteenth Century* (Grand Rapids: Eerdmans, 1992).

[6] K. Barth, *The Epistle to the Romans* (London: Oxford University Press, 6th edn, 1968 [1933]), and *The Teaching of the Church Regarding Baptism* (trans. E.A. Payne; London: SCM Press, 1948).

[7] K. Barth, *Church Dogmatics IV/4. The Christian Life (Fragment)* (Edinburgh: T&T Clark, 1969). This shift is also evident between the earlier volumes in *CD* and *CD* IV/4 and is succinctly summarized by H. Hartwell, 'Karl Barth on Baptism', *Scottish Journal of Theology* 22.1 (March, 1969), 13.

[8] On this connection, see Wallace, *Calvin's Doctrine*.

the promise'. They are an accommodation by God to human inability to discern the spiritual by using 'earthly elements to lead us to himself' (*Inst.* 4.14.3). Since 'a sacrament consists of the word and the sign' (*Inst.* 4.14.4) their purpose is to strengthen the believer's faith in God's promises. God nourishes the faith of believers by means of the sacraments 'whose only office is to make his promises visible to our eye...to be pledges of his promises' (*Inst.* 4.14.12).

Against those who would argue that all that is needed, therefore, is God's word and those things to which the sacramental signs point, Calvin employs an analogy. While an official document's seal is nothing in itself and is pointless if the document is blank, nevertheless it does confirm a genuine document's authenticity. He appeals to Romans 4.11, where Abraham's circumcision was not for justification, which came by the faith that preceded the sign, but an attestation to the covenant (*Inst.* 4.14.5).[9] Later in his defence of infant baptism he uses the example of circumcision to show that it is not necessary that what is signified always has to precede the sign (*Inst.* 4.16.21).

The purpose of both the word and the sacraments is one and the same: 'the office of the sacraments differs not from the word of God' for both 'hold forth and offer Christ to us, and, in him, the treasures of heavenly grace. They confer nothing, and avail nothing, if not received in faith, just as wine and oil...will run away and perish unless there be an open vessel to receive it' (*Inst.* 4.14.17).

'A sacrament is a seal of attestation or promise of God' (*Inst.* 4.19.2), and this leads Peter Lillback to describe Calvin's doctrine of the sacraments as 'saturated with the covenant'.[10] This is signalled from the outset in his definition of sacrament as 'a *testimony* of the divine favour toward us' and in his understanding of the sacraments as including 'all the signs which God ever commanded men to use, that he might make them sure and confident of the truth of his promises' (*Inst.* 4.14.18). However, the new covenant is superior to the old, being richer and fuller:[11] 'the New Testament flows from that covenant which God made with Abraham, and afterwards sanctioned by the hand of Moses. That which is promulgated for us in the Gospel is called the New Covenant, not because it had no beginning previously, but because it

---

[9] Egil Grislis, 'Calvin's Doctrine of Baptism', *Church History* 31 (1962), 51: 'The very center of Calvin's theology of infant baptism rests upon the view that there exists an anagogic relationship between circumcision in the Old Testament and infant baptism in the New Testament', see *Inst.* 4.16.3, which François Wendel, *Calvin: The Origins and Development of his Religious Thought* (trans. Philip Mairet; London: William Collins, 1976), 325, attributes to the influence of Martin Bucer (*Quid de baptismate infantium iuxta scripturas Dei sentiendum* [Strasbourg, 1533]).

[10] P.A. Lillback, *The Binding of God: Calvin's Role in the Development of Covenant Theology* (Texts and Studies in Reformation and Post-Reformation Thought; Grand Rapids: Baker Academic, 2001), 263. See the whole of his discussion of sacraments, 242-63.

[11] See Wallace, *Calvin's Doctrine*, 33.

was renewed, and better conditions added.'[12] For Calvin, "'The sacraments of the Mosaic law foretold Christ, ours announce him'", and "'The sacraments of the old law only promised a Saviour, whereas ours give salvation'" (*Inst.* 4.14.26).

Chief of the Old Testament sacraments, for Calvin, is circumcision, but there were also the various purifications and sacrifices of the Mosaic law. The grounds on which he equates the sacraments of the two testaments is that both have the same end in view, specifically 'to direct and almost lead us by the hand to Christ...like images to represent him and hold him forth' (*Inst.* 4.14.20). Later he insists that the meaning of the covenant does not change in the new covenant (*Inst.* 4.16.10), rather the difference between the sacraments of both testaments is that 'our sacraments [baptism and the Lord's supper[13]]...present Christ the more clearly to us' (*Inst.* 4.14.22).

The young Barth agreed with Calvin that baptism is a sacrament.[14] This is nowhere clearer than on Romans 6.3-5:

> baptism is a sacrament of truth and holiness; and it is a sacrament, because it is the sign which directs us to God's revelation of eternal life and declares, not merely the Christian "myth", but—the Word of God. It does not merely signify eternal reality, but is eternal reality, because it points significantly beyond its own concreteness. Baptism mediates the new creation: it is not itself grace, but from first to last a means of grace. As the question which men put to God is always also His answer to it; as human faith is enclosed invisibly by the faithfulness of God; so also the human act of baptism is enclosed by that action of God on behalf of men which it declares.[15]

But later Barth changed his mind.[16] For the mature Barth there is only one sacrament, Jesus Christ himself.[17] The two editors of *CD* IV/4 explain that for Barth

---

[12] Calvin on Ezek. 16.60, *Ezekiel and Daniel* (Calvin's Commentaries; Grand Rapids: Associated Publishers and Authors, n.d.), 254.

[13] '[A]fter Christ was revealed, sacraments were instituted, fewer in number, but of more august significancy and more excellent power' (*Inst.* 4.14.26, a view he owed to Augustine). Calvin recognizes the laying on of hands and ordination as sacraments, but not as 'among ordinary sacraments', namely baptism and the Lord's supper, on the grounds that they apply only to one part of the church, the clergy (*Inst.* 4.14.20). Calvin rejected the other five sacraments recognized by the Roman Catholic Church: confirmation, penance, extreme unction, orders and marriage (see *Inst.* 4.19.1–37).

[14] E.g., K. Barth, *The Theology of John Calvin* (Grand Rapids: Eerdmans, 1995 [German original, *Die Theologie Calvins* (1922)]), 172-77, 280-83. Here, the young Barth focuses on the 1536 edition of the *Institutes* and Calvin's other early work.

[15] Barth, *Romans*, 192. See also, Barth, *Teaching of the Church*, 12, 16 and 29.

[16] The shift resulted from the work of his eldest son Markus Barth, *Die Taufe—ein Sakrament? Ein exegetische Beitrag zum Bespräch über die kirchliche Taufe* (Zürich: Evangelischer Verlag Zollikon A.G., 1951), whose detailed exegetical study of New Testament baptism convinced his father to abandon the sacramental understanding of baptism which is evident in his earlier work (*CD* IV/4, x) and forms the basis for the detailed exegetical sections which occur throughout *CD* IV/4. For a detailed summary of

'only in the incarnation of the Son of God in the man Jesus is there a real sacramental unity between God and man'. Baptism and the Lord's supper are human responses to Christ and, therefore, 'not themselves sacraments since they are not recurrent actualisations of the incarnation or means through which supernatural power is infused into believers'.[18]

Barth's rejection of the sacramental nature of baptism (*CD* IV/4, 101-30) occurs in the section on the meaning of baptism. Baptism, he announces, is a step towards Christ and a response to the baptism of the Spirit (*CD* IV/4, 101). As a human and not a divine work 'Baptism responds to a mystery, the sacrament of the history of Jesus Christ, of His resurrection, of the outpouring of the Holy Spirit. It is not itself, however, a mystery or sacrament', and as such he opposes the 'ancient and overwhelmingly strong ecclesiastical and theological tradition' which sees it as a sacrament (*CD* IV/4, 102). Barth then critically examines and rejects the various sacramental views of Roman Catholicism, Lutheranism and the Reformed tradition, including Calvin, and their claims to biblical support (*CD* IV/4, 102-107). This he follows with a study of the terms 'mystery/sacrament' (*CD* IV/4, 108-109), concluding that the New Testament never uses the concept of 'mystery/sacrament' to denote baptism, but rather it is used, in the singular and plural, 'exclusively with reference to God's work and revelation in history, not to the corresponding human reactions' (*CD* IV/4, 108). This leads to the conclusion that any sacramental understanding of baptism takes away the freedom of people to respond to God (*CD* IV/4, 106).

In all this, Barth recognizes that we must not oppose scripture and so he seeks to undergird his anti-sacramentalism with a firm exegetical base. This he does by employing two hermeneutical principles: that scripture is its own interpreter and that all exposition is interpretation. Before he turns to his exegesis of the New Testament references and allusions to baptism he sets out three preliminary considerations. First, in the New Testament the act of baptism was so impressive and incisive an event that references to words and concepts such as water, river, pool, fountain, bath or washing would have reminded authors, hearers and readers of baptism. Secondly,

---

Markus Barth's work, see Dale Moody, *Baptism: Foundation for Christian Unity* (Philadelphia: Westminster Press, 1967), 64-71.

[17] J.E. Colwell, 'Baptism, Conscience and the Resurrection: A Reappraisal of 1 Peter 3.21', in S.E. Porter and A.R. Cross (eds), *Baptism, the New Testament and the Church: Historical and Contemporary Studies in Honour of R.E.O. White* (*Journal for the Study of the New Testament*, Supplement Series, 171; Sheffield: Sheffield Academic Press, 1999), 226, describes as a 'quite remarkable reversal' Barth's concern, which is evident throughout the whole of the *CD*, that affirms 'the human and the divine in their connectedness and non-contradiction'. Colwell, 226 n. 58, shows that in *CD* IV/2, 54-55, Barth was happy to speak of 'the one sacrament of the incarnation of Christ as the basis for the "concurrence" of "a divine and human, an outward and inward, a visible and invisible operation and reception of grace in the 'sacramental' actions of baptism and the Lord's Supper"'.

[18] G.W. Bromiley and T.F. Torrance, 'Editors' Preface', *CD* IV/4, v.

references to baptism, with the exception of Matthew 28.19, occur in ethical contexts (note the subtitle of *CD* IV/4 'The Christian Life'). He dismisses the contribution of the references to baptism in Acts as simply serving 'to emphasise and illustrate the story' of the progress of the gospel.[19] Thirdly, he presupposes that the New Testament makes the same distinction he makes between Spirit- and water-baptism (*CD* IV/4, 110-11). Then, following a lengthy examination of the New Testament passages (*CD* IV/4, 111-27), he concedes[20] that 'some of the passages could be taken sacramentally' but this 'is no more than a possibility'. Other passages, however—though notable here by their absence are Acts 2.38 and 1 Corinthians 12.13—'more or less completely' rule out a sacramental interpretation and others force the exegete to a different conclusion (*CD* IV/4, 127-28), namely, that 'baptism is not a sacrament' but rather 'a true and genuine human action which responds to the divine act and word' (*CD* IV/4, 128). In affirming that baptism is a human action and not a sacrament, Barth was aligning himself Huldrych Zwingli. While critical of some aspects of Zwingli's baptismal theology,[21] he sought to ground his own anti-sacramentalism on more firm theological grounds and describes his own position as neo-Zwinglian (*CD* IV/4, 128-30).

The Role of the Holy Spirit

It is the work of the Holy Spirit that makes Calvin's sacramental theology possible. He rejected the prevalent notion that the sacraments are effective *ex opere operato*. While sacraments were instituted by Christ for 'the increase and confirmation of faith', this efficacy is not inherent in them for they only fulfil their intention 'when accompanied by the Spirit, the internal Master'. If the Spirit is absent then the sacraments can achieve no more than sunshine on the eyes of the blind or sounds spoken to the deaf. There is a hint here that the sacraments are only for the elect, those who can see and hear, and this is later used by Calvin in his covenantal argument for infant baptism. Later Calvin quotes with approval Augustine's

---

[19] He follows this with the dubious statement that 'Baptism was plainly an element in the life of the New Testament community *rather than its teaching*' (*CD* IV/4, 111, italics added), not least given its role in Mt. 28.19 in making disciples, and Barth completely ignores the importance of catechesis and the catechumenate in the early church. See, e.g., E. Glenn Hinson, *The Evangelization of the Roman Empire: Identity and Adaptability* (Macon: Mercer University Press, 1981), ch. 12, 'Baptism: Making Disciples'.

[20] In his later discussion of baptism as an act of renunciation and committal (see below) Barth makes another concession: 'Baptism is the oath taken by them [the candidate and the community] in concert. If the original sense of the Latin *sacramentum* is observed, it might be called a sacrament from this standpoint. In baptism they take up their posts in the ranks of the *militia Christi*... In baptism they say to God and to one another that they acquiesce in this, and that, thus equipped and led, they will do the best they can in their different functions. This is the pledge which the Christian has made in baptism in answer to God's pledge to him' (*CD* IV/4, 161).

[21] See n. 26 below.

contention that it is only in the elect that the sacraments accomplish what they represent (*Inst.* 4.14.15): if not received in faith sacraments confer and accomplish nothing. The effective work of the Spirit and the elect are brought together a few sentences later when he asserts, 'The Holy Spirit, whom the sacraments do not bring promiscuously to all, but whom the Lord specially confers on his people, brings the gifts of God along with him, makes way for the sacraments, and causes them to bear fruit' (*Inst.* 4.14.17).[22]

In the thought of the medieval scholastics an inherent power was ascribed to the sacraments whereby they *caused* righteousness and salvation. Calvin refuted this by appealing to Augustine's distinction between the sacrament itself, the sign (Latin *signum*), and the substance/matter (Latin *res*) of the sacrament, and argued that the two must not be confused. The sign points to the substance which he identifies unequivocally as Christ, 'since in him they have their whole solidity, and out of him promise nothing'. Their efficacy lies, therefore, in the way they cherish, confirm and increase 'the true knowledge of Christ, so as both to possess him more fully, and enjoy him in all his richness' and this is the case 'when that which is there offered is received by us in true faith' (*Inst.* 4.14.16).

All the power, then, lies in the Spirit's operation by means of the sacraments: 'I ascribe the whole energy to him, and leave only a ministry to them'. Without the agency of the Spirit this ministry is 'empty and frivolous', but 'when he acts within, and exerts his power, it is replete with energy' (*Inst.* 4.14.9).

From the beginning of *CD* IV/4 Barth makes his position clear in two consecutive and contrasting statements:

> A man's turning to faithfulness to God, and consequently to calling upon Him, is the work of this faithful God which, perfectly accomplished in the history of Jesus Christ, in virtue of the awakening, quickening and illuminating power of this history, becomes a new beginning of life as his baptism with the Holy Spirit.

This he sets in opposition to

> The first step of this life of faithfulness to God, the Christian life, is a man's baptism with water, which by his own decision is requested of the community and which is administered by the community, as the binding confession of his obedience, conversion and hope, made in prayer for God's grace, wherein he honours the freedom of this grace (*CD* IV/4, 2).

Barth, therefore, sees baptism as twofold: a work of God (Spirit-baptism) and a person's work performed in worship (water-baptism). This dichotomy (which will be examined in this and the following section, and which marks a radical departure from

---

[22] Grislis, 'Calvin's Doctrine of Baptism', 57: 'Calvin's doctrine of baptism simply cannot be separated from his doctrine of election without departing from both. In other words, in so far as the doctrine of election is a very central theme of Calvin's thought, the tensions which surround it are consistently reflected also in his other doctrines.' See the whole of this article, 46-65.

the Reformed tradition[23]) is the key to understanding Barth's theology of baptism, and *CD* IV/4 is divided into the discussion of these two baptisms. But it is important to note that water-baptism is dependent on the prior baptism with the Spirit: 'Baptism can and should be administered on the basis of the gift and in reception of the Holy Spirit with a look at the living Christ' (*CD* IV/4, 158).

The first and shorter of the two subsections deals with the baptism of the Spirit (*CD* IV/4, 3-40). Barth separates these two baptisms because of his concern to preserve the freedom and sovereignty of God, along with its corollary that no human action can manipulate the divine work of salvation. For these reasons Barth rejects a temporal coincidence of Spirit- and water-baptism.

As we have said, baptism with the Spirit is the work of God. The new life has its foundation in God (*CD* IV/4, 3-4), more specifically '[i]n the history of Jesus Christ' (*CD* IV/4, 17). This 'divine change in virtue of which the human decision can be made and the Christian life is actually founded' is 'the work of the Holy Spirit'. Barth summarizes these two matters in a single sentence: 'In the work of the Holy Spirit the history manifested to all men in the resurrection of Jesus Christ is manifest and present to a specific man as his own salvation history' (*CD* IV/4, 27). In this work of the Spirit a person 'is liberated to run to the God whom he previously sought to evade, to be faithful to the God to whom he was previously unfaithful' (*CD* IV/4, 28-29). The 'power of the divine change…is the power of their baptism with the Holy Ghost' (*CD* IV/4, 30). The content of this act of God which constitutes the beginning of the Christian life is summed up in five points. First, the beginning of the Christian life 'takes place in a direct self-attestation and self-impartation of the living Jesus Christ, in His active Word of power which goes forth…to specific men in the work of the Holy Ghost'. Here there is a hint of the doctrine of election (*CD* IV/4, 31) and this is followed by mention of the covenant: 'the fact that a man becomes a Christian, and as such a member of the holy people of the covenant, is something which he owes… directly to the Lord of this people, the Master, whom the community and all its members seek to serve… The Church is neither author, dispenser, nor mediator of grace and its revelation.' But

> this divine change at once makes possible and demands the corresponding human decision. Nevertheless, the human decision is not that in and with which, or in virtue of which, the divine change takes place. In other words, the baptism of the Spirit certainly calls for the baptism with water which is requested of the community and administered by it, which is received by the man who accepts the Word of Jesus Christ. *But it is not identical with this, nor is water baptism identical with it.* Baptism with the Spirit does not take place in a man either with or through the fact that he receives water baptism. He also becomes a Christian in his human decision, in the fact that he requests and receives baptism with water. But he does not become a Christian through his human decision or his water baptism… Jesus

---

[23] Old, *Shaping*, 284: 'The Reformers insisted that according to Scripture there was one baptism. To divide the sacrament into a baptism of water and a baptism of the Spirit…was misleading.' See also 178, 222 and 263.

Christ Himself, and He alone, makes a man a Christian (*CD* IV/4, 32-33, italics added).

Secondly, Spirit-baptism is 'a form of the grace of God' which is 'the active and actualising grace of God'. But this cannot be said of water-baptism. The baptism of the Spirit 'is more than a reference and indication through image and symbol. It is more than an offer and opportunity.' It is 'effective, causative, even creative action on man and in man. It is, indeed, divinely effective, divinely causative, divinely creative.' This leads Barth to admit that '[h]ere, if anywhere, one might speak of a sacramental happening in the current sense of the term. It cleanses, renews and changes man truly and totally.' This divine change, a person's baptism with the Spirit, 'is not half grace, or half-adequate grace; it is whole grace and wholly adequate grace' (*CD* IV/4, 33-35).[24]

The Meaning of Baptism

Calvin opens his chapter on baptism with the assertion that it 'is the initiatory sign by which we are admitted to the fellowship of the Church, that being ingrafted into Christ we may be accounted children of God' (*Inst.* 4.15.1). T.H.L. Parker observes that 'by which' agrees in the Latin with 'the sign' not 'initiation' so that it is the substance of the sacrament of baptism not the performance of the rite which admits into the church.[25]

As with the other sacrament, the purpose of baptism is twofold: that it might contribute to the believer's faith in God and be a confession to other people (*Inst.* 4.15.1; cf. 4.14.13). The contribution baptism makes to faith is threefold. First, it has been appointed by God to be a sign and evidence of purification, 'a kind of sealed instrument by which he assures us that all our sins are so deleted, covered, and effaced, that they will never come into his sight, never be mentioned, never imputed'.[26] This washing and salvation are not effected or caused by the water; rather

---

[24] The final three points do not need to detain us long. Thirdly, this grace demands obedient gratitude; fourthly, it incorporates the person baptized in the Spirit into the communion of saints; and, fifthly, it is a new beginning that moves towards the future (*CD* IV/4, 35-40).

[25] T.H.L. Parker, *Calvin: An Introduction to His Thought* (London: Geoffrey Chapman, 1995), 150.

[26] It is interesting that it is here, rather than earlier in ch. 14 when he was discussing his definition of 'sacrament', that Calvin rejects the definition offered by, for example (though not named), Zwingli, of a 'badge and mark by which we profess our religion before men, in the same way as soldiers attest their profession by bearing the insignia of their commander'. This was based on the Latin use of *sacramentum* as an oath of allegiance such as that made by a soldier to his commanding officer on their enrolment and thus was an oath of allegiance to Christ. What Calvin says is lacking in this definition is that it does not include 'the principal thing in baptism; and that is, that we are to receive it in connection with the promise' of Mk 16.16 that whoever believes and is baptized will be saved (*Inst.* 4.15.1). See, e.g., H. Zwingli, *Of Baptism*, in G.W.

it is only 'that the knowledge and certainty of such gifts are perceived in this sacrament'. The 'only purification which baptism promises is by means of the sprinkling of the blood of Christ, who is figured by water from the resemblance to cleansing and washing' (*Inst.* 4.15.1–2).

Secondly, baptism 'shows us our mortification in Christ and new life in him' (so Rom. 6.3-4; cf. Calvin's earlier treatment of baptism as the external means which effects repentance and regeneration, *Inst.* 3.3–7). This involves the imitation of Christ and a dying to one's lusts (*Inst.* 4.15.5). Thirdly, baptism assures us that we are not only ingrafted into Christ's death and life but also 'so united to Christ himself as to be partakers of all his blessings'. Jesus was baptized by John 'that he might have it in common with us as the firmest bond of union and fellowship which he deigned to form with us' and we become children of God as we put on Christ in baptism (cf. Gal. 3.27). The fulfilment of our baptism is Christ who is the 'proper object of baptism' because 'all the divine gifts held forth in baptism are found in Christ alone' (*Inst.* 4.15.6).

However, baptism not only looks back to the saving work of Christ (*Inst.* 4.15.2), but also forward. He declares that those who have been baptized, at whatever time in their life, 'are washed and purified once for the whole of life'. He therefore rejects the medieval belief that post-baptismal sin negates the grace of baptism and the resulting practice of leaving baptism till one's deathbed because of the belief that post-baptismal sin cannot be forgiven. To the contrary, 'as often as we fall, we must recall the remembrance of our baptism, and thus fortify our minds, so as to feel certain and secure of the remission of sins' (*Inst.* 4.15.3).

The second goal of baptism is discussed only briefly and is to serve as a public confession, 'a mark by which we openly declare that we wish to be ranked among the people of God' to worship the one God and 'by which...we publicly assert our faith' (*Inst.* 4.15.13).

From the purpose of baptism, Calvin turns to how it is to be used and received. However much it is given to elevate, nourish and confirm faith it is, above all, to be received 'as from the hand of its author, Christ', fully persuaded 'that it is he himself who speaks to us by means of the sign; that it is he himself who washes and purifies us...; who makes us the partakers of his death, destroys the kingdom of Satan, subdues the power of concupiscence...[making us] one with himself, that being clothed with him we may be accounted the children of God'. Baptism, he states, is an analogy or similitude that 'in corporeal things [the washing of our

---

Bromiley (ed.), *Zwingli and Bullinger* (Library of Christian Classics, 24; Philadelphia: Westminster Press, 1953), 131. On the sacraments in general and baptism in particular, see W.P. Stephens, *The Theology of Huldrych Zwingli* (Oxford: Clarendon Press, 1986), esp. 180-217, and *Zwingli: An Introduction to His Thought* (Oxford: Clarendon Press, 1992), 76-93; U. Gäbler, *Huldrych Zwingli: His Life and Work* (Philadelphia: Fortress Press, 1986), 125-31; and T. George, 'The Presuppositions of Zwingli's Baptismal Theology', in E.J. Furcha and H.W. Pipkin (eds), *Prophet, Pastor, Protestant: The Work of Huldrych Zwingli after Five Hundred Years* (Pittsburgh Theological Monographs, n.s.; Eugene: Pickwick Publications, 1984), 71-87.

bodies and immersion by which we are surrounded in water] we are to see spiritual' things, 'since the Lord has been pleased to represent them by such figures'. In seeing these things 'he leads us to the actual object, and effectually performs what he figures' (*Inst.* 4.15.14).

Calvin then launches an assault on the Anabaptists, many of the arguments of which recur in his 1544 treatise against them.[27] Of the claim that God's promises have to be received by faith which precedes baptism, Calvin agrees and implicitly resorts to his covenant theology, arguing that at the time of their baptism as infants it 'profited us nothing, since in us the offered promise, without which baptism is nothing, lay neglected'. But when by the grace of God they came to repent they then embraced the promise in faith (*Inst.* 4.15.17). Calvin also repudiates the Anabaptists' defence of rebaptism on the basis of Paul's rebaptism of the disciples of John (Acts 19.3, 5; *Inst.* 4.15.18) by arguing that, far from being different from Christian baptism, John's baptism is 'the very same as that which was afterwards delegated to the apostles' (*Inst.* 4.15.7).[28]

Calvin opposes the Donatists of Augustine's day and the Anabaptists of his own[29] who argued that the validity of a sacrament depended on the worthiness of the administrator on the grounds that baptism is received 'as from the hand of Christ', and therefore its 'dignity neither gains nor loses by the administrator' (*Inst.* 4.15.16). Calvin dismisses as absurdities the Anabaptists who rebaptized those baptized by the Roman Catholic Church ('in the Papacy') on the grounds that 'we were initiated not into the name of any man, but into the name of the Father, and the Son, and the Holy Spirit' and 'that baptism is not of man, but of God, by whomsoever it may have been administered', whether they were ignorant of God and piety or despisers. For Calvin it is clear that 'if baptism was of God, it certainly included in it the promise of forgiveness of sin, mortification of the flesh, quickening of the Spirit,

---

[27] J. Calvin, *Brief Instruction for Arming All the Good Faithful Against the Errors of the Common Sect of the Anabaptists* (trans. and ed. B.W. Farley; Grand Rapids: Baker Academic, 1982), 36-158, esp. 'The First Article: On Baptism', 44-55. This was written is response to the Anabaptists' Schleitheim Confession (1527). See Farley's 'Editor's Introduction', 13-35; W. Balke, *Calvin and the Anabaptist Radicals* (trans. W. Heynen; Grand Rapids: Eerdmans, 1981); Karl H. Wyneken, 'Calvin and Anabaptism', *Concordia Theological Monthly* 36.1 (1965), 18-29; and Galen Johnson, 'The Development of John Calvin's Doctrine of Infant Baptism in Reaction to the Anabaptists', *Mennonite Quarterly Review* 73.4 (October, 1999), 803-23. On the Anabaptists in general, including Calvin's dealings towards them, see George H. Williams, *The Radical Reformation* (Sixteenth Century Essays and Studies, 15; Kirksville: Truman State University Press, 3rd edn, 2000), *passim*.

[28] See D.C. Steinmetz, *Calvin in Context* (Oxford: Oxford University Press, 1995), 157-71.

[29] Cf. D.F. Wright, 'Donatist Theologoumena in Augustine? Baptism, Reviviscence of Sins, and Unworthy Ministers' and 'The Donatists in the Sixteenth Century', in D.F. Wright, *Infant Baptism in Historical Perspective: Collected Studies* (Studies in Christian History and Thought; Milton Keynes: Paternoster, 2007), 105-15 and 212-25 respectively.

and communion with Christ'. That baptism 'ought to be celebrated in the assembly of the godly' does not mean it loses its efficacy if it 'is partly defective' (*Inst.* 4.15.16). However, despite these assertions, Calvin categorically rejects the administration of baptism by laymen or women, even in the case of clinical and deathbed baptism (*Inst.* 4.15.20), and he seeks to justify this restriction on the grounds that the administration of both sacraments belong solely to 'the ministerial office', and this is not open to women (*Inst.* 4.15.20-22).

At this point Calvin denies that baptism is necessary even in the case of someone who is in danger of imminent death; for such notions are based on the dogma that baptism is necessary for salvation. This is especially so in the case of '[o]ur children' — by which he means the children of Christians, the elect — for 'God declares that he adopts for his own when he promises that he will be a God to us, and to our seed after us. In this promise their salvation is included' (*Inst.* 4.15.20). So even children who die before 'an opportunity of immersing them in water, are not excluded from the kingdom of heaven'. Unless this position is accepted, he believes 'great injury is done to the covenant of God', for it suggests that the covenant is weak and this cannot be as the covenant's effect is not dependent on either baptism or any accessories. The covenant is antecedent, baptism being added as a seal, not giving efficacy to the promise of God but merely confirming it. It follows, then, that the children of believers are not baptized in order to become God's children, but are received into the church 'by a formal sign, because, in virtue of the promise, they previously belonged to the body of Christ'. Again Calvin asserts the primacy of faith over the secondary sign, baptism: 'When we cannot receive them [the sacraments] from the Church, the grace of God is not so inseparably annexed to them that we cannot obtain it by faith, according to his word' (*Inst.* 4.15.22).[30]

Calvin also briefly discusses the mode of baptism, but he seems to do so reluctantly and his conclusions are pragmatic and practically motivated rather than scripturally based. He confesses that '[i]n regard to the external symbol, I wish the genuine institution of Christ had been maintained'. He then dismisses the traditions of giving a candle, chrism, the use of spittle and 'other follies' as 'theatrical pomp' that 'dazzle the eyes of the simple, and dulls their minds'. They are later and complicating additions to the simplicity of the institution of Christ. 'From our experience of them [these later additions], let us learn that there is nothing holier, or better, or safer, than to be contented with the authority of Christ alone'. There is, here, an inconsistency in Calvin's theology, for while he admits that 'baptize' means 'to immerse' and that this was the form employed in the primitive church, he nevertheless pragmatically declares that whether total immersion is used, once or three times, or whether sprinkling is the mode adopted, 'is not of the least

---

[30] This is wholly consistent with Calvin's theology which is well summarized by Wendel, *Calvin*, 316: 'With whatever insistence Calvin underlines the usefulness of the sacraments, considered as instruments that the Spirit of God makes use of in order to reach us and bring us to Christ, still, the deepest requirements of his theology, which necessitate the rejection of any subordination of the divinity to earthly contingencies, compel him to exclude any essential union between the sacramental elements and grace.'

consequence' for 'churches should be at liberty to adopt either, according to the diversity of climates' (*Inst.* 4.15.19), and this from the man who condemned the Anabaptists for being unscriptural (*Inst.* 4.16.22).[31] It is difficult not to see here an example of special pleading by Calvin who elsewhere insisted that the church is subordinate to the word of God.[32]

With all that we have seen of Calvin's understanding of the meaning of baptism, what he says about the sacraments in relation to the doctrine of the church will make more sense. The church is made up of all the elect and this is witnessed to in baptism. Calvin summarizes Titus 3.5: "'God saves us by His mercy and He has given us a symbol and pledge of this salvation in baptism, by admitting us into His Church and engrafting us into the Body of His Son.'"[33] Ronald Wallace summarizes Calvin's teaching on the sacraments and union with the body of Christ: 'The aspect of the Gospel which the sacraments chiefly bring before our eyes in clarifying for us the promises given in the Word is that of our mystical union with the body of Christ.' The nature of this union is 'such a spiritual mystery...that it is incomprehensible to the natural mind', even to the minds of believers. Therefore God has appointed two sacraments whose chief purpose is 'to depict visibly this particular mystery, so that by their use we may come to know and understand better the nature of our union with Christ'.[34] Christ has done all that is needful for salvation through his incarnation, life, death and resurrection, but these benefits cannot be available unless we are brought into union with his body. This God does

---

[31] Calvin, 'First Article: On Baptism', 45: 'I do not ask antiquity to legitimate anything for us *unless it is founded on the Word of God*' (italics added). The problem for Calvin was that he was not prepared to accept that there are other possible and legitimate interpretations of scripture on baptism as on many subjects.

[32] See Wallace, *Calvin's Doctrine*, 'Scripture as the sole authority in the life of the Church', 99-101, and the examples from Calvin's writings cited there. However, Old, *Shaping*, 264-82, argues that immersion was not the only New Testament mode of baptism and also for the appropriateness of sprinkling. See also I. Howard Marshall, 'The Meaning of the Verb "Baptize"', in Stanley E. Porter and Anthony R. Cross (eds), *Dimensions of Baptism: Biblical and Theological Studies* (*Journal for the Study of the New Testament*, Supplement Series, 234; Sheffield: Sheffield Academic Press, 2002), 8-24, argues that while immersion was the general rule, affusion, and even sprinkling, were also practised.

[33] J. Calvin, *The Second Epistle of Paul the Apostle to the Corinthians and the Epistles to Timothy, Titus and Philemon* (Calvin's Commentaries; Edinburgh: Oliver and Boyd, 1964), 382.

[34] Wallace, *Calvin's Doctrine*, 143-44. For recent detailed discussions of baptism and union with Christ, see Mark A. Garcia, *Life in Christ: Union with Christ and Twofold Grace in Calvin's Theology* (Studies in Christian History and Thought; Milton Keynes: Paternoster, 2008), esp. ch. 4, 'Christ and the Spirit: Sacraments, Salvation, and the Strata of Union with Christ', 149-95, and *passim*; and William B. Evans, *Imputation and Impartation: Union with Christ in American Reformed Theology* (Studies in Christian History and Thought; Milton Keynes: Paternoster, 2008), 7-41.

by his Spirit[35] through his pre̶ ̶ ̶ ̶ ̶g̶race which is received by t̶h̶e̶ elect in faith, and baptism outwardly shows t̶h̶a̶t̶ ̶t̶h̶e̶ ̶p̶e̶r̶s̶on is a member of the body of Christ: 'as far as God is concerned, it always holds true that baptism is an ingrafting into the body of Christ, because everything that God shows forth to us in baptism, He is prepared to carry out, so long as we, on our part, are capable of it'.[36] In short, the nature of baptism is to connect us to the body of Christ.

Along with the other magisterial reformers, Calvin believed that the sacraments were identity-giving; that they were the 'marks of the church' (Latin *notae ecclesiae*). His definition of the visible church is that 'Wherever we see the word of God sincerely preached and heard, wherever we see the sacraments administered according to the institution of Christ, there we cannot have any doubt that the Church of God has some existence' (*Inst.* 4.1.9). Wallace notes that '[s]o closely does Calvin identify incorporation in Christ with incorporation in the Church that he regards the activity of the Church towards its individual members as being identical with the action of Christ towards the individual. The response of the individual to the ministry of the Church is thus identical with his response towards Christ.'[37] The ministry of preaching the word and administering the sacraments, then, are for Calvin the prerogative of the church: 'apart from the body of Christ and the fellowship of the godly, there can be no hope of reconciliation with God'.[38]

Finally, Calvin notes the relationship between the two sacraments are that baptism mainly bears witness to the believer's initiation into the body of Christ, while the Lord's supper is a sign of continuing in this union.[39]

The second and longer of Barth's two sub-sections deals with water-baptism (*CD* IV/4, 41-213). For the greater part of this (*CD* IV/4, 41-164, 195-213), he focuses on New Testament baptism, namely, the baptism of believers (that is, a free and responsible human act), not the later practice of infant baptism, and he presupposes all that he has said on Spirit-baptism. This is important for all that he says on baptism is what is now called believer's baptism and presupposes the prior divine act, Spirit-baptism.

Barth begins by acknowledging the two elements which form the foundation of the Christian life: the objective and the subjective, the former corresponding to Spirit-baptism, the latter to water-baptism. 'Only as (1) the divine change makes

---

[35] *Inst.* 4.17.10: '[W]hat our mind does not comprehend let faith conceive—viz. that the Spirit truly unites things separated by space'.

[36] J. Calvin on 1 Cor. 12.13, *The First Epistle of Paul the Apostle to the Corinthians* (Calvin's Commentaries; Edinburgh: Oliver and Boyd, 1960), 265.

[37] Wallace, *Calvin's Doctrine*, 235. In this sense, Calvin agrees with Cyprian's declaration (*Epistle* 73.21) that 'there is no salvation outside the church' (see Cyprian, 'Letter 73', in S.L. Greenslade [trans. and ed.], *Early Latin Theology: Selections from Tertullian, Cyprian, Ambrose and Jerome* [Library of Christian Classics, 5; Philadelphia: Westminster Press, 1956], 169).

[38] J. Calvin on Isa. 33.24, *Isaiah* (Calvin's Commentaries, 3; Grand Rapids: Associated Publishers and Authors, n.d.), 448.

[39] Wallace, *Calvin's Doctrine*, 150.

possible and demands human decision as conversion from unfaithfulness to faithfulness to God, and only as (2) this human decision has its origin wholly and utterly in the divine change, does there come about the foundation of the Christian life and the existence of a man who is faithful to God.' Neither element should be either separated or confused with the other. Spirit-baptism does not render water-baptism unnecessary, rather it 'demands it', and this, he notes, applies to infant or believer's baptism: 'Whether it looks back to this or forward to it [Spirit-baptism]' (*CD* IV/4, 41).

The beginning of the Christian life is one of obedience and begins with baptism: 'he does it because he is invited and commanded to do it by the grace of God... [H]e does it in obedience, as the first exemplary work of faith' (*CD* IV/4, 43-44). Barth then explains what baptism is: a bodily washing with water; it parallels Jewish proselyte baptism; it is a self-evident custom in the New Testament church; it is not a prominent theme in the New Testament (the only major discussion being that of John's baptism which he equates with Christian baptism[40]), and when it is mentioned it is within ethical contexts; it is indebted to God's work; and it is administered by the community of God's people (*CD* IV/4, 43-50).

Barth's remaining discussion of water-baptism is in three parts. First, the basis of baptism is Christ's command (Mt. 28.19), behind which stands Christ's own baptism by John. Christ's baptism marked the beginning of the fulfilment of his own mission, confessed both God and humanity, and began his work as mediator in obedience to his Father and in solidarity with humanity (*CD* IV/4, 50-68).

Secondly, the goal of baptism (*CD* IV/4, 68-100) lies beyond the act of baptism in water to 'God's act of reconciliation in Jesus Christ through the Holy Spirit, God's act of judgment and grace, of salvation and revelation', namely, Spirit-baptism. 'Baptism is administered in the Christian community with a view to this divine act'. For those 'who newly join the community' it is 'the first concrete step of faith, love, hope and service...by which they publicly and bindingly confess and commit themselves to their recognized and acknowledged Lord as Mediator of the covenant, and also to the mutual fellowship of Christians' (*CD* IV/4, 72).

Barth's final section deals explicitly with the meaning of baptism (*CD* IV/4, 100-213). After rejecting the sacramental nature of baptism, he emphasizes three things. First is the form of the act of baptism. As Christian baptism immersion is 'more properly the indication of such a washing' and a 'reflection of the divine act to which, as a human action, it looks back, from which it comes, to which it looks forward and towards which it also moves'. Integral to it—and which differentiates it from other similar actions—is 'the word which is spoken in it as a response to the deed of the God who acts and speaks in Jesus Christ through the Holy Ghost' and the fact that it takes place publicly (*CD* IV/4, 130; cf. 144: 'As man's conversion to God this is to be done in a way which is visible not only to God but also to his

---

[40] In his extensive discussion of John's baptism (*CD* IV/4, 75-89), however, Barth notes that while the goal of John's baptism is the same as Christian baptism (see below) there are differences between them which can be largely understood in terms of what was promised in the former is now fulfilled in the latter.

people and all men. It is thus to be done as a wholly human act in the human sphere, and it is binding as such').

Secondly, there is the social character of baptism. It 'involves both [the] one who baptises and [the] one who is baptised', the former being an acknowledged member of the community, the latter is being acknowledged as such in the act of baptism (*CD* IV/4, 130-31). Later Barth states that the community and its representatives 'baptise only those who according to their understanding and judgment are appointed and ready for baptism' (*CD* IV/4, 132-33). Thirdly, it is a free action, an act of obedience to God and an act of hope. 'Obedience to God can only be free obedience. Obligatory and enforced hope is not hope in God. Hope in Him can only be free hope' (*CD* IV/4, 131-32).

So what happens in this act that makes it Christian baptism? Corresponding to God's act, but distinct from it, water-baptism, Barth reiterates, is an act of obedience 'from the standpoint of its basis, for in it they obey the divine command', and hope 'from the standpoint of its goal, for in it they grasp the divine promise' (*CD* IV/4, 134). It is also an act of conversion 'in the sense that it gives concrete and binding emphasis to the fact that the community in relation to the candidate, and the candidate in relation to the community, is engaged in leaving an old path and entering upon a new' (*CD* IV/4, 135). But this act of conversion is also to God: 'a man's conversion, and its confirmation in baptism, are his conversion and its confirmation in his relation to God' (*CD* IV/4, 139).

Baptism, then, 'is the first step of the way of a human life which is shaped and stamped by looking to Jesus Christ. It is the first step which the baptised person who has come to see Jesus Christ takes along with the community' (*CD* IV/4, 149) and this is preceded by instruction in the Christian faith and conduct (*CD* IV/4, 151-52). While this instruction in the form of the catechumenate can only be proved from the second century it is, nevertheless, 'materially justifiable, legitimate and imperative on the ground that the New Testament witnesses plainly presuppose it. They count on it that prior to baptism candidates have not only been addressed by the proclamation of the Gospel but also that they have in some measure heard and received it, that they have more or less understood it and take it to heart' (*CD* IV/4, 152).

Barth, then, summarizes what is involved in this free and responsible human act of water-baptism. It is an act of obedience to the baptismal command of Jesus, though this is not to suggest that it is essential to salvation (*CD* IV/4, 153-58). It is also an act of renunciation and committal that responds to Christ's work of remission and renewal (*CD* IV/4, 158-63). He concludes,

> Baptism, then, is the twofold answer of man to the divine justification and sanctification, cleansing and renewal, which have taken place for him and been revealed to him in Jesus Christ. It is the corresponding renunciation and pledge. Hence water baptism, not in and for itself, but as a first model which is to be followed throughout the Christian life, is the human decision which follows the divine change effected for man, and which corresponds to the history of Jesus Christ and baptism with the Holy Ghost (*CD* IV/4, 162).

And all this takes place within 'the sphere of the covenant of grace' in which 'we find dialogue and dealings between two who stand in clear encounter, God on the one side and man on the other, God and all men concerned, so that, while these men can only follow what God says and does, they are all active subjects for their part, and they can and should follow with their own speech and action on the basis of their own responsible decision' (*CD* IV/4, 163).

Barth closes *CD* IV/4 declaring that Jesus Christ 'is both the origin of baptism and also the future opened up beyond it; he is thus the meaning of the act of baptism' (*CD* IV/4, 195). It is a 'human action in which the participants look beyond themselves and what they do into the future' and to Christ. 'The meaning of baptism consists, then, in the fact that the community and its candidates let Jesus Christ be the future of their action, that they act in hope in Him. We have to see that what is really at issue here is the hope of these men in *Him* and their own *action* in this hope. We have to know that what they do in baptism, what is the meaning of baptism as their act. This is why we could not simply refer to the fact that it is commanded'. An 'expectation which is idle, passive and inactive cannot possibly be expectation of Jesus Christ and His action' (*CD* IV/4, 206-208). And finally, Barth sees baptism as a prayer of hope 'which is confident of being heard' and 'means an end of all idle gaping, the strongest possible break with all neutrality or passivity, and going to it with the freest resolution' (*CD* IV/4, 209). It is an epiclesis, a calling on the name of the Lord and '[h]erein and as such it is a saving act' (*CD* IV/4, 212). Barth closes, 'As asking and praying which is ventured in hope in Jesus Christ, in obedience, it is a constitutive action which makes a beginning and which is a model for all that follows. It is truly the first step of the Christian life in retrospect of which ethical reflection and ethical admonition are possible, necessary, permitted and commanded at every step which follows' (*CD* IV/4, 213).

Infant Baptism

Calvin devotes the whole of *Institutes* 4.16 to a defence of infant baptism. Throughout the Anabaptists are in view, 'frenzied spirits' who have raised and continue to raise a 'great disturbance in the Church on account of paedobaptism'. He denounces their claims for the scriptural basis of antipaedobaptism[41] as specious, an introduction of 'human presumption and depraved curiosity' and without 'a thread to hang on', whereas a true sacrament rests 'on the sure foundation of the word of God' (*Inst.* 4.16.1). In short, infant baptism is of divine origin.

---

[41] For various collections of Anabaptist writings on baptism, see George H. Williams and Angel M. Mergal (eds), *Spiritual and Anabaptist Writers* (Library of Christian Classics, 25; Philadelphia: Westminster Press, 1957); Michael G. Baylor (ed.), *The Radical Reformation* (Cambridge Texts in the History of Political Thought; Cambridge: Cambridge University Press, 1991); and Daniel Liechty (ed.), *Early Anabaptist Spirituality: Selected Writings* (Classics of Western Spirituality; Mahwah: Paulist Press, 1994). For an overview, see Rollin S. Armour, *Anabaptist Baptism: A Representative Study* (Studies in Anabaptist and Mennonite History, 11; Scottdale: Herald Press, 1966).

Calvin rejects the Anabaptists' belief in the radical discontinuity between the old and the new covenants, the former being a material covenant, the latter a spiritual one (*Inst.* 4.16.11) and denounces the Anabaptist contention that there is a radical distinction between God's physical children under the old covenant and his spiritual ones under the new (*Inst.* 4.16.12). He then argues that following Christ's resurrection God does not fulfil his promise to Abraham's descendants allegorically but literally so that it is wrong to spiritualize a carnal promise to the point that physical infants merely symbolize newborn infants in Christ, and he thereby maintains his equation of circumcision and infant baptism (*Inst.* 4.16.15). While there are differences between the two they are insubstantial, for behind both signs, circumcision and baptism, lie 'the promise of the paternal favour of God, of forgiveness of sins, and eternal life. And the thing figured is one and the same—viz. Regeneration'. The result of this is that 'everything applicable to circumcision applies also to baptism, excepting always the difference in the visible ceremony'. Therefore, Calvin can say, 'it is incontrovertible, that baptism has been substituted for circumcision, and performs the same office' (*Inst.* 4.16.4, which is based on his prior argument in 4.16.3; see also 4.14.21, 23–24; and his later development of these arguments in 4.16.10–16). As the circumcision of Jewish children shows that they are members of the covenant people of God along with their parents, so, therefore, 'if the covenant remains firm and fixed, it is no less applicable to the children of Christians in the present day, than to the children of the Jews under the Old Testament. Now, if they are partakers of the thing signified, how can they be denied the sign? If they obtain the reality, how can they be refused the figure? The external sign is so united in the sacrament with the word, that it cannot be separated from it... Since, then, the word of baptism is destined for infants, why should we deny them the sign, which is an appendage of the word?' (*Inst.* 4.16.5).

Support for this position Calvin finds in Jesus' blessing of the little children (Mt. 19.13), arguing that though he does not baptize them he says '"of such is the kingdom of heaven"'. This, to Calvin, means that they enjoy what baptism signifies and it therefore makes no sense to him to withhold 'the symbol of our communion and fellowship with Christ' (*Inst.* 4.16.7). He forcefully asserts that infant baptism 'receives strong support from Scripture' and completely rejects the argument that because there is no specific mention of it in scripture it is therefore invalid. Infants, he argues, were not expressly excluded from the accounts of household baptism in Acts (e.g. 16.15 and 32) and neither were women excluded from the Lord's supper, something which is only mentioned in the early patristic rule of faith. He then scornfully proclaims, 'The assertion which they disseminate among the common people, that a long series of years elapsed after the resurrection of Christ, during which paedobaptism was unknown, is a shameful falsehood, since there is no writer, however ancient, who does not trace its origin to the days of the apostles' (*Inst.* 4.16.8).

He follows this with a brief outline of the benefits which result from the observance, both to parents and their infants: the parents are assured that God's covenant promises incorporate their children; it makes the infants the object of greater interest to the rest of the church; and, in adulthood, it urges them to earnestly seek to serve God. Of any who would oppose this teaching, Calvin pronounces that 'God will take vengeance on every one who despises to impress the symbol of the covenant on his child', for such is 'a rejection, and... abjuration of the offered grace' (*Inst.* 4.16.9).

Calvin then counters Anabaptist objections against the continuity of the two covenants by reprising many of the arguments he has already made (*Inst.* 4.16.10–16) and proceeds to an examination of infants and faith. With his covenantal theology and understanding of election behind him, Calvin rejects as inadequate the claim that infants are to be regarded as children of Adam until they are old enough for 'the second birth', for to be children of Adam means that 'they are left in death'. But 'Christ bids them be brought to him...that he may quicken them...[and make] them partners with himself'. And though it is beyond human comprehension, 'infants who are to be saved (and that some are saved at this age is certain) must, without question, be previously regenerated by the Lord' (*Inst.* 4.16.17). This argument is supported by the examples of the Holy Spirit's activity in John the Baptist and Jesus himself, both of whom were sanctified, respectively, 'from his mother's womb' (Lk. 1.15) and 'from earliest infancy' (*Inst.* 4.16.17–18). But while preaching is the normative means by which faith comes, there are those whom God 'has called and endued with the true knowledge of himself, by internal means, by the illumination of the Spirit, without the intervention of preaching' (*Inst.* 4.16.19). Though infants are incapable of repentance and faith because God gave circumcision as 'the sign of repentance and faith' to infants, children are baptized 'for future repentance and faith', so while these 'are not yet formed in them, yet the seed of both lies hid in them by the secret operation of the Spirit' (*Inst.* 4.16.20). Elect children who die in infancy, therefore, having received the sign of regeneration are renewed 'by the incomprehensible energy of his Spirit', while those elect children who do grow into adulthood will 'be animated to greater zeal for renovation, the badge of which they will learn that they received in earliest infancy, in order that they might aspire to it during their whole lives' (*Inst.* 4.16.21).

Calvin then makes a surprising claim, but one which he is forced to because of his argument to date: 'in adults, the receiving of the sign ought to follow the understanding of the meaning, yet...a different rule must be followed with children' (*Inst.* 4.16.21; cf. 4.16.24). Infant baptism, then, is for the children of Christians, while adults coming to faith who were not baptized in infancy are to be instructed in the faith before baptism[42] (cf. *Inst.* 4.16.23). But for those who die without baptism Calvin appeals to John 5.24 and claims that the passage shows that 'we must not deem baptism so necessary as to suppose that every one who has lost the opportunity of obtaining it has forthwith perished' (*Inst.* 4.16.26), and this is possible for him because of what he has previously argued about the importance of the thing signified not the sign itself.

---

[42] Calvin, 'First Article: On Baptism', 46 and 53.

Finally for our purposes,[43] Calvin deals with the objection that infants should no more be given baptism than they should communicate in the eucharist, remarking that scripture drew significant distinctions between the two sacraments. First, baptism is 'a kind of entrance, and as it were initiation into the Church, by which we are ranked among the people of God, a sign of our spiritual regeneration', whereas the Lord's supper 'is intended for those of riper years, who…are fit to bear solid food'. Secondly, in scripture Christ makes no distinction of age for baptism, while he does not admit all to partake of the supper, but restricts it 'to those who are fit to discern the body and blood of the Lord, to examine their own conscience, to show forth the Lord's death, and understand its power' (cf. 1 Cor. 11.28). Thirdly, circumcision, and therefore baptism, was intended for infants, while the Passover, which corresponds to the Lord's supper, was eaten only by those 'of an age sufficient to ask the meaning of it' (*Inst.* 4.16.30; cf. Ex. 12.26).

To this point in *CD* IV/4 Barth has been concerned with what is to be found in the New Testament, namely believer's baptism (though he does not use this term, *CD* IV/4, 164), but now his attention shifts to infant baptism (*CD* IV/4, 164-95[44]). 'From the end of the second century…the picture begins to become blurred and ambiguous with respect to those baptised by the community, and then in and from the 5th century it changes generally, and as a rule unequivocally, into a very different picture'.[45] This point marks a separation between the baptizing community in the persons of the clergy and the candidates, the former baptizing on their own authority, without presupposing or appealing to the responsibility or decision of the latter. This 'ecclesiastical baptism came to resemble less and less the corresponding event at the Jordan and in the New Testament communities'. Candidates were now recruited more and more from the children of 'so-called Christian families' and less so from the pagan world. The result was that '[t]here triumphed the idea of a specific circle of human beings who, as the physical progeny of people now called Christians, could and should be baptised unhesitatingly without asking concerning their desire or their own decision, as though it were simply a matter of disposing of them and marking

---

[43] Calvin devotes the closing sections of the chapter to twenty objections to the work of the anti-trinitarian radical Michael Servetus (*Inst.* 4.16.31–32), in whose execution Calvin was to play a major part, see, e.g., T.H.L. Parker, *John Calvin* (Tring: Lion, 1987), 138–46.

[44] Barth deals with infant baptism in his earlier *Teaching of the Church*, a useful study on which is J.E. Colwell, 'Alternative Approaches to Believer's Baptism (from the Anabaptists to Barth)', *Scottish Bulletin of Evangelical Theology* 7 (Spring, 1989), 13-17.

[45] Barth opposes the defences of infant baptism by O. Cullmann (*Baptism in the New Testament* [Studies in Biblical Theology, 1; London: SCM Press, 1950]), and Joachim Jeremias (*Infant Baptism in the First Four Centuries* [Library of History and Doctrine; London: SCM Press, 1960], and *The Origins of Infant Baptism: A Further Study in Reply to Kurt Aland* [Library of History and Doctrine; London: SCM Press, 1963]), implicitly agreeing with the refutation of such arguments for the New Testament practice of infant baptism by Kurt Aland (*Did the Early Church Baptize Infants?* [Library of History and Doctrine; London: SCM Press, 1963]).

them at will... In this practice the baptised person has his place as an object of the community's action but there can be no question of any renunciation and pledge as an act of his own free decision. Hence he has no function, no active part. He is not a subject, and baptism cannot be understood seriously as a common work' (*CD* IV/4, 164-65). Such an historical development is clearly at odds with Barth's theology of baptism in which '[t]here has to be resolve, decision. There has to be the will and act of those who take part. There has to be a transition which in that knowledge is taken freely and responsibly' (*CD* IV/4, 138). This cannot be taken for a person by the church or godparents, but only by the person him- or herself.

Barth states that a proper defence of infant baptism requires four things. First, its necessity must be shown and he believes both Luther and Calvin fail to do this. He shows that Calvin's doctrines of baptism and infant baptism are two different series of reflections and arguments which give the 'almost unavoidable impression that the doctrine of infant baptism is not an original element in the organism of theological knowledge but is contingent to it', and he notes that the fourth book of the *Institutes* is not consistent with book three (*CD* IV/4, 169-70).

Secondly, any defence of infant baptism needs to be presented calmly, unlike Luther and Calvin (*CD* IV/4, 170-71). It is here that Barth asks of Calvin, 'How does it come about that the Reformer has more than twice as much to say about infant baptism than he has in exposition of baptism itself?' The answer lies in his fierce denunciations of infant baptism's opponents, and he adds, 'anger and abuse are a fairly sure sign that a man is not certain that he is right' (*CD* IV/4, 171).

Thirdly, defenders of infant baptism should not abandon the premises from which they start (*CD* IV/4, 171-75). Calvin is strongly criticized for doing this. According to his own arguments, baptism is a work of grace in so far as it mediates knowledge, is a visible pledge which makes the faith of those taught by the Holy Spirit certain, and it strengthens and increases faith. Barth points out that Calvin's defence of infant baptism is also inconsistent with his 'full definition of faith': 'it is a firm and sure knowledge of the divine favour toward us, founded on the truth of a free promise in Christ, and revealed to our minds, and sealed on our hearts, by the Holy Spirit' (*Inst.* 3.2.7; cf. 3.2.4). In order to defend infant baptism Calvin has to qualify his position on faith's origin in the hearing of God's word (cf. Rom. 10.17). Now he adds the qualification that this is only the ordinary means alongside of which there may be other ways, which include the faith of parents and sponsors, and that there is within children a seed of repentance and faith by virtue of the operation of the Spirit.[46] Calvin further entangles himself in difficulties by defining both a sacrament and baptism as a two-sided event involving God and people. The final inconsistency is when Calvin introduces the understanding of baptism in terms of circumcision, something that is not even mentioned in *Inst.* 4.15, and in so doing he obliterates completely the active human side of baptism. Barth rounds off with a stinging indictment: 'It does not speak too well for the theological integrity of the cause that so great a theologian can aid himself at the decisive point only by forgetting,

---

[46] See also Barth's rejection of this argument from Calvin, *CD* IV/4, 187.

passing over, or at any rate keeping silence on his own presuppositions' (*CD* IV/4, 173-75). Earlier Barth had severely criticized another inconsistency in Calvin's thought:

> It should be noted that in addition to its significance as a divine work and gift Calvin also sought to ascribe to baptism a complementary meaning of a very different kind, namely, as the initial act which attests, pledges and confesses the Christian faith before God, angels and men. He developed this aspect, however, with surprising brevity, and when he was concerned to establish or defend infant baptism he usually preferred not to speak of it at all (*CD* IV/4, 105).

Fourthly, infant baptism should prove what it has to prove and not something else (*CD* IV/4, 175-78). While Barth agrees with Calvin on the 'material unity of the old and new covenants in spite of their formal distinction' and that, as Lord of both economies, Christ is Lord of both circumcision and baptism, there are also differences between the covenants.[47] For example, unlike Israelite circumcision, Christian baptism cannot be based on the physical descent of the candidate: 'That it can and should be, is what had to be proved. But Calvin has not proved it. He, too, has evaded or skipped proving the decisive minor premiss, which is in his case that everything which applies to circumcision applies also to baptism' (*CD* IV/4, 177-78). Later, Barth accepts that the children of Christian parents are privileged, but rejects any ideas of 'cheap grace' for they, too, 'have still to enter in at the strait gate and tread the narrow way. No one is a true and living member of this people...merely by living in its midst'. This only happens when a person is awakened by the Spirit who is the power of the work and word of Christ, when they are born again, created anew: 'the Christian life will and can begin only on the basis of their own liberation by God, their own decision' (*CD* IV/4, 183-84).[48] '[T]he personal faith of the candidate is indispensable to baptism' (*CD* IV/4, 186).[49]

---

[47] See Petrus J. Gräbe, *New Covenant, New Community: The Significance of Biblical and Patristic Covenant Theology for Contemporary Understanding* (Milton Keynes: Paternoster Press, 2006), 203.

[48] Barth also dismisses the appeal to Jesus' blessing of the infants in Mk 10.14 and par. as justification for infant baptism. Rather, 'Why should not even genuinely pious parents be content with the promise which is given to them and their children? Why should they not stick to the fact that the "Suffer the little children"...applies to their children too?' (*CD* IV/4, 193; cf. also 176: 'Jesus promised in advance to all children access to Himself and therewith to the kingdom of God, and that as the Saviour of all He blessed and embraced all children—certainly the children of Christian parents, but not these alone').

[49] Barth agrees then with Tertullian's dictum, 'People are not born Christians, they have to be made into Christians', *Apology* 18. Barth, *CD* IV/4, 184: 'The Christian life cannot be inherited as blood, gifts, characteristics and inclinations are inherited. No Christian environment, however genuine or sincere, can transfer this life to those who are in this environment. For these, too, the Christian life will and can begin only on the basis of their own liberation by God, their own decision.' Barth opposes the covenantal

Barth then launches into his criticisms of Reformation teaching. The exegesis of New Testament passages do not provide explicit evidence for infant baptism (*CD* IV/4, 179-85); notions of vicarious faith and real infant faith have little cogency (*CD* IV/4, 185-89); and while infant baptism might well declare the objectivity and omnipotence of God's grace this is not sufficient for its continuation (*CD* IV/4, 189-90). There is, according to Barth, a 'crisis in baptism' which is 'the crisis in infant baptism. The doctrine of infant baptism is forced to try to think through the relation between baptism and faith. But when it does, no matter how it twists and turns, it inevitably finishes up in hopeless blind alleys. The one obscurity and confusion calls forth the other, and follows the other' (*CD* IV/4, 189).

After dismissing other minor arguments used to support infant baptism (*CD* IV/4, 190-94), Barth exclaims, 'Enough of this matter!... Theology...cannot share with the Church the responsibility which the Church has taken on itself by introducing this practice, and which it constantly takes on itself by maintaining. *This practice is profoundly irregular!*' A few sentences later he remarks, 'even theology has not yet realised by a long way that infant baptism is an *ancient ecclesiastical error*' (*CD* IV/4, 194, italics added).

While Barth comes out strongly against the indiscriminate practice of infant baptism and calls for its reform (*CD* IV/4, x-xi) and systematically disassembles the argument for it, he nowhere either contests or rejects the validity of infant baptism.[50]

Conclusion

It is clearly neither necessary nor possible to engage with Calvin and Barth on every issue, but some attempt must be made to comment on their views in the light of and contribution to contemporary research and to do so on the four main issues we have studied.

The Sacramental Nature of Baptism

The major weakness of Barth's anti-sacramentalism is that his study is based on the radical distinction between Spirit- and water-baptism and, in this regard, his study simply demonstrates what it presupposes.[51] While he strives to be exegetical and theological his failure to show convincingly that sacramentalism has no or, at best,

---

view of Calvin that the children of Christian families are legitimate candidates for infant baptism on the basis of that fact. He observes (*CD* IV/4, 165), 'There triumphed the idea of a specific circle of human beings who, as the physical progeny of people now called Christians, could and should be baptised unhesitatingly without asking concerning their desire or their own decision...'

[50] Cf. Hartwell, 'Karl Barth on Baptism', 27.

[51] See John E. Colwell, *Living the Christian Story: The Distinctiveness of Christian Ethics* (Edinburgh: T&T Clark, 2001), 149-57.

only a shaky biblical foundation is unconvincing.[52] As we have seen, his position is undermined by his strategic omission of Acts 2.38 and 1 Corinthians 12.13[53] at a key stage in his exegetical justification of anti-sacramentalism. Barth might well dismiss the contribution of the book of Acts to a doctrine of baptism, but its importance and interpretation sacramentally has recently been demonstrated by Stanley E. Porter.[54] Other important studies of the New Testament passages have also demonstrated the legitimacy of sacramental interpretations.[55] And while the distinction of Spirit- and water-baptism has been advocated in the biblical studies of James Dunn and Gordon Fee,[56] the argument to the contrary continues to be overwhelming and, to my mind, convincing.[57] Herbert Hartwell questions Barth's distinction between the two baptisms: 'seeing that in [Spirit-baptism] man's co-operation is required in respect of the receiving and accepting of the Holy Spirit and in [water-baptism] man cannot make his free responsible decision except by faith and thus only by God's grace and in the power of the Holy Spirit'. Further, '[e]ven if Barth's premise is accepted that faith must precede Baptism, man also needs faith to make the decision demanded by Barth as an integral part of Baptism and that faith is the work of the Holy Spirit in man and thus God's work.'[58] In the end, then, Barth was not able to free himself from the sacramental significance of baptism.

---

[52] The most thorough exegetical study of New Testament baptism in the last fifty years and which continues to be of great value, is G.R. Beasley-Murray, *Baptism in the New Testament* (Exeter: Paternoster, 1972 [1962]), who concludes that 'The Apostolic writers...view the [baptismal action] as a symbol with power, that is, a sacrament', 263.

[53] To deny that 1 Cor. 12.13 is a text which supports a sacramental understanding of baptism on the basis that the New Testament only witnesses to the separation of Spirit- and water-baptism is simply to beg the question.

[54] S.E. Porter, 'Baptism in Acts: The Sacramental Dimension', in A.R. Cross and P.E. Thompson (eds), *Baptist Sacramentalism* (Studies in Baptist History and Thought, 5; Carlisle: Paternoster Press, 2003), 117-28.

[55] E.g., Beasley-Murray, *Baptism*, 93-125; L. Hartman, *'Into the Name of the Lord Jesus': Baptism in the Early Church* (Studies of the New Testament and its World; Edinburgh: T&T Clark, 1997), 127-45, e.g., 139, where he concludes that the author of Luke-Acts is 'among other New Testament theologians to whom baptism is the sacrament of faith'; and S.K. Fowler, *More Than a Symbol: The British Baptist Recovery of Baptismal Sacramentalism* (Studies in Baptist History and Thought, 2; Carlisle: Paternoster Press, 2001), 178-95.

[56] J.D.G. Dunn, *Baptism in the Holy Spirit: A Re-examination of the New Testament Teaching on the Gift of the Spirit in Relation to Pentecostalism Today* (London: SCM Press, 1970), e.g., 127-31; and G.D. Fee, *God's Empowering Presence: The Holy Spirit in the Letters of Paul* (Peabody: Hendrickson, 1994), 176, 180 and 854.

[57] See Cross, 'Spirit- and Water-Baptism in 1 Corinthians 12.13', in Porter and Cross (eds), *Dimensions of Baptism*, 120-48; E. Ferguson, *The Church of Christ: A Biblical Ecclesiology for Today* (Grand Rapids: Eerdmans, 1996), 193-94 n. 45; K. McDonnell and G.T. Montague, *Christian Initiation and Baptism in the Holy Spirit: Evidence from the First Eight Centuries* (Collegeville: Liturgical Press, 2nd edn, 1994).

[58] Hartwell, 'Karl Barth on Baptism', 28-29; see *CD* IV/4, 212-13, on baptism as an epiclesis.

Of greater relevance today, then, is Calvin's sacramentalism. It is only possible to examine several aspects of this and the subjectivity of doing so has not escaped me. While Barth's neo-Zwinglianism appeals to many, for example, many baptists,[59] there are, however, an increasing number of baptist scholars who see in baptism, and other sacramental acts (the eucharist, preaching, ministry and ordination) the working of God by his Spirit in believers' lives and the church.[60] For instance, Stanley K. Fowler demonstrates that Barth's objections to baptismal sacramentalism on the grounds of the objectivity and finality of the work of Christ in his death and resurrection are false 'because no form of sacramentalism asserts that baptism saves apart from, or in the same sense as, the events of the gospel. The debate over sacramentalism is not about the ultimate cause of human salvation; it is about the instrumental cause(s), specifically the role of baptism as an instrument.'[61]

But perhaps the most eloquent defence of this position has been made by Emil Brunner who coined the term 'the divine–human encounter'. Brunner contends that the subject–object antithesis originated in Greek philosophy and is a misunderstanding of the New Testament.

> In baptism it is God, first and sovereign, who acts, who forgives sin, who cleanses man and regenerates him. But man too acts in baptism. He allows this cleansing of himself to take place, he lets himself be drawn into the death of Christ, he confesses his faith and his attachment to Christ. Baptism is not merely a gift to man, but also an active receiving and confession on the part of man. Indeed baptism, precisely as this free confession of man, is the stipulation for the individual's joining the Church. Baptism is not only an act of grace, but just as much an act of confession stemming from the act of grace.

When baptism is enjoined in the New Testament it is regarded as a 'two-sided happening' which involves what Brunner terms 'personal correspondence'. Baptism is not merely a gift to humanity, but also an active receiving and confession on the part of humanity.[62]

---

[59] The term 'baptists' is used here in the sense of those inheritors of the Radical Reformation, otherwise known as the Free Church or Believers' Church, see J.W. McClendon, *Systematic Theology: 1. Ethics* (Nashville: Abingdon, 1988), 19, and, therefore, not just those commonly denominated as Baptists. K. Roy, *Baptism, Reconciliation and Unity* (Carlisle: Paternoster Press, 1997), 11-12, among others, uses the term credobaptists.

[60] See A.R. Cross, *Baptism and the Baptists: Theology and Practice in Twentieth-Century Britain* (Studies in Baptist History and Thought, 3; Carlisle: Paternoster, 2000); Fowler, *More Than*; and Cross and Thompson (eds), *Baptist Sacramentalism* and the forthcoming second volume also edited by Cross and Thompson, *Baptist Sacramentalism 2* (Studies in Baptist History and Thought, 25; Milton Keynes: Paternoster, 2008).

[61] Fowler, *More Than*, 193.

[62] E. Brunner, *The Divine–Human Encounter* (London: SCM Press, 1944), 128.

The Role of the Holy Spirit

Much has already been said or intimated about the role of the Spirit in baptism, but it is the recognition of this role which allows us to see baptism as an instrumental means of grace. Calvin's sacramental theology majored on the work of the Spirit, while the mature Barth obfuscated it by his separation of the divine and human actions. But the role of the Spirit has recently been taken up by Clark Pinnock who, rejecting any dualism of matter and spirit, notes that today we tend to 'perceive Spirit as something ghostly, intangible, impalpable, numinous, lacking concreteness. There is resistance to linking the Spirit to the material' with the result that many 'shy away from physical manifestations of the divine presence and expect intangible, not real-life effects of the Spirit'.[63] It must not be thought that baptism is an empty sign. Calvin argues that though administered by the hands of men, the baptism of water is not a vain act 'because Christ who ordered that to be done will do His part to baptize us with the Spirit'.[64] Ronald Wallace comments that the sacraments are not merely 'speaking symbols' but signs 'not merely of something that happened once in the past but of a present activity of God which is taking place in the midst of, and alongside, the human action'.[65] This has great relevance to theology and the church today and opens further avenues of exploration of God's immanental work by his Spirit.

The Meaning of Baptism

Early on in Calvin's discussion of sacraments he says they are an accommodation by God to humanity's inability to discern spiritual things.[66] Much contemporary thought on the sacraments has lapsed into a form of gnosticism with its matter–spirit dualism, which is to be found in the writings of both Zwingli and

---

[63] C.H. Pinnock, *Flame of Love: A Theology of the Holy Spirit* (Downers Grove: InterVarsity Press, 1996), 119, and esp. his discussion of 'Spirit and Church', 113-47. See also A.R. Cross, 'Being Open to God's Sacramental Work: A Study in Baptism', in S.E. Porter and A.R. Cross (eds), *Semper Reformandum: Studies in Honour of Clark H. Pinnock* (Carlisle: Paternoster Press, 2003), 355-77.

[64] J. Calvin on Acts 1.5, *The Acts of the Apostles 1–13* (Calvin's Commentaries; Edinburgh: Oliver and Boyd, 1965), 28.

[65] Wallace, *Calvin's Doctrine*, 160.

[66] Cf. Calvin, *Inst*. 4.15.14: 'in corporeal things we are to see spiritual', though Calvin immediately qualifies this, 'not that such graces are included and bound in the sacrament, so as to be conferred by its efficacy, but only that by this badge the Lord declares to us that he is pleased to bestow all these things upon us'. However, Fowler, *More Than*, 194, sees the connection between the divine and human actions in baptism more closely while still avoiding any notions of *ex opere operato*: 'If the Spirit is given to all those who believe, as both Jesus (John 7:37-39) and Paul (Rom. 8:9) affirm, and baptism is the vehicle by which faith comes to expression, then it is appropriate to think in terms of the bestowal of the Spirit *through* baptism', italics added.

Barth.⁶⁷ The rediscovery of God's use of the material as a means of grace has been taken up and developed to great effect by a number of scholars, including Pinnock⁶⁸ and Paul Fiddes. Fiddes recognizes that sacraments are 'pieces of earthly stuff that are meeting places' with God. They are 'outward and visible signs of an inward and spiritual grace', and as such there is no need to think of 'grace' as 'a kind of substance or divine fluid, but as God's gracious coming and dwelling with us. They are signs which enable us to participate in the drama of death and resurrection which is happening in the heart of God.' Fiddes' aim is to enable us to see 'that the world is a sacrament in the sense of being a place of encounter with God'.⁶⁹

In recent years the issue of baptism has come increasingly to be subsumed under the discussion under the broader topic of 'conversion-initiation'. This particular term was coined by James Dunn,⁷⁰ but applies to a change in emphasis that can be traced back to the mid-twentieth century.⁷¹ Here baptism is seen as part of the process of becoming a Christian, a journey or process.⁷² While neither Calvin nor Barth discuss this, Calvin's appeal to metonymy as a way of understanding baptism is an important observation which can help us understand New Testament baptism. For example, in John 1.32 Calvin notes that the dove does not merely represent the Spirit but is called 'the Spirit'. This is an example of metonymy by which 'the name of the thing is suitably transferred to the sign'.⁷³ On Galatians 3.27, F.F.

---

⁶⁷ E.g., Barth, *CD* IV/4, 129.

⁶⁸ Pinnock, *Flame*, 120: 'Sacraments exist simply because we are bodily creatures inhabiting a material world... Created reality is richly imbued with sacramental possibilities', and this leads him to conclude that 'anything can mediate the sacred' with the result that '[t]here is in theory no limit to the number of [sacraments]'; and his 'The Physical Side of Being Spiritual: God's Sacramental Presence', in Cross and Thompson (eds), *Baptist Sacramentalism*, 8-20.

⁶⁹ P.S. Fiddes, *Participating in God: A Pastoral Doctrine of the Trinity* (London: Darton, Longman and Todd, 2000), 281 and 292 respectively. See also his 'Baptism and Creation', in P.S. Fiddes (ed.), *Reflections on the Water: Understanding God and the World through the Baptism of Believers* (Regent's Study Guides, 4; Oxford: Regent's Park College, 1996), 47-69 (also in his *Tracks and Traces: Baptist Identity in Church and Theology* [Studies in Baptist History and Thought, 13; Carlisle: Paternoster Press, 2003], 107-24).

⁷⁰ Dunn, *Baptism*, 4.

⁷¹ See A.R. Cross, '"One Baptism" (Ephesians 4.5): A Challenge to the Church', in Porter and Cross (eds), *Baptism*, 173-75.

⁷² See P.S. Fiddes, 'Baptism and the Process of Christian Initiation', *Ecumenical Review* 54.1 (January–April, 2002), 48-65, and the literature cited there.

⁷³ J. Calvin on Jn 1.32, *The Gospel according to John 1–10* (Calvin's Commentaries; Edinburgh: Oliver and Boyd, 1959), 34, and especially his comment that 'this symbolism [metonymy] is usual in the sacraments'; cf. *Inst*. 4.14.12. Wallace, *Calvin's Doctrine*, p. 162, explains: 'The elements in the earthly action are spoken of as being identical with the heavenly realities which they represent, and what is done by man in figure is spoken of as being simultaneously done by God in reality.' On metonymy, see also *Inst*. 4.14.12. Jaroslav Pelikan, *Reformation of Church and Dogma (1300–1700)*

Bruce writes, 'If it is remembered that repentance and faith, with baptism in water and reception of the Spirit, followed by first communion, constituted one complex experience of Christian initiation, then what is true of the experience as a whole can in practice be predicated of any element in it. The creative agent, however, is the Spirit.'[74] Recognition of this also helps us to understand the lack of any standardization in Luke's accounts of conversions in Luke-Acts.

While both Calvin and Barth appeal to covenantal theology in support of their theologies of baptism, for Calvin, where it is more prominent, it in fact forms the basis for his defence of infant baptism. This, however, has been challenged by, among others, Paul Jewett who criticizes the argument from the covenant on the grounds that 'it stresses the covenant idea as the unifying concept of redemptive history to the point of suppressing the *movement* of redemptive history, a movement from the age of anticipation and promise to the age of realization and fulfillment'. While he applauds paedobaptist affirmations 'of the centrality and perpetuity of the covenant concept as a fundamental category of biblical revelation' he nevertheless cautions that it must not overshadow the truth that 'the old covenant made with the Jewish people has now become the new covenant in Jesus Christ'.[75]

In his discussion of the contribution of baptism to faith Calvin states that it shows us our mortification in Christ. This ethical dimension is also highlighted in Barth's title for *CD* IV/4 'The Christian *Life*' and he rightly points out that references to baptism in the New Testament almost always occur in ethical contexts. This dimension of baptism is important and will profit both baptists and infant baptists in their thinking about baptism. So, for example, Brian Haymes writes,

> in baptism the believer is united with Christ, and all other believers in the Church, and from this there follow moral implications. It is an act of faith with moral

---

(The Christian Tradition: A History of the Development of Doctrine, 4; Chicago: University of Chicago Press, 1984), 194: 'To Calvin it was an "axiom" that "whenever sacraments are being dealt with, it is usual for the name of the things signified to be transferred by metonymy to the sign." [see J. Calvin, *Replies to Joachim Westphal* 1, *CR* 37:36]. Metonymy, he explained, is not the same as parable or allegory, but implies that God is representing himself "truly" by it.' For other discussions of Calvin's use of metonymy, see Lillback, *Binding of God*, 244-45 on the sacraments, and 259-60 on the presence of Christ in the eucharist.

[74] F.F. Bruce, *The Epistle to the Galatians: A Commentary on the Greek Text* (New International Greek Testament Commentary; Exeter: Paternoster Press, 1982), 186. In my 'Spirit- and Water-Baptism', 137-48, and 'The Evangelical Sacrament: Baptisma Semper Reformandum', *Evangelical Quarterly* 80.3 (July, 2008), 195-217, I have refined this and argue that synecdoche is the more accurate term, though the two tropes are frequently identified.

[75] P.K. Jewett, *Infant Baptism and the Covenant of Grace* (Grand Rapids,: Eerdmans, 1978), 235-36. It is also worth noting that Jewett has also, to the minds of many, successfully dispelled the equation of circumcision and baptism, see 85-104, 229-30 and 238-40. See also John P.W. Hunt, 'Colossians 2:11-12, the Circumcision/Baptism Analogy, and Infant Baptism', *Tyndale Bulletin* 41.2 (November, 1990), 227-44.

consequences. The believer is baptized in the name of the Trinity, into the life and mission of God revealed in Christ. This is a work of God, before baptism, at baptism and following baptism. Therefore baptism is more than a moral act alone, a particular expression of following Jesus. The consequence of baptism implies further moral obligations. Yet they are not reduced to a moral 'ought' but rather spring from the fundamental relationship which baptism asserts. It would be reducible to that if there were no corresponding work of God. But, in fact, salvation is a moral miracle of faith, a work of God and humankind.[76]

In the work of both Calvin and Barth the whole issue of hermeneutics is essential. Barth is convinced that the passages he examines (though as we have noted he conveniently omits two key passages) demonstrate the anti-sacramentalism of the New Testament, though he has to concede the possibility that some texts could be interpreted sacramentally. Calvin, on the other hand, was not prepared to accept that there are other possible and legitimate interpretations of scripture on baptism as on many subjects. This is nowhere clearer than in his condemnation of the opponents of infant baptism, of whom the Reformation historian William Estep writes: 'Within the Reformation no group took more seriously the principle of *sola Scriptura* in matters of doctrine and discipline than did the Anabaptists.'[77] The reason behind Calvin's rejection of the Anabaptists' hermeneutics was not primarily due to their exegesis but because of their rejection of three core doctrines in his theological system: free will, predestination and the cause of salvation.[78] There is, here, a salutary note for contemporary paedobaptists and antipaedobaptists and the need for a greater respect to be shown to those of other traditions whose interpretation of scripture differs from their own.

Infant Baptism

This brings us to infant baptism. Neither Calvin's nor Barth's theologies of infant baptism follow on from their expositions of New Testament baptism. On this, Calvin is less consistent than Barth (see the latter's criticisms of the former[79]),

---

[76] B. Haymes, 'The Moral Miracle of Faith', in Porter and Cross (eds), *Dimensions*, 328. See also M.O. Fape, *Paul's Concept of Baptism and Its Present Implication for Believers: Walking in Newness of Life* (Toronto Studies in Theology, 78; Lewiston: Edwin Mellen Press, 1999). That teaching on Christian lifestyle and moral instruction occupied a key position in pre-Constantinian baptismal catechesis (but that from the fourth century onwards the teaching became increasingly doctrinal), see E. Ferguson, 'Catechesis and Initiation', in A. Kreider (ed.), *The Origins of Christendom in the West* ((Edinburgh: T&T Clark, 2001), 229-68

[77] W.R. Estep, *The Anabaptist Story* (Grand Rapids: Eerdmans, rev. edn, 1975), 140.

[78] So Farley, 'Editor's Introduction', 26.

[79] D.F. Wright, 'Development and Coherence in Calvin's *Institutes*: The Case of Baptism (*Institutes* 4:15–4:16)', in *Infant Baptism*, 226-37, argues for a more coherent interpretation of the relationship between Calvin's theology of baptism and his defence of infant baptism.

though Barth does not carry through his dismantling the case for it nor does he offer realistic ways for it to be reformed, other than to imply that indiscriminate infant baptism should be abandoned. This poses the challenge to advocates of infant baptism to provide stronger theological arguments for its continuation.

Historically Calvin is inaccurate when he claims that infant baptism was practised in the New Testament: 'there is no writer, however ancient, who does not trace its origin to the days of the apostles' (*Inst.* 4.16.8). He can only do this by appealing to the likes of Irenaeus, Origen, Cyprian, Ambrose and Augustine,[80] omitting reference to, for example, Tertullian who rejects it, something he would not do if it were in the New Testament.[81] The justification of infant baptism, then, needs to be grounded on other bases other than a falsely claimed historical foundation.[82] David F. Wright has convincingly argued that infant baptism developed out of child believers' baptism[83] and he has also shown that the introduction of infant baptism was not

---

[80] See Balke, *Calvin and the Anabaptist Radicals*, 103 n. 29.

[81] So P. Bradshaw, *Early Christian Worship* (London: SPCK, 1996), 31: 'It is not at all certain when baptism began to be extended to infants as well as older children and adults. The first undisputed reference to the custom occurs in North Africa at the beginning of the third century in the writings of Tertullian [*On baptism* 18], who disapproves of it.' Many scholars now agree with, e.g., N.P. Williams, *The Ideas of the Fall and of Original Sin: A Historical and Critical Study* (London: Longman, Greens, 1929), 550, that New Testament baptism's recipients 'are adults, and that the disposition required in them are those of conscious and deliberate renunciation of sin and idols, and of personal faith in and allegiance to Christ'. However, 552, 'It must suffice to state that in the author's view the argument *a praxi ecclesiae* is the only, but also a sufficient, ground for affirming the legitimacy and laudability of Paedo-baptism' (italics orginal). David F. Wright *What has Infant Baptism done to Baptism?: An Enquiry at the End of Christendom* (Didsbury Lectures; Milton Keynes: Paternoster, 2005), 80-82, defends the legitimacy of infant baptism even though he accepts that it was a development of New Testament baptism. See, also, his 'Recovering Baptism for a New Age of Mission', in *Infant Baptism*, 374-76.

[82] There is little early evidence that Jesus' blessing of the infants in Mk 10.13-16 and par. was associated with infant baptism. See D.F. Wright, 'Out, In, Out: Jesus' Blessing of the Children and Infant Baptism', in *Infant Baptism*, 149-65. In his *What has Infant Baptism done?*, 8-9, Wright has shown that infant baptism early on adopted the theology and practice of faith-baptism, which, he shows, was the norm, 14-15 and 77 (cf. the more cautiously worded *Baptism, Eucharist and Ministry* [Faith and Order Paper, 111; Geneva: World Council of Churches, 1982], 4, 'baptism upon personal profession of faith is the most *clearly attested* pattern in the New Testament documents' [italics added]). On pp. 46-47, Wright states, 'Not far short of a millennium after infant baptism became the more or less universal form of baptism in the West, infants were still being baptized by an awkward adaptation of a rite formulated for the baptism of responding believers—and long after the use of that order of service for persons speaking for themselves had fallen into desuetude.' He, however, defends the legitimacy of infant baptism on other grounds, see *passim*, but e.g., pp. 80-82, and *Infant Baptism*, 374-76

[83] D.F. Wright, 'The Origins of Infant Baptism—Child Believers' Baptism', in *Infant Baptism*, 3-21.

controversial.[84] This latter historical observation needs to be taken on board by baptists and should dissuade them from continuing to make sweeping, and often intemperate, denunciations of infant baptism of the kind that have too often blighted their apologetic and polemical writing on baptism. More in line with Christian respect and worthy of note, in this regard, is the conclusion of the last published work of one of the leading Baptist writers on baptism, George Beasley-Murray: 'I make the plea that churches which practise believer's baptism should *consider* acknowledging the legitimacy of infant baptism, and allow members in Paedobaptist churches the right to interpret it according to their consciences.' He notes the variations in baptismal experience recorded in Acts (2.37-38; 8.14-17; 10.44-48; 11.1-18; 18.24–19.6) and states, 'The great lesson of those variations is the *freedom of God* in bestowing his gifts.'[85]

In Concluding

The above issues are clearly subjective and selective and many other issues that are raised by the writings of Calvin and Barth on baptism could easily have occupied our attention. But the preceding shows that the contributions of both theologians continue to demand our attention and interaction and this will only benefit the biblical, historical and theological study of Christian baptism, the importance of which is shown, whether in paedobaptist or baptist traditions, in its place at the beginning of the Christian life, a person's entry into union with Christ and into his body, the church.

---

[84] D.F. Wright, 'How Controversial was the Development of Infant Baptism in the early Church?', in *Infant Baptism*, 22-43.
[85] G.R. Beasley-Murray, 'The Problem of Infant Baptism: An Exercise in Possibilities', Faculty of Baptist Theological Seminary, Rüschlikon (ed.), *Festschrift Günther Wagner* (Berne: Peter Lang, 1994), 13-14, italics added.

PART THREE

ATONEMENT

CHAPTER 4

Karl Barth's Narrative Doctrine of Substitutionary Atonement

Neil B. MacDonald

Introduction

It may be said without too much equivocation that, in the minds of most Reformed congregations, Calvin's thought, as expressed in the *Institutes of the Christian Religion* in particular, defines to a greater or lesser extent *what* Reformed theology is, the identity of Reformed theology one might say. As James T. McNeill put it in his book *The History and Character of Calvinism* 'The *Institutes* became for three centuries the essential textbook of theology in the Reformed churches.'[1] And, no matter that, in the nineteenth century the Reformed church itself provided from its own ranks an alternative to Calvin in the form of Schleiermacher – one influence among many such that it could be said that the Calvinism of Dort or Westminster was 'discarded or altered almost beyond recognition' during this century – the fact remains that, when one speaks today of the Reformed doctrine of salvation or creation or the eucharist, it is more often than not Calvin's own doctrines which will be meant.[2] Or: if we wish to follow Richard Muller's advice that, from a sixteenth-century perspective Calvin should only be understood as teaching the Church's doctrines and not his own since such possessive individualism is an anachronism, we might put it this way: what the (Reformed) Church taught in the sixteenth century has become definitive for the identity of Reformed doctrine such that what we find on the pages of Calvin's *Institutes* is the touchstone, the measure of the truth of any doctrine purporting to be 'Reformed.' Calvin remains this great primal force of the Reformed Church.

And yet, according to Barth himself, the one presupposition of Reformed doctrine was not that it necessarily be identified with those doctrines endorsed by the pen of Calvin; the one presupposition was that it adhere to the scripture-principle. It was this that made Reformed *theology Reformed* theology. In his 1922 lectures on Calvin Barth spoke of the objective of the 'Reformed' Reformation as being 'the establishment of the Word of God contained in the Bible as the norm of faith and life.'[3] In 1923 he delivered a lecture entitled 'Reformed Doctrine: Its Essence and

---

[1] J.T. McNeill, *The History and Character of Calvinism* (New York: OUP, 1954), 234.
[2] McNeill, *The History and Character of Calvinism*, 409.
[3] K. Barth, *Die Theologie Calvins, 1922* (ed. Hans Scholl; Zurich: TVZ, 1993), 2.

Task' in which he said that 'every doctrine must be measured against an unchangeable and impassable standard': the Word of God, 'discoverable in the Scriptures.'[4] And in what has become known as the *Göttingen Dogmatics* – a set of lectures Barth delivered under the title of Calvin's *Institutes of the Christian Religion* in the winter semester of 1923-24 – he wrote that the Bible is a 'norm' of faith, a 'ruler or plumb line or rule.'[5] In these judgements Barth thought he had support from the history of Reformed theology itself: notwithstanding the common perception, the old Reformed theologians had held the scriptures to be the measure of truth and not any particular interpretation of them by pious men of the past, even though their names should be Calvin or (even) Zwingli.

Therein lies the rub for Barth: it will be said by those who adhere to Calvin that it is *precisely because* the latter has adhered to the scripture-principle that he has had the position of priority among the Reformed faithful as the very identity of the Reformed faith. By implication Barth cannot be granted any such status. He clearly has not so adhered since his doctrines of, for example, election and atonement differ in essentials from those of Calvin. This would not of itself be fatal for Barth except that according to those in agreement with Calvin, the Bible does teach a double decree of predestination and election, and it does teach limited atonement. No matter Barth's intention to be guided by *sola scriptura* some extraneous factor or other has intervened to lead him astray in these doctrines since we find neither in the corpus that is Barth's work.

My point of departure in this chapter will not be to answer these charges head-on as it were. That is: I am not going to begin by examining whether the Bible does teach limited atonement and in the light of the answer, ask whether Barth teaches what the Bible teaches. Rather: what I intend to do is to follow an indirect route toward vindicating Barth in the eyes of the Reformed faithful. I call the route or strategy indirect because I want to begin with what I believe is the most powerful and persuasive version of the biblical doctrine of the atonement. The greatest story so far of this great doctrine, if you will. I then want to show how very close Barth comes to affirming this very doctrine, how very much of it is in fact Barth's own understanding of the atonement in *Church Dogmatics* IV/1 (hereafter referred to as *CD* in the references). To be sure: the fact that this account goes *beyond* Barth's own account of the atonement will reveal what I consider to be the locus of a deficiency in Barth's theology. Nevertheless, it will also enable us to show how Barth affirmed a doctrine that did three monumental things in an age that has ceased to find atonement credible as an intellectual construction.

First, the doctrine succeeds in passing any criterion of common-sense rationality one cares to name; which is to say: it does not take recourse to special pleading in a manner not unknown to epistemically weaker theological conceptions! The Enlightenment's attitude toward the doctrine of the atonement as exemplified by such

---

[4] Barth, 'Reformed Doctrine: Its Essence and Task', in K. Barth, *The Word of God and the Word of Man* trans., D Horton (New York: Harper, 1957), 240-241.

[5] K. Barth, *Göttingen Dogmatics* vol 1, ed. H Reiffen, trans. G W Bromiley (Grand Rapids: Eerdmans, 1991), 212, 216.

as Kant is unwarranted. This means, among other things, that Barth's doctrine is at least equal, if not superior, to any version of the doctrine advanced by such as critical-historical methodology. I include in this the version you find in Tom Wright's hugely influentially *Jesus and the Victory of God* and will accordingly say something in the fashion of a comparative argument at the end of the essay.[6]

Second, the doctrine meets the demands of the scripture-principle, and indeed remains true to the canonical shape of the biblical canon – what also might be called the 'final form of the text.' Barth discerns, as we shall see, a doctrine of *substitutionary* atonement to be objectively present in the narratives that are the synoptic Gospels; and does not affirm atonement as a matter of Pauline 'interpretation.' We therefore have a happy coincidence: Barth's version of the atonement is scriptural *and* can be preached without fear of any kind of dismissive rejection characteristic of the modern age. It is not often acknowledged how concerned were theologians such as Augustine and Calvin to avoid bringing the Gospel into ridicule in the eyes of the educated classes of their respective times. I want to claim that Barth's doctrine – suitably supplemented – is the best, most persuasive, doctrine the *one holy apostolic catholic church* has available, not merely the most powerful the Reformed church has to hand.

Third, his doctrine has within itself the potential to inspire an unrivalled pulpit performance of 'preaching the Gospel' as a triumph of dialectic and imagination, even in the modern age. It goes without saying how important this is to a church such as the Reformed churches, which rightly places great emphasis on the witness and proclamation of the Bible. It is often said of Barth that he is the first great narrative theologian. That is correct; but what is underplayed in making this assertion is that Barth also discerned the following: what made the narrative a *Gospel* narrative is a crucial, dynamic *kerygmatic* dimension. This kerygmatic dimension calls for a *faith-decision* of a certain sort (in a manner not unreminiscent of Bultmann!) on the part of the church congregation, and indeed, beyond its walls. Barth's doctrine brings the listener – or reader, for that matter – into a dynamic faith-relation with the text. God addresses us – you and me – in the text! I therefore found it unsurprising that I was able to explicate this dimension in terms of the art-form peculiar to the modern age, and the twentieth century in particular: cinematic film.

I will not be in the business of proving each of these claims as it were in consecutive sections. But I hope that each will have emerged in the body of the essay in an utterly logical and convincing fashion by its journey's end.

YHWH, the God of Israel, who takes His own Judgement on Himself (in the Form of His Son, Jesus of Nazareth)

Let me start my argument with what I think is the most cogent interpretation of the Gospel narrative. I think the fundamental thematic of the narrative is this. It is the story of YHWH, the God of Israel who takes His own judgement on Himself – in

---

[6] N.T. Wright, *Jesus and the Victory of God* (London: SPCK, 1996).

the form of His son, Jesus of Nazareth. I recognise that to say YHWH takes His judgement on Himself, and then to add – 'in the form of His son' – is to court semantic anomaly if not downright inconsistency and contradiction. (How can YHWH really take His own judgement on Himself if it is in fact taken on the shoulders of His son?) It is a question – one that recurs in different forms throughout the history of doctrine - that discerns an apparent tension inherent in speaking of a monotheism which yet includes the man Jesus. Let us however put this historic critique to one side for the moment and consider another criticism, which comes from yet another angle. This criticism goes as follows. Whatever else the Gospel narrative is about, isn't it much more about Jesus Christ (also of course Jesus of Nazareth) and less about YHWH, the God of Israel? To be sure, Jesus speaks of God all through the Gospel but, still, it is Jesus and not this God who is the central figure in the narrative. The Old Testament is about YHWH the God of Israel, yes, but the New Testament, like the new covenant, is about Jesus Christ, His only Son. A straightforward and simple demarcation!

I would argue that this demarcation is too simple, especially if it is employed as a framework with which to view the relation between the Old and New Testament. To be sure, the demarcation is undergirded by a very venerable tradition that has Jesus or Christology writ large, as it were, interpret the Old Testament. Jesus or Christology interprets the Old Testament as a book of typology or prophecy or even allegory. One may reads the Old Testament for its plain sense as it were, as one's first hermeneutic; but then, in the light of one's reading of the New Testament, one re-reads the former for its Christological sense, the second and primary hermeneutic.[7] As regards the primary hermeneutic, one may describe the relation between the two testaments as a 'front-to-back' model in the sense that one reads the New Testament first, then 'reads' the Old Testament as it were behind it rather than the other way around. One may also describe the relation of New to Old by an automobile metaphor, as a 'front-wheel drive' model. One reads the Old Testament from the context or perspective of the New Testament and, in particular, the Christ event, and in the light of this, one deems to pull the Old Testament along, behind you as it were. (Someone like Marcion might be described as one who didn't want to pull much of this part of scripture along with him, didn't think there was much point in wasting time pulling along what wasn't necessary for his and the Church's spiritual journey).

Now as I say this is a most venerable tradition. It informed the Patristic period, dominated mediaeval theology (especially with its tendency toward the allegorical mode of biblical interpretation), and remains – even given the emphasis on the plain sense of scripture – the prevalent mode of biblical interpretation today. Yet – to my mind – it poses something of an obstruction to stating the doctrine of atonement in its most cogent form, that which I have outlined above in which the primary agent

---

[7] Francis Watson's *Text, Church, and Truth* (Edinburgh: T& T Clark, 1998), ch. 5, is an preeminent example of this kind of trinitarian-christological interpretation of the Old Testament.

is YHWH the God of Israel. The alternative position, which I should say has been gaining currency in recent times – and arguably has a precedent in the apostolic fathers and the early church –[8] is one I describe in an opposite manner to this 'front-to-back' or 'front-wheel drive' model. It is a *'back-to-front'* model or a *'back-wheel drive'* model: one reads the Old Testament for its plain sense in order to identify who the God of Israel is: who it is that acts in Israel's history, His divine identity, as it were, construable as a historical identity. One then attempts to read the Gospel narrative as the story of this same divine identity. Clearly, to the extent that the narrative can be read as this story, it is read in terms of one's plain-sense reading of Old Testament narrative. The New Testament is, as it were, read from the context or perspective of the Old Testament, rather than as Christian convention has it (though not necessarily the scripture-principle) the other way round. It is not then that Jesus interprets the Old Testament; rather, he or his story is interpreted in terms of the Old Testament. In particular, the Jesus of Nazareth as rendered in the Gospel narratives – especially the synoptic narratives – is read in terms of the divine identity of YHWH as rendered in Old Testament narrative. He is read in terms of that identity as it is manifest: initially in the exodus narrative, centrally in the Deuteronomistic narrative, but also before and after these narratives – in both the primeval and in the post-exilic history. As Brevard Childs puts it, paraphrasing some of the seminal work of Hans von Campenhausen, 'the problem of the early church was not what to do with the Old Testament in the light of the Gospel, which was Luther's concern, but rather the reverse. In the light of the Jewish scriptures which were acknowledged to be the true oracles of God, how were Christians to understand the good news of Jesus Christ?'[9]

This God of Israel is the one identified in the Old Testament, and principally in Old Testament narrative, as essentially a *soteriological* identity. The God of Israel reveals Himself to be a judging yet desisting, forbearing, and saving historical identity. To be sure, He is 'the one who releases Israel from the bondage of Egypt' in the exodus narrative, and as we know 'the one who released Israel from the bondage of Egypt' is a key identifying description of the God of Israel in the Old Testament. Nevertheless this definite description is not sufficiently comprehensive to be descriptive of His identity in the later narratives. It does of course remain true of Him at the time of the Deuteronomistic history for example as in above, but it is not the identity that ties all these narratives together in terms of the sameness of divine identity. The divine identity that does this is precisely the God of Israel understood as a *judging yet (ultimately) desisting, forbearing, saving God*. The God of Israel is this in the exodus narrative. But He is also this – paradoxically – in the narrative that in modern times goes by the name of the Deuteronomistic history and which culminates in the downfall of the (southern) kingdom of Judah and Babylonian exile early in the sixth century BCE, having already testified to the demise of the (northern) kingdom of Israel in 772 BCE. YHWH is also this in the post-exilic

---

[8] See Hans von Campenhausen, *The Formation of the Christian Canon* (London: SCM Press, 1971).

[9] See B.S. Childs, *Biblical Theology* (London: SCM Press, 1992), 226.

period. And most pointedly, He is this in the very words of Ezra who, when speaking of the return from exile under the beneficence of Cyrus the great from 536 onwards, experiences YHWH as 'having punished us less than our iniquities deserve, and has given us such deliverance as this' (Ezra 9.13). Even though Judah is to be no more a kingdom, the return from exile is still the action of a gracious and merciful God who saves His people Israel more than they deserve. And Ezra recognises this.

It is this personal historical identity that, I would argue, manifests himself in the Gospel narrative. The God of Israel who I said above takes His own judgement on Himself in the form of His son is YHWH, the judging yet desisting and forbearing historical identity, the God who is decisively identified in Old Testament narrative as this personal identity.

Barth: 'Front-Wheel Drive' or 'Back-Wheel Drive' Theologian?

Though it could be argued that Barth does understand the Gospel narrative in terms of YHWH the God of Israel who takes His own judgement on Himself in the form of his son, Jesus of Nazareth, I am inclined to think that his 'christocentric concentration' (as it was called by von Balthasar) led him to a overly christocentric conception of the God of Israel whose 'refusal to give His name'[10] is finally known only in the revealed identity of Jesus Christ. Barth to my mind puts insufficient emphasis on the fact that the God of Israel has a *prior* identity to that of Jesus of Nazareth. Instead of understanding Jesus in terms of the prior identity of YHWH the God of Israel, Barth's christocentric focus reverses the relation and subordinates the identity of the latter to that of the former.

But paradoxically, though Barth puts too light a stress on the independent witness and plain sense of the Old Testament as regards his conception of the identity of YHWH, he was almost unerringly right when it came to the relation between Jesus and YHWH in the New Testament, and the plain sense of the synoptic narratives in particular. Any judgement of Barth as a 'front-wheel drive' theologian must be tempered by this observation. As regards the synoptic narratives, Barth was a 'back-wheel drive' theologian in the sense that *he puts much more emphasis on the presence of YHWH in the synoptic Gospels than is customary for a theologian of his christocentric orientation.* Though the Gospel narrative does in fact appear to be much more about Jesus of Nazareth and less about YHWH, the God of Israel, this is not in the least incompatible with the view that the narrative is in fact about YHWH taking His own judgement on Himself. It was Barth who made the crucial breakthrough as regards how the narrative could be understood in this way.

The most powerful version of the atonement is one that understands Jesus of Nazareth in terms of the identity of YHWH, the God of Israel, not the other way round. *But the precise way in which YHWH does this involves most intimately*

---

[10] For some sterling criticism of the evacuation of the identity of the God of Israel from Christian doctrine in modern times, see K Soulen, 'YHWH the Triune God', *Modern Theology* 15 (1999), 25–54, esp. 37–39. See also K Soulen, *Christian Theology and the God of Israel* (Minneapolis: Fortress Press, 1996).

Jesus of Nazareth substituting himself in place of Israel and the world, and undergoing YHWH's judgement in their stead. Barth's careful formulation of the mechanics of this substitution is in fact his signal contribution to the doctrine of atonement.

There are four crucial steps to understanding Barth's doctrine of substitutionary atonement. The first two steps are to do with literary form and content. The *first* focuses on Barth's preference in this respect for the synoptic narratives over the Johannine one. The *second* draws attention to the essential three-part structure of the literary shape of the synoptic narrative. The *third* step involves foregrounding what Barth calls the *judicial framework* of the first two parts of this narrative. Jesus declares the eschatological judgement of God in the first part of the narrative and is himself judged by the ruling Jewish body, the Sanhedrin, and then most decisively by the governor and procurator of Judaea, Pontius Pilate: As Barth puts it the passion narrative is best described within a judicial framework: '... an arrest, a hearing, a prosecution in various courts, a torturing, and then an execution and burial' (*CD* IV/1, 226). The *fourth* step is the really significant one. In the light of Jesus' resurrection appearances after his death on the cross, The evangelist invites his 'readers' or 'audience' to discern in Pontius Pilate's judgement the divine judgement at work. In this way is the merely human judicial framework transformed into a theological drama of substitutionary atonement.

The question is this: is the story simply about a man who proclaimed the judgement of God on Israel and the world and then died an inglorious failure on a cross outside the gates of Jerusalem at the hands of the ruling Roman authorities? Was Pilate's judgement on Jesus merely the judgement of one man (no matter how powerful) on another? Or is the narrative about YHWH taking His own judgement on Himself in the form of His son, Jesus of Nazareth? In other words, is the narrative about inglorious failure or is it about substitutionary atonement? Let me take these four steps in turn.

Step One: The Locus of Barth's Doctrine in the Synoptic Narratives

The locus of Barth's doctrine of substitutionary atonement is in fact the Gospel narratives at the head of the canonical shape of the New Testament, the synoptic narratives: Matthew, Mark, and Luke. (For Barth this locus is evidence that substitutionary atonement is in fact the most important doctrine of the New Testament).

A short historical note would be worthwhile at this juncture. In *Church Dogmatics* IV/1 Barth notes how Luther's preference was for the Johannine Gospel over the synoptics. In making this preference Luther belonged to a tradition that stretches preeminently back to Origen and continued up from Augustine through the mediaeval period to Luther's own time.[11] The reason for this is precisely the overtly

---

[11] Indeed John's Gospel only cedes its pre-eminence in this respect in the wake of the results of historical – and source-criticism, and, in particular – in the course of the

'pedagogical' or 'doctrinal' nature of the figure of Jesus in John's Gospel, which makes the Gospel a different genre of narrative. This is why Calvin thought that one should read John's Gospel first and then turn to the synoptics afterwards. He writes that the Gospel of John is 'a key to open the door to the understanding of the others. For whoever grasps the power of Christ as it is here graphically portrayed, will afterwards read with advantage what the others relate about the manifested Redeemer.' And later in the same paragraph he writes: 'As to John being put fourth in order, it was done because of his order in time. In reading them a different order will be better.'[12] As is known, Calvin took his own advice in when it came to exegesis, the commentary on John appearing in 1553, followed by the *Harmony of the Synoptic Gospels* in 1555. Calvin sums up the difference between the two genres in a way that is characteristic of the how the whole classical tradition viewed the difference. John's Gospel 'emphasised more the doctrine in which Christ's office and the power of His death and resurrection are explained' than the synoptics which simply 'narrate the life and death of Christ' but as it were 'more fully.'[13]

Now, in the paragraph in *CD* IV/1 in which Luther's preference is noted, Barth expresses his agreement with the judgement of tradition on the synoptic narratives. He writes: 'It is obvious in these Gospels there is little express mention of the significance of the Christ event which took place there and then' (*CD* IV/1, 224). Instead, it 'is content simply to tell the story - this is how it was, this is how it happened. There is interpretation only in the lightest and sometimes rather alien strokes' (*CD* IV/1, 227). And later on in IV/1 he says: 'The Gospel story [expressed in the synoptics]...does not offer any theological explanation. It says hardly anything about the significance of the event' (*CD* IV/1, 239).

Yet the strange fact presents itself to us that it was in the synoptic narratives - where just the kind of 'doctrinal explanation' of which Calvin spoke was precisely lacking – that Barth found his doctrine of substitutionary atonement.[14] He persevered to find it precisely in the historicity of the narrative itself rather than being content with the more doctrinal affirmations of John 1.29 or 3.16, passages that, as we know, speak more *directly* of atonement or reconciliation. Utterly paradoxically: it is the narrative's very reticence bordering on silence as regards *the presence of YHWH in the passion narrative* that is *indicative* of the very doctrine of substitutionary

---

nineteenth century – the general acceptance of the historical priority of Mark. Hitherto, a great nineteenth-century theologian like Schleiermacher had taken the view that this gospel carried the greatest historical weight due to the fact it had been written by 'the beloved disciple,' John himself – unlike Mark's Gospel.

[12] Calvin, *Gospel of John, 11–21* (trans. T.H.L. Parker, ed. D.W. Torrance and T.F. Torrance; Edinburgh: Oliver & Boyd, 1961), 6.

[13] Calvin, *Gospel of John, 11–21*, 6.

[14] This is why Barth writes that when we 'consider this history carefully once more' we see 'how radically puzzling and therefore significant it is just as it stands, factually and without any great attempt to draw attention to it, in its simple character as history', *CD* IV/1, 224.

atonement that Barth is after. I mention this now because this feature is of seminal importance when we come to step four.

Step Two: The Literary Shape of the Synoptic Narrative – the Three Essential Parts

The early twentieth-century German theologian Martin Kähler famously characterized Mark's Gospel as a passion narrative with an extended introduction. This description is now taken to be too simplistic a characterization of the Gospel; and one implication would be that one has to give *equal* weight to both Jesus' ministry and his passion history, instead of 'privileging' the latter and the expense of the former. What has not been rejected is something like a consensus view to the effect that Mark's Gospel has three essential parts to it when the sequel to Jesus' death on the cross – the resurrection-appearances history – is added. (We might add to this the contemporary view that Mark is made of two essential sources [when we set aside the resurrection tradition]: units of tradition arranged by the evangelist constitutive of Jesus' ministry; and a pre-Markan passion narrative which achieved a self-contained literary form at an early stage in the tradition).

We therefore have three parts if we restrict ourselves to the synoptic Gospel that is Mark's. To be sure, both Matthew and Luke prefix an infancy narrative to their Gospels; hence, we cannot conclude without qualification that the literary shape of the synoptic narrative *per se* is three-part in structure. Notwithstanding this however, *in the context of Barth's doctrine of substitutionary atonement*, there are three essential parts to the synoptic narrative.

Barth locates the division between the first part and the second part in the following way:

> The sections from the record of the entry into Jerusalem up to and including the last supper can be regarded as belonging to the first or the second part, or as the transition from the one to the other. But from the description of Gethsemane [onwards] at any rate the second part forms a self-contained whole' (*CD* IV/1, 226).

Jesus' agony in the Garden of Gethsemane is in fact the key moment in the narrative when the man who had hitherto proclaimed the eschatological judgement of YHWH's kingdom, now himself begins to undergo the judgement of the religious and civil authorities (the Jewish and Roman authorities respectively) culminating in his execution on the cross. Judgement takes place in the first part of the synoptic narrative and judgement takes place in the second part of the synoptic narrative. For this reason Barth provides an exposition of the first two parts of the historicity of the synoptic narrative in terms of a *judicial framework*.

In other words, mere literary appreciation of the synoptic narrative as *narrative* does not suffice. It does not suffice because we must come to terms with the *historicity* of the first two parts of the narrative. The judicial framework does just that; and in doing so brings us a step nearer *divine* substitutionary atonement, which is the fundamental theme of the Gospel. So Barth.

Step Three: The First Two Parts are to be Understood in Terms of a Judicial Framework

It is a commonplace observation of New Testament scholars that Paul's letters evince very little interest in the historical Jesus, preferring to know Jesus/Christ 'after the flesh' (2 Cor. 5:16). Bultmann saw in Paul's remark (as he saw in John's Gospel) the first stage in the process of demythologising the mythical Jesus into a Christ-figure accessible to modern philosophical if not theological categories.

In contrast Barth sees in Paul's lack of concern with the historical Jesus precisely a *lack of reference to the historical contents outlined in the first part of the synoptic narrative*. Since Barth understands Paul as offering essentially a theological interpretation of the passion narrative – the second part of the narrative – in terms of a 'theology of the cross', this is not of itself a major shortcoming. For one thing it dovetails perfectly with Barth's understanding of the canonical shape of the New Testament where Paul provides, among other things, a commentary on Jesus' death on the cross.

Yet as a child of the nineteenth century, Barth knew that the great book which had brought to an end the first quest for the historical Jesus – Albert Schweitzer's *The Quest of the Historical Jesus* – had made a great deal of *the Jesus of the first part of the synoptic narrative*.[15] By the end of the nineteenth century the historical priority of Mark had superseded the earlier traditional belief that this status be awarded to John, the Gospel of the 'beloved disciple' who had known Jesus personally (as opposed to the other evangelists) and therefore had first-hand knowledge of Jesus' life. Schweitzer's book reflected this reversal of priority. More importantly, Schweitzer detected in the first part of Mark – and therefore in Matthew and Luke (both of whom he rightly thought reliant on Mark) – a Jesus-figure who remains a pivotal influence on New Testament studies even today.[16] The Jesus Schweitzer discerned in the first part of the synoptic narratives was no less than *an eschatological Jesus who had declared God's final judgement on Israel and the world*. Not for Schweitzer the picture of Jesus as a mere teacher of ethics for a future world religion!

Barth was not unaware of the rationality, even probable historicity, of Schweitzer's apocalyptic Jesus. Paradoxically, he had no compunction in concurring with Schweitzer's depiction of Jesus since it is essentially what he too discerned in the first part of the synoptic narrative *reading it as a theologian reading scripture. Barth agreed that something like Schweitzer's Jesus was a valid reading of the first part of the synoptic narrative*. Moreover he agreed that the first part must be just as determinative for the identity of Jesus of Nazareth as the second part, the passion narrative: the part traditionally taken since Paul to be in the end the sole criterion of the identity of Jesus. As Barth put it: we 'must understand the first part of the story

---

[15] Albert Schweitzer, *The Quest of the Historical Jesus: A Critical Study of Its Progress from Reimarus to Wrede* (London: Black, 3rd edn, 1945)

[16] I speak most obviously of Tom Wright's *Jesus and the Victory of God*, more of which will be said at the end of the chapter.

as a commentary on the second, and *vice-versa*' (*CD* IV/1, 235). This stress on the first part of the synoptic narrative as equally important in the determination of a doctrine of substitutionary atonement was a new phenomenon in the history of systematic and dogmatic theology and heralded Barth's desire to play the critical-historical school at its own game!

Ironically, it is precisely because of this demand (of reciprocity of commentary) that Barth had other ideas than the ones proffered by Schweitzer as regards the passion narrative. Paradoxically, where Schweitzer saw nothing but a romantic, tragic hero dying an inglorious and deluded death on a cross (Jesus had proclaimed the end of the world but had died an unfulfilled failure in this respect), Barth discerned a certain commonality of motif in the passion narrative corresponding precisely to the motif of judgement implicit in the first part of the narrative, to Jesus' proclamation of the eschatological judgement of YHWH on Israel and the world. Just as Jesus judges in the first part then so he is judged in the second part. The passion narrative corresponds to a sequence of events Barth describes as: '... an arrest, a hearing, a prosecution in various courts, a torturing, and then an execution and burial' (*CD* IV/1, 226). In other words, Jesus judges in the first part of the narrative and he is judged in a judicial context – firstly by the Jewish authority in Jerusalem, the Sanhedrin – and then most importantly by Pontius Pilate, the governor and procurator of Judaea.[17] As we will see, Pilate's judgement is most important – not merely because his is the judgement that leads inexorably to Jesus' execution on the cross, but because it is the locus of the real identity the evangelist perceives at work in the narrative: YHWH's judgement on Israel and the world falling instead on Jesus himself.

There is no doubt that the judicial framework that Barth employed to great effect in his exegesis of the literary structure of the synoptic narrative was inspired by the Reformed doctrine of the judicial work of Christ, and by Calvin's version of this doctrine in particular. I have dealt with the historical roots of this aspect of Barth's doctrine of substitutionary atonement at some length elsewhere.[18] Suffice to say that Barth chose the 'forensic' framework over the traditional patristic and mediaeval understandings of Christ's death of the cross – sacrificial or cultic, military, financial or feudal – because, as he put it himself, he found that he was able to see the narrative 'better and more distinctly and more comprehensively' under the judicial framework than would be possible had he committed himself radically, for example,

---

[17] Conversely, though Pilate's judgement on Jesus occurs in the nexus of the events leading from Gethsemane to the cross, it also has a context beyond the passion narrative itself. This context is precisely the *first part* of the narrative. Pilate's judgement on Jesus does not take place in a vacuum. It takes place precisely in a narrative context in which Jesus has previously – already – proclaimed YHWH's own judgement on Israel and by extension the world (since God's judgement occurs within the context of God's imminent reign on earth ('as it is in heaven').

[18] Neil B. MacDonald, *Karl Barth and the Strange New World within the Bible: Barth, Wittgenstein, and the Metadilemmas of the Enlightenment* (Carlisle: Paternoster, rev. edn, 2001), ch. 11.

to the priestly framework (*CD* IV/1, 275). The reason Barth is so intent on emphasizing the judicial framework of the passion narrative – in preference to the presence of the priestly or sacrificial work of Jesus – is that it in turn corresponds to the larger judicial framework that also encompasses the first part of the synoptic narrative. In contrast, the 'priestly' or 'sacrificial' motif is largely if not completed limited to the passion narrative, the second part. Hence in the context of narrative historicity it is not able to construe the passion narrative as a commentary on the first part of the narrative. The great strength of the judicial framework is that it does.

Moreover, the manner in which it delivers a doctrine of substitutionary atonement to the Church in nowise depends on the believer's subjective act of faith that Jesus' death on the cross was a sacrifice. To be sure, Jesus did die for us on the cross as Paul explicitly says, but the grounds for this assertion emerge at bottom from the objective truth-claims one finds in the judicial framework of the synoptic narrative itself. The assertion is not based, as it were, exclusively on the ingenious theological meaning which Paul provides in his epistles as an interpretation of Jesus' death on the cross. Indeed, Barth would say that Paul's sacrificial metaphors can only be understood with the context of the canonical shape of the New Testament. Only if we observe the canonical priority of the synoptic narrative in this sense are we able to see that the concept of sacrifice constitutes a commentary on the judicial work of Jesus of Nazareth narrated in the passion rather than vice-versa.

Before we proceed to the crucial fourth step in the exposition of Barth's doctrine of substitutionary atonement, let me recapitulate the three steps that we have just covered. First, we noted that Barth's preference is for the synoptic narratives over the Johannine one. Next, we drew attention to Barth's emphasis on the essential three-part structure of the literary shape of the synoptic narrative. The *third* step foregrounds what Barth calls the *judicial framework or shape* of the first two parts of this narrative. Jesus declares the eschatological judgement of God in the first part of the narrative and is himself judged by the ruling Jewish body, the Sanhedrin, and then most decisively by the governor and procurator of Judaea, Pontius Pilate: the passion narrative is best described within a judicial framework: '… an arrest, a hearing, a prosecution in various courts, a torturing, and then an execution and burial' (*CD* IV/1, 226).

What is common to each of these steps is that none of them presupposes any kind of faith-stance or extra-naturalistic assumption on the part of the reader of scripture. This observation is especially pertinent to the third step – the most controversial as far as biblical scholars would be concerned. Though there are biblical scholars such as Dominic Crossan who argue that it is circumstantially, historically unlikely that an encounter between Pontius Pilate and Jesus actually took place – far less that this encounter took the form of the dialogue narrated in the Gospels – equally there are biblical scholars who, again on historical grounds, want to affirm just this historical truth-claim. N.T. Wright for example implies that it is just as rational to affirm that the encounter took place as to say it didn't. Whether one wants to query the accuracy of the Gospel account of the actual words they spoke to each other, one would at the very least hold that, whatever happened, Pilate did issue a judgment on Jesus that led to Jesus' execution by crucifixion. The latter to Barth's mind is a rational claim to make.

But note well. A biblical scholar like Crossan isn't arguing a point about theology. In particular, he isn't arguing a point of whether substitutionary atonement is true or rational to believe. He is arguing over the strictly naturalistic-historical point about whether Jesus ever stood in front of the governor and procurator of Judaea, Pontius Pilate. Insofar as he rejects the latter, he rejects the validity of the judicial framework as a means of understanding the synoptic narrative. But it seems – if we take another biblical scholar like N.T. Wright as our guide – that it is just as rational to affirm the judicial framework as it is to reject it. Barth would agree. But, again, *note well*: the affirmation of the judicial framework, inclusive of the encounter between Pilate's judgment and Jesus' execution, is entirely compatible with Schweitzer's view of Jesus' passion and death as expressive of tragic and essentially ignoble failure. Neither God nor theology necessarily belong in the judicial framework that Barth discerns in the synoptic narrative.

Step Four: The Resurrection and the Identity of Jesus of Nazareth

What makes the decisive difference is seeing the judicial framework in the light of the resurrection appearances. The first two parts must be understood from the perspective of the third part, Jesus' appearances after his death on the cross to those who had known him during his pre-Easter life. Barth takes the view that, outside of the context of the resurrection appearances, Jesus' life did indeed end in failure on the cross, no matter the presence of a judicial thematic across the first two parts of the narrative. The synoptic witness in the passion narrative is that the disciples were completely at sea, unable to comprehend what was at work in what was happening to Jesus after Gethsemane (and indeed largely oblivious to his words at the Last Supper); accordingly, Peter denied, Judas betrayed, and every last one of the disciples scattered after the crucifixion.[19]

But inside the context of the resurrection-appearances history, Jesus of Nazareth reveals Himself to be included within the identity of YHWH, the God of Israel. For Barth it is not coincidental that the New Testament's confession of Jesus' divinity or his inclusion within the divine name of YHWH is always coupled with reference to his exaltation in his resurrection from the dead (Matthew 28.19-20 In particular the New Testament's confession at John 20.28 and at Philippians 2.9-11 that Jesus is to be included within the divine name of YHWH.

But as Barth says of these witnesses [of the apostolic church], 'it is not they who have given him this name, but God.' And Barth goes on to say: 'God has given him this name by exalting him above all things (Phil. 2.9) out of and after his death on the cross' (*CD* III/2, 450). That is: YHWH has included Jesus in His own divine

---

[19] See Werner Georg Kümmel, *Theology of the New Testament* (London: SCM Press, 1974), 68–69.

identity, His own divine soteriological identity by giving Jesus his own name *by* exalting or *in that* He exalted Jesus above all things through resurrecting Him from the dead. YHWH is the one who raised Jesus by raising him from dead *and thus* exalting him above all things.[20] How it is rational to claim this, Barth would say, is because of Jesus of Nazareth's resurrection appearances as narrated in the Gospel narratives. The resurrection-appearances history *presupposes* Jesus resurrection from the dead (*CD* III/2, 447). I have dealt with Barth's exegesis of this history elsewhere and in particular how it is rational to affirm its historicity without falling foul of Troeltschian rationality as manifested, for example, in Troeltsch's famous principle of analogy.[21]

What Barth is effectively saying is that YHWH includes Jesus within His own divine soteriological identity *by* giving Jesus His own name. And He gives Him this name precisely *by* raising him from the dead, which is to say, exalting him above all things in heaven and on earth.

The implication is to be drawn: outside the resurrection-appearances history, the first two parts of the synoptic narrative – even inclusive of a compelling judicial pattern of motif – end in inglorious unfulfilled deluded failure with the man Jesus' death on a cross. Inside their context, however, *the first two parts – inclusive of the same judicial framework - are to be included within the divine soteriological identity of YHWH*.[22] In other words, *the judicial framework itself is to be understood within the soteriological identity of YHWH.*

Barth's Theological Move: The Judicial Framework as Substitutionary Atonement

The crucial step in Barth's doctrine of substitutionary atonement is upon us. The question is this: how is the judicial framework of the synoptic narrative to be

---

[20] In this context it is not difficult to deduce the significance Anselm's revealed name for God 'that than which a *greater* [my italics] cannot be conceived' had for Barth. 'Greater' is almost a synonym for 'higher.' Jesus effectively reveals Himself to have this name – which proves his existence within the divine existence – in his resurrection appearances from the dead.

[21] I again refer to my book *Karl Barth and the Strange New World within the Bible* and, in particular, ch. 8 though see also ch. 6. The key passage in this respect in the *Church Dogmatics* is *CD* IV/2, 144-48.

[22] The resurrection appearances confer on Jesus' person or identity inclusion in the divine soteriological identity of YHWH. But Jesus' appearances also reveal that the risen Jesus is the same person as the one the disciples had encountered in his pre-Easter existence and history: Jesus' resurrection appearances reveal that the risen Jesus declares himself *in identity and continuity with* 'the one previously followed and who had died on the cross and been buried' (*CD* IV/2, 144). This is why Barth says that an alternative way of saying the same thing is to say that the name 'YHWH' is 'inseparable from [Jesus'] person, and His person inseparable from his name' (*CD* III/2, 450). The resurrection appearances tell us that the Jesus of the first two parts of the synoptic narrative is no less to be included in the divine soteriological identity of YHWH.

understood within the soteriological identity of YHWH? Barth understands the Easter story as 'the commentary on the Gospel story in the unity and completeness of its first two parts' (*CD* IV/1, 228). In this context, Barth says, we 'must understand the first part of the story as a commentary on the second, and *vice-versa*' (*CD* IV/1, 235). In other words: unless we affirm the resurrection-appearances history then, we cannot understand the first two parts – Jesus proclaiming the eschatological judgment of God in Galilee and being judged and executed in and around Jerusalem – to be the *theological* unity which the evangelists understands them to be.

The corollary of this question is the following: how is someone like Schweitzer's Jesus – the Jesus of *the first part of the judicial framework* – to be understood within the divine identity of YHWH? For as we have noted: this Jesus who in Schweitzer's view declared the eschatological judgment of YHWH on Israel and the world *is* himself precisely the one who is to be included in the soteriological identity of YHWH. This means that Jesus is to be understood as included in the soteriological identity of YHWH even as he declares YHWH's own eschatological judgment on Israel and the world.

For Schweitzer Jesus' life ends in tragic vain death on a cross. And this remains true: even if Jesus' proclamation of YHWH's judgement in the first part of the narrative corresponds in particular to the Roman procurator Pontius Pilate's judgment of Jesus which leads ultimately to his execution on the cross as an 'enemy of Rome'; even if the passion story culminating in Jesus' death is best described within the judicial framework of: '… an arrest, a hearing, a prosecution in various courts, a torturing, and then an execution and burial' (*CD* IV/1, 226).

But what if, Barth asks, the evangelist wants to say that what is perhaps the most famous encounter between two people in western civilisation, story, and history *was in fact really an encounter between Jesus and YHWH, the God of Israel*? What if the evangelist wanted to say that the judgment of Pilate on Jesus that had ultimately led to his execution on the cross *was in fact YHWH's own judgment on Jesus*?

Then, Barth said, we would not be reflecting on the historically insignificant datum of a Jewish man's death on a cross, but rather on a theological drama of substitutionary atonement, which involves *most intimately Jesus of Nazareth substituting himself in place of Israel and the world, and undergoing YHWH's judgment in their stead*. And we would be reflecting on this not as mere (subjective) interpretation of the narrative but as a historical truth-claim *objectively present in the narrative*.

The Theological Identity of Pilate's Judgement: YHWH's Judgement on Jesus

Before I proceed to the explanation of how the strictly theological identity of Pilate's judgement on Jesus could motivate the conclusion of a narrative 'doctrine' of substitutionary atonement, I want to say something about the source of Barth's claim. It is most likely that the inspiration as regards the theological identity of Pilate's judgement was from Calvin. Barth lectured on the 1536 *Institutes* in his

1922 lectures on the theology of Calvin, and he was also extremely well acquainted with the 1559 edition. In both places Calvin construes Pilate's judgement of Jesus from his judgement seat (John 19.13) as a prefigurement of the judgement that would have awaited us at God's heavenly judgement seat on the Last Day had Jesus not substituted himself in place of us and taken on our impending judgement in his way to the cross. In the 1536 edition Calvin writes:

> He suffered ... under Pontius Pilate, condemned indeed by the judge's sentence, as a criminal and wrongdoer, in order that we might, by his condemnation, be absolved before the judgement seat of the highest Judge.[23]

And more expansively in the 1559 edition, Calvin writes:

> The curse caused by our guilt was awaiting us at God's heavenly judgement seat. Accordingly Scripture first relates Christ's condemnation before Pontius Pilate, governor of Judea, to teach us that the penalty to which we were subject had been imposed upon this righteous man. We could not escape God's dreadful judgment. To deliver us from it, Christ allowed himself to be condemned before a mortal man – even a wicked and profane one ...

He continues:

> To take away our condemnation, it was not enough for him to suffer any kind of death: to make satisfaction for our redemption a form of death had to be chosen in which he might free us both by transferring our condemnation to himself and by taking our guilt on himself. If he had been murdered by thieves or slain in an insurrection by a raging mob, in such a death there would be no evidence of satisfaction. But when he was arraigned before the judgement seat as a criminal, accused and pressed by testimony, and condemned by the mouth of the judge to die – we know by these proofs that he took the role of a guilty man and evildoer.[24]

If we look at Barth's exegesis on Pilate's judgement we see that he follows Calvin's emphasis on the importance of the 'judicial' aspects in the details of the narrative. Like Calvin, Barth foregrounds the significance of the 'narrative' fact that Pilate acts as a judge sentencing a man as in a court of law. Barth would agree with

---

[23] J. Calvin, *Institutes of the Christian Religion* (1536 ed.) (edited by F.L. Battles; Atlanta: John Knox, 1975), 54.

[24] Calvin, *Institutes* (1536), 509. It is also worth pointing out that a similar idea is expressed in his 1555 Harmony of the Gospels. Calvin describes the encounter between Jesus and Pilate in these terms: 'The Son of God wished to stand bound before an earthly judge and therefore submit to the death sentence, that we might not doubt that we are freed from guilt and free to approach the heavenly throne of God ... God's Son stood trial before a mortal man and suffered accusation and condemnation, that we might stand without fear in the presence of God' Calvin, *A Harmony of the Gospels, Matthew, Mark, Luke* (trans. A.W. Morrison, ed. D.F. Torrance and T.F. Torrance; 3 vols; Edinburgh: St. Andrew Press, 1972), 179.

Calvin that, had Jesus been 'murdered by thieves, or slain in an insurrection by a raging mob' the theological interpretation of his death would have to be quite different from the one generated in a judicial context. In other words, *Barth's perception that the synoptic evangelists wanted to identify Pilate's judgment on Jesus as God's judgement on Jesus is very probably to be traced to Calvin.*

There is however a very significant and very interesting difference. This difference, in my opinion, made a decisive contribution to Barth's claim that substitutionary atonement was objectively in the synoptic narrative. It is not merely that Calvin thought God had providentially predestined this most famous encounter in human history, nor that he thought God had done this from eternity.[25] To be sure, according to Calvin and indeed the whole classical tradition from Augustine to Aquinas, God acted in history from eternity as it were. *But this did not of itself preclude the possibility that God had decreed from eternity that Pilate's judgement of Jesus be His own judgement.* Such a position was clearly conceivable even given Calvin's understanding of God's relation to time. But Calvin did not draw this conclusion. Rather, he drew the conclusion from the plain sense of scripture that Jesus' encounter with Pilate remains merely and unalterably *an encounter between Christ and a mere man.* To be sure, the encounter constituted both a prefigurement of Jesus' intercession for us before the heavenly judgement seat of God; and of our standing before the same judgement but without fear of judgement since Jesus had taken it on himself in our stead. But Pilate's judgement is never in Calvin the presence of God's judgement then and there – whether real and *de facto* or providentially predestined from God's vantage-point in eternity.

It is quite otherwise with Barth. In contrast to Calvin, Barth thought that Pilate's judgement was *actually and really* God's judgement on Jesus then and there, occurring then and there in time, in historical time.[26] He thought that the synoptic narrative witnessed to the unspoken identity of God in time. It was this insight that enabled him to make the seminal breakthrough to the idea of a doctrine of substitutionary atonement right there at the centre of the synoptic narratives. He realised that if Pilate's judgement then and there was in fact YHWH's judgement then and then – that this was what was narrated in the second part of the narrative – then he effectively had a doctrine of substitutionary atonement. How did he come to

---

[25] Note what Calvin says in his 1553 commentary on John's Gospel: '... if we want to read the story of Christ's death with profit, the chief point is to look to Christ's eternal counsel. The Son of God is before the judgement seat of a mortal man. If we think this was done by men's will and do not raise our eyes to God, our faith must needs be put to shame and confounded.' Calvin, *Gospel of John, 11 – 21* (trans. T.H.L. Parker, ed. D.W. Torrance and T.F. Torrance; Edinburgh: Oliver & Boyd, 1961), 165.

[26] According to Barth God was in history acting in history. He had been in history ever since the seventh day of creation when he had determined Himself to be within the spatial and temporal constitution of the world, the very same world He had created beforehand. For Barth this self-determination was sufficient for it to true that God had spatially located Himself within the world. This was what was meant by saying that 'God was in heaven.' It was no mere mythological conception for Barth! See *CD* III/1, 226-28.

see this? *The answer is to do with how Barth interpreted the first part of the narrative.*

The Two Narrative Conditions of Substitutionary Atonement

Barth asked two crucial questions. He asked the question: *what if the narrative is saying that YHWH's judgement on Jesus executed through Pilate in the passion narrative is the self-same judgement that Jesus declared on Israel and the world in the first part of the narrative?* And he asked the question: what if the narrative is saying that this is true because YHWH *made it true*: made his own judgement – Pilate's judgement – on Jesus *the very same* judgement that Jesus himself had previously declared in Galilee? In other words, what if it were the case that not only is Pilate's judgement on Jesus God's own judgement on Jesus, but also that this judgement of God's – expressed through Pilate's – is the very same judgement that Jesus declared in the first part? And that both were true because God made it so?

Then, Barth says: we have a doctrine of substitutionary atonement in the first three Gospels at the head of the New Testament canon. It is there objectively in the narrative. As he puts it in *Church Dogmatics* IV the Gospel story in its 'unity and completeness' narrates a story in which

> the divine subject of the judgement on man as which Jesus appears in the first part of the evangelical record becomes the object of this judgement from the episode of Gethsemane onwards. If this judgement is fulfilled at all – and that is what the Evangelists seem to be trying to say in the second part of their account – then it is with this reversal (*CD* IV/1, 238).

Barth indeed calls this reversal at a 'curious reversal of fortune'. Implicit in the above passage is the fact that Jesus becomes the object of the *self-same* eschatological judgement in the second part of the Gospel story that he issued in the first part of the Gospel story. But he can only become the subject of the same judgement if his own judgement (God's judgement) coincides with Pilate's judgement (God's judgement). This is indeed what Barth says. According to Barth, the rationale behind the narration of Jesus' agony in Gethsemane is precisely that the good will of God is absolutely at one with the evil will of the Sanhedrin and of Pilate. Gethsemane marks the beginning of the forsakenness of God that culminates in Jesus' cry of dereliction on the cross. 'The Lordship of God is concealed under the lordship of evil and evil men' (*CD* IV/1, 269). This is what will imminently bear down on Jesus once the sequence of events are set in motion by his arrest in Gethsemane. In the 'judicial' context this means that:

> It was a matter of the divine judgement being taken out of the hands of Jesus and placed in those of His supremely unrighteous judges and executed by them upon Him (*CD* IV/1, 271).

This is a crucial claim. The self-same judgement that Jesus had declared in the first part of the Gospel narrative is 'taken out of the hands of Jesus' and placed in the hands of pre-eminently Pilate's. Since the identity of Jesus' judgement is precisely 'the divine judgement' then so too is Pilate's judgement identical with 'the divine judgement.' Pilate's judgement on Jesus coincides with God's judgement – Jesus' eschatological judgement – exercised in the first part of the Gospel story. Or more precisely perhaps: Pilate's judgement in the second part *is* Jesus' judgement in the first part.

The divine judgement therefore remains constant, remains the same across the first two parts of the synoptic narrative. What changes across the two parts is the object of judgement. In the first part Israel and the world constitute the object of judgment. In the second part, Jesus constitutes the object of judgment. It is because this truth holds that Jesus comes to be in the passion story the *object of his own judgement – his own judgement being the one that he had declared on Israel and the world in the first part of the narrative.* This is because the God of Israel had made *His* judgement on Jesus – identical with Pilate's judgement on Jesus – also identical with Jesus' judgement.[27] Therefore, I repeat: *Jesus becomes the object of his own judgement.* Were it not the self-same judgement, Jesus – God – could not have taken our place. For then it would be the case that Jesus had suffered a different judgement. And if he suffered a different judgement he could not have taken our place as the object of the judgement declared in the first part of the Gospel story. This is the deep literal sense of the story of Barabbas' release (Mk 15.6-15). As Barth puts it: '…a murderer is in every respect acquitted instead of Jesus, and Jesus is condemned to be crucified in his place' (*CD* IV/1, 224). More expansively, Barth writes: '…the accusation, condemnation, and punishment to which [the second part of the Gospel story] refers all fall on the very One on whom they ought to fall least, and not at all on those on whom they ought to fall' (*CD* IV/1, 224). But Barth can only say this because he understands Pilate's judgement on Jesus as identical to – continuous with – the eschatological judgement that Jesus proclaims in Galilee.

Same judgement, different object of judgement equals *substitutionary atonement*. Jesus takes the place of Israel and world. Jesus takes *our* place, whether Jew or Gentile.

There is an oft-quoted passage in *Church Dogmatics* IV/1 in which Barth writes:' The atonement is, noetically, the history about Jesus Christ, and ontically, Jesus Christ's own history. To say atonement is to say Jesus Christ. To speak of it is to speak of his history' (*CD* IV/1, 158) I contend that the exposition that I have provided of Barth's doctrine of substitutionary atonement constitutes the fundamental reason behind that claim. The identity of Jesus of Nazareth is precisely the realisation of identity in the encountering of circumstance. And these circumstances are best interpreted in terms of Jesus the divine bearer of YHWH's judgement who

---

[27] Note also it is not *Jesus* who makes Pilate's judgement his own judgement. Whether or not he could have done this given his divine status, he did not. It is YHWH the God of Israel who did.

becomes the object of his own judgement. Accordingly, atonement is itself objectively in the historical event that corresponds to the identity of Jesus of Nazareth; it is not a matter of a subjective interpretation of Jesus' death.

Jesus takes His own Eschatological Judgement on Himself

But the judgement Jesus takes on himself is not just any kind of judgement, it is *eschatological* judgement that he takes on himself. Jesus takes his own eschatological judgement on himself. Barth utterly ironically concurs with the critical-historical tradition that follows in the wake of Weiss and Schweitzer (and in our own time, N.T. Wright). Jesus declares eschatological judgement on Israel and the world in the first part of the synoptic narrative and he becomes the object of this same judgement in the second part. Pilate's judgement is not merely God's judgement, it is God's eschatological judgement on Jesus.

What does it mean to be the object of eschatological judgment? The central theme is this. For Jesus to be the object of eschatological judgement in place of Israel and the world – us – is not merely to undergo death; it is to undergo *eschatological death* as in the *deuteros thanatos*, the *'second death'* referred to in Revelation 20.14.[28] Hence: not only is God's will indistinguishable from the will of evil men, the will of God is 'indistinguishably one with the evil will of men and the world and Satan. It was a matter of the triumph of God being concealed under that of His adversary, of that which is not, of that which is supremely not' (*CD* IV/1, 271). This is precisely why Barth perceives that what is bearing down on Jesus at Gethsemane, in the form of pre-eminently Pilate's judgement and execution of Jesus by crucifixion, must also be expressed in terms of satanic will or radical evil.

To suffer God's eschatological judgement is to live and die *apart from God*, or YHWH, the God of Israel, precisely because God has turned away from us.[29] This is the central meaning of the cry of dereliction on the cross: 'My Lord, my Lord, why hast thou forsaken me?' For God to turn away from Jesus in his death on the cross *is what it means to say* that Jesus in death has 'descended into hell.'

---

[28] Indeed, it is often overlooked that in Barth's later theology, Jesus is not merely resurrected from the dead, but from the 'second death.' Accordingly, he is raised from this death as an act of self-justification on the part of God.

[29] I am inclined to think that this concept of 'turning away' is fundamental to Barth's conception of *das Nichtige* as he understands it in the context of Genesis 1.2. For Barth seems to want to understand 1.2 retrospectively from the perspective of 1.3. It is God's *turning away* from the chaos described by 1.2 that is constitutive of the reality of *das Nichtige*. In other words, His utterance of the words 'Let there be light …' constitutes a turning away from chaos See also Barth's discussion in *CD* IV/1, 253 where he says that 'My turning from God is followed by God's annihilating turning from me.' Any attempt to evaluate Barth's understanding on these points must pay attention to Barth's conception of divine epistemology in II/1, and in particular, his view that God's knowledge does not depend on there being, as it were, objects of knowledge. See *CD* II/1, 543-560.

Ordinary death is a death that does not separate us from the love of God (and therefore does involve the concept of hell): 'If we live, we live to the Lord, and if we die, we die to the Lord; so then, whether we live or whether we die, we are the Lord's. For to this end Christ died and lived again, that he might be the Lord of both the living and the dead (Romans 14.8-9). One might think that this is cold comfort: death is still death. But Barth would say that it is Jesus' death – the 'second death' – that constitutes the criterion of *what it is* ordinary death is. This death – the death that Jesus died – is indeed a 'casting into outer darkness' since it is a dying apart from God. This 'withdrawal' of the divine self is achieved by the simple yet devastating 'apocalyptic' action of God determining himself to be the one who withdraws, who sets Himself apart, from Jesus. Eschatological death is a privative concept: it is the absence of God. 'Hell' and 'satan' are also representative of privative concepts in this sense. God's judgement on Jesus is precisely that He wills to be apart from Jesus during the passion and pre-eminently in his death.

Again, as in the case of the theological identity of Pilate's judgement, it was Calvin who had the greatest influence on Barth's thinking about eschatological death. Almost certainly it was Calvin's exposition of Christ's descent into hell in the apostle's creed, which provided the essential impetus to Barth's thought. As Calvin says: '…we ought not to omit [Christ's] descent into hell, a matter of no small moment in bringing about redemption.'[30] Barth would have agreed wholeheartedly; and he would have done so on behalf of the historical figure of Jesus who declared God's eschatological judgment on Israel and the world, and became the object of this same judgement culminating in the cross.

Calvin noted that 'there are some who think that nothing new is spoken of in this article, but that it repeats in other words what had previously been said of his burial, the word 'hell' often being used in Scripture to denote a grave.'[31] (This view was held by Bucer and probably by Beza.) The best reason that Calvin gives for thinking such a position untenable is the simple one to the effect 'it is not likely that a useless repetition could have crept into this summary [the creed].'[32] Instead, he proposes the following interpretation. The death that Jesus submitted to in place of us is one in which he had to 'bear and suffer all the punishments that they ought to have sustained… No wonder that is said to have descended into hell, for he suffered the death that God in his wrath had inflicted on the wicked.'[33] Calvin continues: 'The point is that the Creed sets forth what Christ suffered in the sight of men, and then appositely speaks of that invisible and incomprehensible judgment which he underwent in the sight of God in order that we might know not only that Christ's body was given as the price of our redemption, but that he paid a greater and more excellent price in suffering in his soul the terrible torments of a condemned and forsaken man.'[34]

---

[30] Calvin, *Institutes* (1559), 512.
[31] Calvin, *Institutes* (1559), 513.
[32] Calvin, *Institutes* (1559), 513.
[33] Calvin, *Institutes* (1559), 515-16.
[34] Calvin, *Institutes* (1559), 516.

Again, as in the case of Pilate's judgement, the de   influence on Barth's concept of eschatological death seems to have been Calvin.

The 'Directorial Eye' of the Evangelist

As was seen: Calvin followed the literal sense of the synoptic narrative and saw in Jesus' encounter with Pilate an encounter between the Christ and the governor of Judea, a very powerful man to be sure, but no more than a man. Now, notwithstanding what I have said above about the difference between Barth and Calvin on this, what I deliberately avoided saying is that Barth disagreed with him on this specific point. This *was* what the literal or plain sense of the narrative was saying. But Barth thought that the evangelist himself was saying more than that contained in the literal plain sense. In that sense he did not think that the literal sense exhausted the meaning of the narrative.

I want to backtrack to something I said about a certain aspect of the literary form of the synoptic narrative. You will remember Barth's claim, expressing his agreement with the judgement of tradition, that the synoptic narratives express 'little mention of the significance of the Christ event which took place there and then' (*CD* IV/1, 224). Instead, it 'is content simply to tell the story – this is how it was, this is how it happened' (*CD* IV/1, 227). And finally: 'The Gospel story [expressed in the synoptics]... does not offer any theological explanation. It says hardly anything about the significance of the event' (*CD* IV/1, 239).

I think these remarks applied most pointedly to the encounter between Jesus and Pilate in the passion narrative. It is the passion narrative's very reticence bordering on silence as regards the presence of YHWH at the locus of Pilate's judgement that is indicative of the very doctrine of substitutionary atonement that Barth sees in the synoptic narrative. The very part of the synoptic narrative in which YHWH seemed most absent – the passion narrative – He was in fact most present (though He is also present – again 'invisibly' but most potently – in the raising of Jesus). But this could only be perceived through, as it were, the 'directorial eye' of the evangelist. It was not something that was said explicitly in the course of events related in the narrative; rather it was intimated indirectly, insinuated, indirectly communicated. To use a Wittgensteinian concept, it was shown, not said. What do I mean by all this? In particular, what do I mean by the 'directorial eye' of the evangelist?

The answer can be best illuminated by what the writer Graham Greene called the quintessential art-form of the twentieth-century: cinematic film. Many have been the attempts to render the Gospel narrative in celluloid. My judgement on each of them is this. *They have all been failures if measured by what I call the 'directorial eye' of the evangelist in the synoptic narrative.* Nicholas Ray's *The King of Kings*, George Stevens' *The Greatest Story Ever Told*, Pier Paulo Pasolini's *The Gospel According to St Matthew*, Franco Zefferelli's *Jesus of Nazareth*, Martin Scorsese's *The Last Temptation of Christ*, a number of animated films including the recent *The Miracle-Maker* – all in some way or another fail to recognise and include the 'directorial eye' of the evangelist in the Synoptic Gospels.

It is therefore not merely that some have failed to be faithful to what is on the page of the Gospel if measured by the key events of the Gospel story. To be sure, when measured by the criterion of verisimilitude to the narrative in this sense, some of the films have exhibited quite striking disparities. Moreover, in these cases, the explanation is quite obvious. Scorsese's film *The Last Temptation of Christ* is based on Kazanzakisis' novel of the same name. But as Hans Frei pointed out almost thirty years ago in *The Identity of Jesus Christ*, this novel is not really about the personal identity of Jesus Christ as identified in the Gospels at all. By this he meant that the Jesus rendered in Kazanzakisis' novel – no less than some kind of Nietszchean superman – contradicts the Jesus rendered in the Gospels. Excepting some kind of [exceptionally] sophisticated harmonisation tantamount in fact to sophistry, the two accounts cannot meaningfully be reconciled. But this means that Scorsese's film – insofar as it is a faithful account of Kazanzakisis' novel – cannot be a faithful account of the Gospel story. Pasolini's *The Gospel According to St Matthew* is also susceptible to a similar kind of judgement in that its Marxist–motivated/inspired presentation leaves us with a Christ selectively seen through the eyes of a director who has revolution and perhaps the beatitudes continually to mind. Notwithstanding the cinematic aesthetic beauty of this film – in the realm of religious film-making, Pasolini's comes to mind immediately as a masterpiece - its vision of Christ is more Pasolini than the Gospel.

It may be said that, granted Scorsese's and Pasolini's films owe more to extraneous artistic and political sources than to the Gospels for their respective visions, surely many of the other films are direct accounts of the Gospels? Whatever the personal or idiosyncratic sensibilities or intentions of the director, surely Ray's film, Stevens' film, and even more plainly Zefferelli's film, are faithful renderings of the Gospel as we have it? Both Stevens' and Zefferelli's respective films for example have not excised the resurrection from their cinematic accounts in the supposed name of realism or credibility but have unashamedly included reference to it. Indeed, they include most if not all of the key events of the Gospel history. But this is not my criticism. Nor is it that the films have failed – or omitted - to depict what we understand as Jesus' divinity. There are a number of animated versions of the Gospel story – most recently the *Miracle-Maker* – directed from an unashamedly Christian and proselytising perspective that clearly emphasise this aspect of Jesus' identity.

Yet I would argue that none of these features are in themselves sufficient to guarantee a faithful rendering of the synoptic narrative. Ironically, faithfulness in the strict sense exclusively to what is communicated or told us directly by what is 'on the page' is not enough. Indeed, I would say that the great irony at work is that in all the cases where the director's primary concern is getting the ostensive reference of the Gospels – resurrection included – on to the screen, the consequence will be a vision cut asunder from that of the 'directorial eye' of the evangelist. This is because it is to present us with a vision that is *ultimately at odds with the Gospel. It is to create a film that, though not without great emotional content, will focus on the key events of the narrative – cross, resurrection – without any kind of sensitivity to those details in the narrative which, though less directly communicated than these key events, provide for the narrative's deepest interpretative key*. Unless one includes in one's cinematic vision what is communicated merely indirectly, or only subtly insinuated, or in a word, *shown* by the narrative – and not only what is directly communicated or unequivocally said - *theological discrepancy will have intruded to vitiate the fundamental objective of the Gospel's own vision*. For if one merely depicts what is unequivocally stated what is on the page, one will omit what is merely equivocally conveyed on the page – which is to say, one will be retelling the narrative without looking at it through the directorial lens of the evangelist.

And this, Barth would say, means that you will not discern what the 'directorial eye' of the Evangelist sees in Pilate's judgement on Jesus, namely YHWH's judgement on Jesus. And without this you lack the essential point of departure for discerning in the narrative what Barth would say is in the narrative: namely, a doctrine of substitutionary atonement.

The 'Eye of Faith': The 'Directorial Eye' that becomes Your 'Eye'

Let us suppose that Barth is right to imply that substitutionary atonement is the central doctrine of the New Testament canon. The intriguing question arises, why the evangelist did not say this explicitly, why he did not say directly in the plain sense of scripture that Pilate's judgement on Jesus is in fact YHWH's judgement on Jesus. Why does he only insinuate, intimate it? Why is there this 'degree of freedom' built into the Gospel such it is 'left open' to you to decide whether you affirm what it is you see through the 'directorial eye' of the evangelist?

Let us reflect once again on this most famous of encounters. If Barth is right about the presence of the 'directorial eye' of the evangelist then one has to acknowledge (as has implicitly been done) that it is not a moment that has been caught especially well by a film-camera because more often than not the scene has been emptied of its theological significance. However, fortunately, it has been painted more than once by the great classical artists. One of these was the great sixteenth-century Venetian artist Tintoretto. If you ever get the opportunity to see his canvas in the flesh in the *Scuola San Marco*, the question you want to pose is not the famous question in the Gospel that Jesus asks the disciple Peter as in: 'who do you say I am?' (Mark 8:29) The pertinent question here is not about the identity of Jesus. Rather: the question is about the identity of Pilate's judgment on Jesus: precisely 'Who do you say Pilate's judgement is?' Is it merely his own so that Jesus' death is a consequence of the power of the secular and religious authorities alone – or is it in reality and really – though physically embodied in individuals such as Pontius Pilate – really and ultimately – God acting in history and therefore God's own judgement on Jesus. The directorial eye of the evangelist sees not only Pilate's judgement on Jesus in this scene, he also sees God's judgement on Jesus.

Clearly, your answer to this question is constitutive of a *faith-decision*. If you answer in the affirmative, you have responded to what I would call the essential and objective *kerygmatic* locus in the Gospel narrative. You have effectively defined yourself as a participant in the narrative precisely as one of those who have been saved. Our affirmation of the evangelist's perception at this point in the narrative is crucial to our identity as Christians and as members of the Christian community. If we affirm the perception and see Pilate's judgement as God's judgement then we in effect define ourselves as one of those who have been saved by Jesus' substitutionary action. We participate in the story in the sense that we make a faith-decision of a definite sort. In this sense it can be said that Barth's understanding of the manner in which the narrative indirectly communicates the doctrine of substitutionary atonement has within itself the potential to inspire an unrivalled pulpit performance of 'preaching the Gospel' as a triumph of dialectic and imagination, even in the modern age.

The answer one gives to Jesus' famous question effectively defines one as an 'insider' – insofar as one repeats Peters answer (the Messiah, the son of God, etc) – or as an 'outsider' if one rejects Peter's answer. *As has been said, a very similar idea is operative in the question the evangelist asks about Pilate's judgement.* The question whether Pilate's judgement in the narrative is in fact also God's judgement leading to 'judicial' execution by crucifixion, or whether what we have here is a purely human tragedy of an innocent man sentenced to death – will define whether you are an 'insider' and therefore Judao-Christian, or an 'outsider' who rejects this kind of theological conception of history at work in the narrative.

Conclusion

It is submitted that Barth's account of atonement is preferable to Calvin's view of atonement principally because the narrative historicity it presupposes is rational to affirm by the standards of the Enlightenment. This makes it eminently suitable for mission in our modern times. For Calvin, the atonement is concentrated on the cross interpreted as the wrath of God poured out on the man Jesus. Barth, writing this side of the Enlightenment, develops an account which subversively takes advantage of the Enlightenment's advocacy of the eschatological, apocalyptic Jesus as the real historical person - in order to once more affirm a thoroughly theological yet factual description of the passion narrative lost from view in the wake of the Enlightenment legacy. Nevertheless, it is a doctrine of *substitutionary* atonement and this would seem to render it unhistorical in the eyes of the New Testament scholar, N T Wright. Wright writes,

> The categories of the sixth or fifth or fourth centuries, and those of the sixteenth or subsequent centuries C.E., are not necessarily good guides for our understanding of Jesus. Listening to the debate between substitution and representation, in however a sophisticated and nuanced fashion it may be carried on, leaves me as a historian with the same feeling I have when I meet people – as I don't, fortunately, very often

– for whom the key question in the New Testament is whether the Rapture comes before or after the Tribulation.[35]

I reject the implicit claim that all accounts of substitutionary atonement are necessarily non-historical accounts. This is because it seems to be that Barth has an account of the life of the historical Jesus that places substitutionary atonement at the centre of that life as a rational, historical truth-claim. Indeed, Barth's account is ironically decidedly more sceptical than Wright's regarding Jesus' intentions in his ministry even though it advocates a 'classical' theory of atonement involving a claim to divine action. According to Wright, Jesus saw his own coming to Jerusalem as YHWH's long awaited return to Zion as king. In his person he enacted the "forgiveness of sins" as the return from exile, which latter had been longed for since the exile in 587 BC. Jesus sees his final journey as the return of YHWH as king involving the messianic woes akin to the suffering servant of Isa. 52:13 – 53.10.[36] In keeping with this view, Wright holds that 'Jesus…went up to Jerusalem not just to preach, but to die…Jesus believed that the messianic woes were about to burst upon Israel, and that he had to take them upon himself, solo.'[37] In other words, there is a continuity of intention between Jesus' ministry and passion: Jesus goes to Jerusalem to die, and does. In contrast, the view espoused here – which agrees with Barth on many of these matters (Barth is surprisingly modern!) – is that Jesus went up to proclaim the imminence of God's direct reign (YHWH as king: 'Your God reigns!' Isa. 52:7). Jesus goes up to preach, not necessarily to die; he identifies himself as 'the Son of Man' who will be eschatological judge and ruler[38] vouchsafed by the irresistible reign of God, 'coming with the clouds of heaven' (Dan. 7:13). But events take a different turn from his 'triumphal entry into Jerusalem' such that the self-realization of Jesus' identity is as a different self-determining subject who understands that what is bearing down on him – in the form of the evil people who will judge and execute him – is really God's judgement. This is what he perceives to be the true nature of the events from Gethsemane onwards ('Abba, Father…not what I will, but what you will' [Mark 14:36]), and perhaps indeed from the Last Supper onwards. This is what he submits to as a self-determining subject in the encountering of the historical circumstances that constitute the passion. Bultmann writes that the 'Son of Man' motif in the earliest tradition did not speak of a 'Son of Man' who would come as in a second coming, *deutera parousia*, after death and resurrection.[39] Rather, the Son of Man is one who would rule and judge (from

---

[35] N.T. Wright, 'The Servant and Jesus', in William H. Bellinger, Jr, and William R. Farmer (eds.), *Jesus and the Suffering Servant: Isaiah 53 and Christian Origins* (Harrisburg: Trinity Press International, 1998), 295.

[36] Wright, *Jesus and the Victory of God*, 651.

[37] Wright, *Jesus and the Victory of God*, 609.

[38] See G. Theissen and A. Merz, *The Historical Jesus: A Comprehensive Guide* (London: SCM Press, 1998), 553.

[39] See R. Bultmann, *Theology of the New Testament*, vol. 1 (London: SCM Press, 1952), 29.

Jerusalem) under the aegis of a new dawn and age, precisely God's direct reign. This is utterly consonant with a Jesus who, self-determining subject that he is, goes to the cross in such a way that substitutionary atonement is at the heart of the historical Jesus: God takes his own eschatological judgement on himself – in the form of Jesus of Nazareth. God the King. God the Messiah (Jesus the Messiah).

The moral of this story is that Barth's account of substitutionary atonement has a central role to play in the Reformed Church's mission in the modern age, not least because it is rational by philosophical and indeed (I would argue) historical standards of rationality. Indeed, given that both Barth and Calvin on the atonement presuppose in equal measure the scripture-principle (and satisfy, each in its own way, the creedal statements of the historic Church), it is precisely because *inter alia* Barth's view does not flinch from the consequences of the truth of the eschatological Jesus that it has a greater claim to the mantle of the Church's account of atonement today than does Calvin's doctrine.

But like Calvin's view of the atonement, Barth's account is more conservative than Wright's in one respect, and that is it affirms the reality of divine action – God acting – in the life of Jesus, especially during the passion narrative. It may be that Wright's position doesn't presuppose such an action. Wright may think that is one of its many undoubted methodological strengths. But I think that this is a weakness; and that perhaps Wright should embrace a more inclusive species of historical rationality ('the historical critics must become more historical to suit me!', Karl Barth!)

CHAPTER 5

Calvin, Barth, and the Subject of Atonement

Myron B. Penner

Introduction

John Calvin's 1559 version of his *Institutes of the Christian Religion*[1] defines an entire tradition of Reformation theology, and his treatment there of the Christian doctrine of atonement remains an immensely influential analysis of the Christian teaching regarding God's redemption in Christ. Karl Barth's 'Doctrine of Reconciliation,' presented in his *Church Dogmatics* volume IV.1–4[2] in the middle of the twentieth century, is at once a creative and provocative re-thinking of Calvin's concept of God's free grace in Jesus Christ. In this chapter I wish to explain Calvin's doctrine of atonement in the *Institutes* in the light of some of Barth's important objections to and innovations on it in the *Dogmatics*.[3] My central thesis is that Calvin's theology of atonement contains elements that are indispensable to a thoroughly Reformed and scripturally faithful account of atonement. Barth's doctrine of atonement can be adopted, then, only if it is amended to include these. Barth's doctrine of atonement may at many points be a creative and powerful re-thinking of

---

[1] John Calvin, *Institutes of the Christian Religion* (ed. John T. McNeill, trans. F.L. Battles; 2 vols; Philadelphia: Westminster, 1960). Hereafter *Inst*.

[2] See Karl Barth, *Church Dogmatics* (4 vols, 13 tomes; Edinburgh: T. & T. Clark, 1956–69). Hereafter *CD*.

[3] I am limiting myself almost exclusively to the theologies expounded in Calvin's *Institutes* and Barth's *Dogmatics* for two reasons: first, these two works represent the mature theological exposition of each – they represent a distillation of their mature thought, if you will; and secondly, these are the works that are widely known and have influenced the tradition. I do not make any pretenses to exhaustively treat their theological positions in terms of historical development, nor am I even making the case to have represented Barth's and Calvin's personal positions. I am simply limiting myself to their respective teaching in these two works. I recognize, in especially Calvin's case, that my attempt here may be quite foreign to their intentions. See, for example, Richard Muller's stern warnings about accommodating 'the historical Calvin' to 'modern theological programs', in his *The Unaccommodated Calvin* (Oxford: Oxford University Press, 2000), 4ff. My design, however, is less to reproduce anything like 'the historical Calvin' – or Barth for that matter – than it is to discuss the inner logic of the positions reflected in these two significant pieces of theology. In so doing I believe that one is able to derive a basic understanding not far removed from Barth's and Calvin's personal views.

the Reformation concept of God's free grace in Jesus Christ, but his method of centering the atonement on the person of Jesus Christ leads him ultimately to jeopardize a key element of Reformation theology, and indeed the biblical account of human salvation.

I will argue this by laying out the essential structure of Calvin's theology of atonement so that its merits are apparent. My assumption is that Barth's doctrine of atonement shares some structural similarities to Calvin's and therefore I am not going to discuss Barth's doctrine of atonement with the sort of attention it deserves. I will limit my discussion of Barth's doctrine of atonement to his significant departures from Calvin. This will allow me to accentuate how, despite possessing a basic structure similar to Calvin, Barth's different methodological presuppositions produce a theology of atonement with significant and ill-advised differences from Calvin's.

Calvin on Atonement

The theology of John Calvin, especially as presented in his final 1559 version of the *Institutes*,[4] is widely regarded as setting the standard in Reformed theology for several centuries and still functions in that capacity in many quarters of the Reformed tradition today. It is fairly safe to say, then, that an account of atonement that radically deviates from Calvin does so at the peril of leaving behind the distinctives of Reformed theology. This is not to say that only those who mimic Calvin's theology are properly called 'Reformed.' I mean that while Calvin may (and perhaps should be) disagreed with, it is only with the deepest respect and after working through his position to a new one that supercedes Calvin's ability to meet his own goals – goals that he shares with the rest of the Christian tradition.[5] One could say, I suppose, that to disagree with Calvin and yet remain 'Reformed', one must produce a discourse that is more 'Calvinist' than Calvin's. However, it is not Calvin's various doctrinal formulations *per se* that I believe define Reformed theology, so much as his theological and methodological commitments – such as the so-called Scripture-Principle, which asserts (roughly) that the revelation of God in Scripture governs the scope and task of theology. These commitments also include Calvin's christological

---

[4] Calvin's first effort at writing his *Institutes* was in 1536. There were several versions of the *Institutes* in the intervening years until the final version appeared in Latin as *Instutatio christianae religionis* in 1559. See Richard Muller's 'Establishing the *Ordo docendi*: The Organization of Calvin's Institutes, 1536–1559,' in *The Unaccommodated Calvin*, ch. 7, 118-39, for a thorough discussion of the development of Calvin's thought throughout the different versions.

[5] While I do not have space to develop it here I would contend that Calvin does not see himself as creating a new theology. He is very careful to ground his theology in both apostolic and patristic sources, and even scholastic theology as well. Thus Calvin's relationship with tradition is quite complex. It is much more sanguine than a first glance at the *Institutes*, with its pronouncements that the Christian needs only the Scriptures and the Holy Spirit, would suggest.

view of Scripture (discussed below), his commitment to a covenant of grace, and his adherence to the other '*solas*' of the Protestant Reformation: *sola Scriptura* ('Scripture alone' as a rule for theology), *soli Christo* (salvation through 'Christ alone'), *sola fide* (justification by 'faith alone'), and *sola gratia* (righteousness by 'grace alone').

Barth, at any rate, is careful to learn from Calvin and his doctrine of atonement bears some close comparisons to Calvin's. I want to sketch Calvin's doctrine of atonement by way of three elemental theses that display the core of his teaching.

Christ our Redeemer

Let me begin with the touchstone proposition of Calvin's doctrine of atonement. Calvin believes:

1. THE ATONEMENT IS CENTERED ON THE PERSON AND WORK OF JESUS CHRIST

Calvin's allegiance to Scripture as the normative source of authority for theology is renowned. Wilhelm Niesel observes that it is obvious from the first sentence of the *Institutes*[6] that 'Calvin in fact begins to expound...the sum of what God teaches us in Holy Scripture.'[7] Thus, for Calvin any adequate doctrine of theology must be drawn directly from the teaching of Scripture. That said, what is sometimes overlooked is the relationship between Christ and Scripture in the *Institutes*. Two points are critical in this regard. First, in Book IV of the *Institutes* Calvin makes a very clear connection between the revealing activity of God and the person of Jesus Christ such that (following Mt. 11:27 and 2 Cor. 3:18) the revelation of God is completely dependent upon, and comes only through, the direct activity of Jesus Christ.[8] Calvin's position seems to be that the Scriptures are the *words* of God mediated or revealed through Christ, who is the supreme *Word* of God and definitive self-revelation of God.[9] Second, Calvin is convinced that the trajectory of the entire

---

[6] *Inst.* I.1.1 begins: 'All sacred doctrine consists in two things: knowledge of God and of ourselves.'

[7] Wilhelm Niesel, *The Theology of John Calvin* (trans. H. Knight; Ann Arbor: Baker Book House, 1980), 22. See also *Inst.* I.6.3 where Calvin argues that, 'Without Scripture we fall into error.'

[8] '[I]nasmuch as all divinely uttered revelations are correctly designated by the term "word of God," so this substantial Word [i.e., Jesus Christ] is properly placed at the highest level, as the wellspring of all oracles.' Calvin also makes much the same point in *Inst.* IV.8.5.

[9] Cf. Calvin's statements in *Inst.* I.4.2 regarding Scripture as the Word of God, his point in *Inst.* I.4.2, II.7.2, and III.2.6, that Christ is 'the end of the law,' with those just noted in I.13.7 and IV.8.5 that Christ is the sole revealer of God. As Niesel, *The Theology of Calvin*, 33, observes, Calvin seems dedicated to the proposition that there is a strong distinction to be made between the Word of God as the incarnate *Logos*, and

Bible points to God acting as the Creator and Redeemer of humankind.[10] The Christian Scriptures in their *entirety* speak of and towards God's atonement in Jesus Christ. In sum: for Calvin, Scripture takes precedence over all other sources as the normative source for a theology of atonement, but Scripture directs our thinking of atonement to the person and work of Jesus Christ.

Thus, the basic structure of Calvin's doctrine of atonement is places a theology of the person of Christ at the center. Calvin's focus on the person of Christ affects the development of Calvin's view of the atonement in two important ways. First, Calvin insists that *the atonement is intelligible in and through the Scriptures only in light of the incarnation of Christ*. Calvin's grammar of atonement is organized around his understanding of the person of Christ *as the one who meets the specific demands placed on the one who would be 'the Mediator' between God and humanity.* The incarnation of Christ 'the Mediator' is central to Calvin's doctrine of atonement.[11] There is no speaking about the atonement without also speaking of Christ's incarnation as fully God and fully human. The focal point of Calvin's discussion of atonement is found in Chapter 12 of Book II of the *Institutes* where Calvin discusses the reasons why it was 'necessary' that Christ became human to fulfill the office of mediator. Calvin begins this section by focusing our attention on the nature of Christ as 'our Mediator': 'Now it was of the greatest importance for us that he who was to be our Mediator be both true God *and* true man' (*Inst.* II.12.1, my italics). Calvin believes that only orthodox, Chalcedonian (two-natures) christology sufficiently accounts for Christ's atoning work as presented in Scripture.

There is not sufficient space here to discuss in full detail Calvin's argument for the 'necessity'[12] of Christ's two natures to atonement, but in short it runs as follows. On the one hand, the mediator must be fully human in order to atone for expressly *human* sin and to accomplish distinctly *human* salvation; but on the other hand, he must also fully be God in order to perform the monumental tasks of spanning the moral and ontological gap between God and humanity, heaven and hell,

---

the words of Scripture. This creates, of course, a latent tension in Calvin's theology over which is properly regarded as 'the Word of God' (Christ or the Bible?) – a tension that Barth takes up with some dramatic improvements.

[10] Calvin argues in *Inst.* II.10.1-23 that the Old and New Testaments are united in their focus on the covenant of God in Jesus Christ. He therefore comes to argue in *Inst.* II.11.1 that, 'there will be nothing to hinder the promises of the Old and New Testaments from remaining the same, nor from having the same foundation of these very promises Christ!' Thus François Wendel *Calvin: The Origins and Development of His Thought* (trans. P. Mairet; London: Collins, 1963), 215, notes that for Calvin, 'The Biblical witness as a whole is to be regarded as witness to Jesus Christ, and theology has no other purpose than guiding believers in this quest of the Christ through all the Biblical writings.'

[11] See *Inst.* II.12-13. Cf. R Peterson's claim that the incarnation is the pre-requisite to Calvin's doctrine of atonement, *Calvin's Doctrine of Atonement* (Ross-shire: Mentor, 1999), 11ff.

[12] Calvin sees this as a so-called 'hypothetical-necessity,' that does not coerce God from outside of his free choice, rather than an 'absolute necessity.'

as well as conquering sin and death.¹³ The atonement is not incidental to Christ's incarnation but is the sole purpose of it. It is in fact for this very reason that God in Jesus Christ became human.¹⁴

> True, as Calvin notes, it was human sin that creates the conditions that require atoning, but, for Calvin, the atonement is not an accident of history; it is part of God's purposes for the universe from eternity. Drawing on John 1:1, Calvin is clear that Christ is the mediator *before* the creation of Adam and Eve and their subsequent fall into sin. Christ's incarnation reveals the purposes of God for humanity from creation and is *gospel* – quite literally the 'good news' – for in the incarnation we have revealed that God has always loved us in Jesus.

Calvin writes,

> For it was not after we were reconciled to him through the blood of his Son that he began to love us. Rather, *he has loved us before the world was created*... The fact that we were reconciled through Christ's death must not be understood as if his Son reconciled us to him that he might now begin to love those whom he had hated. Rather, *we have already been reconciled to him who loves us*, with whom we were enemies on account of sin (*Inst.* II.16.4, my italics).

The incarnation reveals that Christ's atonement springs from the eternal love of God who has chosen us in Christ. As Calvin makes clear in *Institutes* III.22.7, Christ not only is the *instrument* of God's eternal election of believers; he is also the *source* of our election.¹⁵ In other words, contrary to some of his critics (including Barth),¹⁶ Calvin has a thoroughly christological understanding of election that does *not* separate Jesus Christ from the triune Godhead.¹⁷ It is sometimes suggested that

---

¹³ See *Inst.* II.12.2: 'His task was to make of the children of men, children of God; of the heirs of Gehenna, heir of the Heavenly Kingdom...we trust that we are sons of God, for God's natural Son fashioned for himself a body from our body, flesh from our flesh, bone from our bones, that he might become one with us... It was also imperative that he who was to become Redeemer be true God and true man. It was his task to swallow up death. Who but the Life could do this?'

¹⁴ See *Inst.* II.12.4: 'In short, the only reason given in Scripture that the Son of God willed to take our flesh, and accepted this commandment from the Father, is that he would be a sacrifice to appease the Father on our behalf.'

¹⁵ In addition 5 Calvin teaches in *Institutes* III.24. that it is in Christ that we properly 'contemplate our own election.' Note as well that in *Institutes* II.13.4 and IV.17.30 Calvin argues what is sometimes called the *extra calvinisticum*: that the all of Jesus' divinity was fully incarnate, but that Jesus cannot be limited to his incarnate bodily form. There is, in other words, an *extra* to Jesus in his incarnation. The fullness of God is present in Jesus of Nazareth, but there is more to Jesus of Nazareth than is present in his human form.

¹⁶ See *CD* II/2, 111.

¹⁷ Niesel makes this argument in *The Theology of John Calvin*, 159-69; see esp. 164. See also Stephen R. Holmes *Listening to the Past: The Place of Tradition in Theology*

Calvin understands election to be the Father's decision to elect believers in Christ, but, while this is not totally false, for Calvin election *in* Christ is also election *by* Christ. But more to my purposes here, Calvin's understanding of atonement in the light of the incarnation and its correlative christological character of election, means that Calvin's theology of atonement is a proclamation of God's totally free and unconditioned grace in Jesus Christ to sinful humanity (*Inst.* II.17.1). To use more typically Barthian language, God's revelation to us in Jesus Christ is a 'Yes,' for Calvin, despite the negative side of election.[18]

The above point is important in rebutting a couple of rather prosaic – but also rather frequent – objections to Calvin's teaching on atonement. These objections claim that conceptions of atonement that emphasize Christ's sacrificial death are psychologically unhealthy and/or unethical because they either glorify violence by endorsing the victimization of innocent scapegoats, or they make God out to be spiteful and vindictive (or both). The trouble with these sorts of objections is that they depend on a too-strict separation between the Father and Jesus. When Christ is not regarded as the author of his own election he is perceived as a victim of a vindictive, avenging Father. Thomas F. Torrance's clarification in this regard applies equally to Calvin: 'Propitiation has nothing to do with propitiating God as though he needed to be placated in order to reconcile himself to us, but with the two-way movement on the part of God who in his prevenient love freely draws us near to himself on the ground of the atoning self-sacrifice of Christ offered for us.'[19] Calvin's view depends upon Christ's freedom in the atonement, so that the proper category through which to understand it is not victimization, but self-donation or self-sacrifice.[20]

One effect of Calvin's Christ-centered doctrine of atonement, as I just showed, is that Calvin grounds the formal question of the atonement (i.e., the theological framework for the atonement) on a two-natures theology of the person of Christ. The second result of his Christ-centered approach to atonement is that Calvin explains the material dimension (i.e., *how* the atonement was accomplished) in terms atonement in Christ's fulfillment of the three scriptural offices of Christ's ministry: prophet, priest, and king. This claim places me at slight odds with Robert A. Peterson who claims that Calvin viewed the three-fold offices of Christ and the various biblical metaphors describing atonement as alternate ways of explaining the

---

(Carlisle: Paternoster Press, 2002), 125, who, in fact, extends this christological understanding of election to the whole of 'Reformed Orthodoxy' from Beza onward.

[18] There is much more to say about this, of course, particularly in regards to the extent of the atonement, as anyone who is familiar at all with Calvin's theology is well aware. I will return to this subject below.

[19] Thomas F. Torrance, 'The Atonement. The Singularity of Christ and the Finality of the Cross: The Atonement and the Moral Order', in Nigel M. de S. Cameron (ed.), *Universalism and the Doctrine of Hell* (Carlisle: Paternoster Press, 1992), 242.

[20] See *Inst.* II.16.5.

meaning of the saving work of Christ.[21] Rather than viewing them as alternate and equal ways of explaining the atonement, there is a definite logical priority between them in Calvin's thought. In *Institutes* II.12-14 Calvin's scriptural logic of atonement emphasizes the incarnation of 'the Mediator', and this, he claims, is to be understood in terms of Christ's three ministerial offices prophet, king, and priest.[22] Calvin appears to view these three offices as inhering in the very nature of Christ as those aspects of his person that procure atonement for us. In this case, the biblical metaphors function to further illumine what the being of Christ in these three modes accomplishes for us.

Christ's fulfillment of the three biblical offices establishes 'a firm basis for salvation in Christ' (*Inst.* II.15.1) and fleshes out (literally) for Calvin how Christ accomplished atonement. In treating Christ's atonement in terms of his three offices, Calvin understands *all* of Christ's life, each aspect of his incarnation – life, death, and resurrection – as pertinent to our atonement. As *prophet* Christ is the fulfillment of the Old Testament prophetic teaching regarding the Messiah and came preaching 'useful doctrine sufficient for salvation.'[23] The significance of Christ's prophetic office for atonement lies in Christ's incarnational proclamation (as the Word of God in the flesh) of the Gospel – the good news of God's love and redemption (*Inst.* II.15.1). This office emphasizes Christ's earthly and historical ministry as a human being whose obedient *life* testified to the veracity of his message, setting an example that we should follow (*Inst.* II.16.5). Christ is *king* by virtue of his anointing by the Holy Spirit, which signals that Christ's kingdom is both spiritual and eternal (*Inst.* II.15.3-5). The kingly office stresses Christ's triumph over the powers of evil by his *resurrection* and exaltation the Father (*Inst.* II.16.13). As our king, Christ is always for us from eternity and is therefore the eschatological guarantor of our salvation. Christ's atonement is able to save completely those who believe because as king he is authorized to send the Holy Spirit, who, in turn, indwells believers and endows them with eternal life and spiritual gifts (*Inst.* II.15.4.5).

The crux of our atonement, however, lies in Christ's role as our *priest*, which, according to Calvin, performs two primary functions: reconciliation and intercession (*Inst.* II.15.6). Calvin sums up the significance of Christ's priestly office saying that in this capacity Christ acts 'as a pure and stainless Mediator' in order 'to reconcile us to God' (*Inst.* II.15.6). The emphasis in Christ's priestly service is his unique ability to mediate between sinful humanity and a righteous God, whose 'righteous curse

---

[21] Peterson, *Calvin's Doctrine of Atonement*, 27. I will return to the topic of the biblical metaphors below.

[22] See *Institutes* II.15: 'To know the purpose for which Christ was sent by the Father, and what he conferred, upon us, we must look above all at three things in him: the Prophetic Office, Kingship, and Priesthood.'

[23] *Institutes* II.15.1. My intention at this point is not to exposit Calvin's teaching on the offices in detail, but simply to note briefly how he explains the atonement by means of them. For such a detailed exposition, I refer the reader to Peterson, *Calvin's Doctrine of Atonement*, 27-39. Peterson provides a very helpful commentary on Calvin's teaching on Christ's *munus triplex*.

bars us access to him' and who, 'in his capacity as judge is angry toward us' (*Inst.* II.15.6). The key, then, to Christ's priestly work is his sacrificial *death on the cross*. Following Heb. 9:22 Calvin summarizes: 'The priestly office belongs to Christ alone because by the sacrifice of his death he blotted out our own guilt and made satisfaction for our sins' (*Inst.* II.15.6). On the basis of this first aspect of his priestly work, the reconciliation of believers to God through his death on the cross, Christ is also capable of completing his priestly intercession for believers. Christ's reconciling work on the cross makes us priests with him so that we are able to persevere in a reconciled state with God and offer our own prayers before him, because Christ always lives to intercede for us (*Inst.* II.15.6, and II.16.16). In summary: in his priestly role, Christ's death on the cross offers a propitiatory sacrifice that fulfills the demands of the Law, appeases the Father's wrath against sinful humanity, makes satisfaction for human sin, provides the blood that washes away our guilt, and obtains grace for us thereby giving us access to God. In his priestly ministry we have the union of Christ's earthly and heavenly ministries: in his death Christ offered his humanity in place of ours, and in his resurrection and exaltation he lives always to intercede for us.

Delineating the atonement in terms of Christ's three offices in the context of Christ's two natures corrects a common misunderstanding of Calvin's teaching on atonement. The biblical accounts of the atonement revolve around a singular event – the life and death of Jesus of Nazareth on a cross under Pontius Pilate, Governor of Judea in Palestine during the first century A.D. Scripture itself, however, employs a variety of very different metaphors to describe Christ's atonement.[24] Henri Blocher, for example, identifies the five key biblical metaphors of atonement as punishment, sacrifice, ransom, victory, and Passover.[25] There are other metaphors, though, and classic theories of atonement tend to identify one of the metaphors or small set of metaphors as the central or grounding metaphor for the biblical account, and then interpret Christ's atonement through its lens. The theory most often associated with Reformation theology (and Calvin) is the so-called 'Penal-Substitution Theory' that

---

[24] For a detailed analysis of the relation of biblical metaphors to Christ's atonement, see Colin E. Gunton, *The Actuality of Atonement: A Study of Metaphor, Rationality, and the Christian Tradition* (Grand Rapids: Eerdmans, 1989).

[25] Henri Blocher, 'The Sacrifice of Jesus Christ', *European Journal of Theology* 8 (1999), 30. However, Trevor Hart, 'Redemption and Fall', in Colin E. Gunton (ed.), *The Cambridge Companion to Christian Doctrine* (Cambridge: Cambridge University Press, 1997), 194-95, arranges the various biblical metaphors differently, into three typological groups: metaphors of release, metaphors of transformation, and metaphors that refer to a new, confident and joyful access to God. Joel B. Green and Mark D. Baker, *Recovering the Scandal of the Cross: Atonement in New Testament and Contemporary Contexts* (Downer's Grove: InterVarsity Press, 2000), 25-29, also identify five biblical themes of atonement, with some overlap with Blocher: the court of law, the world of commerce, personal relationships, worship, and the battleground; cited in Kevin J. Vanhoozer, 'Guilt, Goats, and Gifts: The Atonement in Postmodernity', in Charles E. Hill and Frank James III (eds), *The Atonement: Essays Presented in Honor of Roger Nicole* (Downers Grove: InterVarsity Press, 2004).

emphasizes the metaphors of legal punishment and sacrifice to describe Christ's atonement in terms of his bearing the penalty for sin (death) through his death on the cross, by which he satisfied God's wrath and suffered God's punishment in the place of sinful humanity.[26] Calvin's emphasis on the person of Christ and his work (performed through his three offices) reveals the inadequacy of that label. One may find all the elements of penal-substitution[27] – sacrificial death, legal substitution, imputed righteousness, and so on – in the *Institutes*, but these do not exhaust Calvin's understanding of the subject. If Calvin limited his discussion of the atonement to the priestly ministry of Christ, with its focus on the cross and Christ's sacrificial death, perhaps the penal-substitution label would be a sufficient description of Calvin's doctrine of atonement. However, despite the centrality of the cross for atonement, Christ does not atone for us through his priestly oblations alone – such an understanding of atonement does not sufficiently grasp the incarnational Word of God in Jesus Christ as revealed in Scripture, and remains a partial account of our reconciliation. The priestly ministry office of Christ is augmented and completed by the other two offices, which taken as a package, constitute the gamut of the material aspect of atonement.[28]

The virtue of Calvin's approach is its thoroughly incarnational theory of atonement that explains the atoning effects of every aspect of Christ's incarnation – his life and resurrection, in addition to his death. In so doing Calvin attempts to speak from the framework of the whole of Scripture, as he is convinced that the

---

[26] There are other theories of atonement, though, such as the 'Satisfaction Theory,' which explains the atonement in terms of the metaphor of Christ's satisfaction of God's wrath and justice, or the 'Atonement as Victory' theory, which interprets the atonement principally as a payment or ransom to Satan for human sin, and a triumph over the powers of evil. There is also the 'Atonement as Moral Example' theory, according to which Christ's obedient life and death are the supreme example of God's love and function to move us to repentance for our sins. The 'Governmental Theory' of atonement, however, regards Christ's death through the metaphor of a legal transaction and argues that Christ did not bear the punishment for our sins, but upheld the judicial system God put in place ('if you sin, you will die') and in so doing preserved the conditions for a just and moral society. Whatever the case may be, the plurality of biblical metaphors leaves us hardly any closer to giving a theological account of the atonement through a straightforward appeal to biblical texts. What *is* clear in Scripture, however, is that the life, death and resurrection of Jesus Christ is crucial to any biblical understanding of atonement and that this is the central element of the Christian faith. Christian theologians are left, however, with the task of formulating theories of the atonement in an attempt to describe what the biblical teaching of Christ's atonement means and how it works.

[27] See especially, *Inst.* II.12.3, 'Only he who was true God and true man could be obedient in our stead;' and II.17.4, 'The substitution of Christ.'

[28] Cf. 'Now someone asks, How has Christ abolishes sin...? To this we can in general reply that he has achieved this for us by the whole course of his obedience... In short, from the time when he took on the form of a servant, he began to pay the price of our liberation. Yet to define the way of salvation more exactly, Scripture ascribes this as peculiar and proper to Christ's death.' *Institutes* II.16.5.

Scriptures in their entirety speak of and toward Christ. Calvin's commitment to biblicity means, of course, that he must articulate his discussion of human redemption in terms of the biblical metaphors for atonement,[29] but he does not single out a principal metaphor to operate as the interpretive key for atonement, and in fact he does not even identify the atonement primarily in terms of the metaphors. For Calvin it is 'the whole course of Christ's obedience' as summarized in the Apostle's Creed that presents the best summation of the biblical teaching on atonement, for it 'passes at once in the best order from the birth of Christ to his death and resurrection, wherein the whole of perfect salvation consists. Yet the remainder of the obedience he exhibited is not excluded' (*Inst.* II.16.5). Calvin structures the closing sections of his discussion of the material aspect of atonement in *Inst.* II.16.5–II.16.19 according to the lines of the Apostle's Creed, and closes that section asserting that we find 'Christ alone in all the clauses of the Creed.'

The proper way to think of the biblical metaphors of the atonement in Calvin's *Institutes*, then, is to view them as grounded in the incarnation of Christ and the work that he accomplished through his life, death, and resurrection in the performance of his prophetic, kingly, and priestly ministries. Calvin might say that the biblical metaphors *accommodate* God's salvation of us in Christ to our understanding, so that while they fail to encapsulate an exhaustive explanation of a concept or reality, the metaphors roughly express in terms that we can understand the essential truth about the concept or reality.[30] The metaphors can thus be understood to be expressions that variously explain the multi-faceted meaning of God's atonement of us through Christ's ministry in terms that are comprehensible by us. It is therefore no surprise that they ultimately offer conflicting accounts of the meaning of Christ's atonement when any particular one (set) of them is reified, so to speak, and used to try and ground the others. Such an approach, which the classical theories use, always remains open to the criticism that some important aspect of the biblical account of atonement has been ignored or under emphasized. For Calvin, however, all the parts of our redemption must be comprehended in Christ:

---

[29] For a thorough exposition of Calvin's discussion of atonement in terms of the biblical metaphors, see chs 4–9 in Peterson, *Calvin's Doctrine of Atonement*, 40-82.

[30] Although Calvin never invokes the category of accommodation in relation to the atonement, I believe it would be entirely fitting for him to do so. For a fairly plain statement of how Calvin thinks of accommodation, see his comments in *Inst.* I.17.13, where he describes accommodation as 'modes of speaking that describe God for us in human terms. For because our weakness does not attain to his exalted state, the description of him that is given to us must be accommodated to our capacity so that we may understand it. Now the mode of accommodation is for him to represent himself to us not as he is in himself, but as he seems to us.' For more on Calvin's concept of accommodation, see Ford Lewis Battles, 'God was Accommodating Himself to Human Capacity', *Interpretation* 31 (1977), 19-38 [also reprinted in *Interpreting John Calvin* (Grand Rapids: Baker, 1996), 117-38], and Paul Helm's chapter on accommodation in his *John Calvin's Ideas* (Oxford: Oxford University Press, 2004). I will return to the topic accommodation in relation to atonement below.

We see that our whole salvation *and all its parts* are comprehended in Christ [Acts 4:12]... If we seek strength, it lies in his dominion; if purity, in his conception; if gentleness, it appears in his birth. For by his birth he was made like us in all respects [Heb. 2:7] that he might learn to feel our pain [cf. Heb. 5:2]. If we seek redemption, it lies in his passion; if acquittal, in his condemnation; if remission of the curse, in his cross [Gal. 3:13]; if satisfaction, in his sacrifice; if purification, in his blood; if reconciliation, in his descent into hell; if mortification of the flesh, in his tomb; if newness of life, in his resurrection; if immortality, in the same; if inheritance of the Heavenly Kingdom, in his entrance into heaven; if protection, if security, if abundant supply of all blessings, in his Kingdom; if untroubled expectation of judgment, in the power given to him to judge (*Inst.* II.16.19, my italics).

For whom did Christ die?

Calvin's doctrine of atonement begins with and is grounded in the incarnation of Jesus Christ, in both its formal and material elements. The picture I just sketched of this, though, is only a partial and in many respects inadequate portrait of Calvin's theology of atonement. To remedy this I will also explore two important subsidiary theses that follow from Calvin's Christ-centered approach to the atonement, which further illuminate Calvin's theology of atonement. Though by no means providing us with a comprehensive exposition, this will provide at least a more nuanced understanding of Calvin's doctrine of atonement.

Thus the second thesis in Calvin's doctrine of atonement:

2. CHRIST RECONCILES HUMANS TO GOD BY RESTORING THE IMAGE OF GOD LOST BY ADAM'S SIN

Calvin teaches that the Old Testament Law reveals that human beings were created in God's image but are ontologically, epistemologically, and morally separated from God by an infinite chasm because of Adam's sin (*Inst.* II.1 and II.6-7). In other words, Adam's sin has left humanity in a state of total alienation from God: God's image in us is severely damaged without repair (ontological), we no longer possess knowledge of God or even ourselves (epistemological), and we are thoroughly unrighteous (moral). The incarnation of Christ in Scripture depicts Christ's action as the one who completes the Old Testament revelation of the Law (*Inst.* II.7) and reverses the effects of Adam's sin by restoring the image of God in us that was originally present in Adam at creation.[31] Calvin uses Paul's statements in Rom. 5:

---

[31] See *Inst.* I.15.4: '[T]he beginning and recovery of salvation is in that restoration which we obtain through Christ, who also is called the Second Adam for the reason that he restores us to true and complete integrity... [F]or the end of regeneration is that Christ should reform us to God's image.' See also *Inst.* II.12.7 and III.3.9: 'Accordingly, we are restored by this regeneration through the benefit of Christ into the righteousness of God; from which we had fallen through Adam.'

12-21 and 1 Cor. 15:45-49, which compare Christ to Adam, to identify Christ as 'the Second Adam.' Adam and Christ are 'the two roots' of the human race: Adam of sinful humanity, and Christ of the elect who are redeemed and restored to full humanity.[32]

I have been skirting a difficult issue in Calvin's teaching on atonement, concerning Calvin's understanding of the atonement and his view of election in Christ. But before I tackle that issue, it will be helpful to examine an objection Barth launches in *Church Dogmatics* to the effect that Calvin's understanding of humanity is insufficiently Christ-centered. This charge reveals a significant difference in Calvin's and Barth's respective theologies of atonement, and will serve to highlight for us Calvin's view of humanity in relation to atonement. Barth observes that when Calvin discusses our knowledge of God the Creator, he emphasizes that humanity can only know itself properly through God's self-revelation (in Scripture and in Jesus Christ). Barth's trouble with this is that Calvin then seems to posit 'a general antithesis: God on one side and man on the other' (*CD* IV/1, 367), without referring to the mediation of Christ. In other words, Barth believes that Calvin teaches that humans exist in some significant way, over and against God, without the mediation (ontological or epistemological) of Jesus Christ. Barth continues on to note that in the *Institutes* when Calvin speaks of the Old Testament saints' knowledge of God – and even in the New Testament – 'he seems to have regarded it as self-evident that for the moment we cannot and ought not to speak of man in his confrontation with Jesus' (*CD* IV/1, 367). Barth views this as an irremedial flaw in Calvin's theology, for Barth thinks that we can only speak properly of humanity if we speak of Jesus Christ first and always.

We shall return to Barth's assessment of Calvin below, but for now it is enough to note that he is essentially correct and has identified a critical difference between his view of atonement and Calvin's. For Calvin there is real sense in which humans stand, by God's grace, over and against God in their reprobation, and that this is prior to and independent of their direct ontological (creaturely) or epistemological (knowledge) dependence on Jesus Christ for salvation and self-knowledge. Calvin does think that there is a kind of knowledge of God (and self) in the Old Testament Law without explicit reference to Jesus (rather there is what he refers to as 'the promise of the Mediator'), and what is more, he believes that there was an image of God in the Old Testament patriarchs that is not directly linked to their being in Christ. In Calvin's *Institutes* the link between Old Testament saints and Christ is eschatological by virtue of their faith in 'the Mediator' of the covenant (*Inst.* II.16.2-4). There is no explicit knowledge of or connection to Jesus Christ. Calvin holds this position because he believes that there is also an incipient image of God that remains in humans after the fall (though marred through the fall) and prior to

---

[32] Calvin makes this point in *Inst.* I.15.4, and II.12.3 and 7, although, as Peterson notes, it is made more forcefully in Calvin's commentary on 1 Cor. 15:45, where Calvin explicitly states that, 'Adam and Christ are, therefore, as it were, the two origins, or roots of the human race. That is why there is every justification for calling Adam the first man, and Christ the last.' Quoted in Peterson, *Calvin's Doctrine of Atonement*, 41.

Christ's resurrection that is derived from Adam. On Calvin's theology of atonement, then, Christ both restores the image of God lost at the fall and completes the Old Testament concept of salvation promised in the Law.

Now to the difficult issue mentioned above. Are all humans, then, included in the atonement? How does Christ mediate the benefits of his atonement? To whom does it apply? More to the point, how does Calvin account for the reprobate? Who are they and how does one become reprobate? My final thesis of Calvin's doctrine of atonement takes up these questions:

3. THE BENEFITS OF CHRIST'S ATONEMENT ARE EFFECTUAL ONLY FOR INDIVIDUALS BY FAITH THROUGH THE HOLY SPIRIT

There is first a logical problem that Calvin anticipates in his doctrine of atonement, which concerns his assertion that, God 'loved us before the world was created' (*Inst.* II.16.4), while also maintaining that, 'God's wrath and curse always lie upon sinners until they are absolved of guilt' (*Inst.* II.16.1). Calvin puts the problem this way: '[H]ow could [God] have given in his only-begotten Son a pledge of love to us if he had not already embraced us with his free favor? Since, therefore, some sort of contradiction arises here, I shall dispose of the difficulty' (*Inst.* II.16.2).

But what exactly is Calvin's dilemma here? Paul Helm identifies the two horns of the dilemma as arising from the fact that Calvin seems to support both

> God was our enemy until we were reconciled in Christ.

and

> God has already embraced us with his free favor.[33]

The crux of this problem for Calvin is that the change that apparently takes place in God once he ceases to regard us as his enemies is at odds with the love God has of us from eternity. There is an apparent conflict between the atemporal language of God's love (he loves us from 'eternity' with an 'eternal' love) and the temporal language Calvin (following Scripture) uses to describe our being reconciled (we are reconciled at some particular point in time). Or yet again, Calvin seems to describe a transition that takes place in time that constitutes the moment at which we are reconciled to God, yet he continues to insist that God's reconciliation of us is the product of a free, unconditioned election in Christ from eternity.

How does Calvin propose to slip through the horns of this dilemma? Calvin's answer in a word is 'accommodation':[34]

---

[33] See Helm, *John Calvin's Ideas*. My discussion of Calvin's wrath-love dilemma is heavily dependent on Helm's manuscript.

[34] Helm correctly disputes Peterson's claim, *Calvin's Doctrine of Atonement*, 22, that accommodation is only a 'partial answer' to this dilemma for Calvin. Helms points out that Calvin very strongly implies that this is the *whole* answer to the dilemma.

Expressions of this sort have been accommodated to our capacity that we may better understand how miserable and ruinous our condition is apart from Christ. For if it had not been clearly stated that the wrath and vengeance of God and eternal death rested upon us, we would scarcely have recognized how miserable we would have been without God's mercy, and we would have underestimated the benefit of liberation (*Inst.* II.16.2).

Calvin's method of resolving the tension between God's eternal love of humans and his wrath against human sin is to treat the expressions of the transition from wrath to reconciliation as expressions that do not convey the whole truth of our situation. More specifically, it is the idea of a temporal change in our relation to God, and not in His relation to us, that is accommodated to us. Calvin's position seems to be that the truth about the atonement has to be represented to us as if it implied a change in God when in fact the change takes place only in us. God's love of us is eternal, as we have seen, and based on his free election of us in Christ, and there is therefore no transition in him. What is more, Calvin insists that the scriptural texts that speak of God's wrath against us are actually overstatements of the truth designed to teach us the horror of our sin (*Inst.* II.16.3). So, again, no change takes place in God – although this in no way diminishes the reality of God's anger at sin.[35] Instead, *we* undergo a change in time, as Helm notes, not from wrath to grace, but from our belief that we are under wrath to our belief that we are under grace. God, however, remains constant in his love of us from eternity. Calvin passes through the horns of the dilemma of the wrath-love dilemma, then, by invoking the category of accommodation to say that statements (A) and (B) do not represent states of affairs that are strictly true. There is therefore no real contradiction between them. (A) and (B) nevertheless affirm something true about our situation. Statement (A) confirms the horror of our situation apart from Christ and teaches us that we must embrace Christ and be reconciled to God in time; whereas (B) indicates that God is always for us in Jesus and that there is nothing we can do either to merit or forfeit God's free grace in Christ.

So, what does this tell us about Calvin's doctrine of atonement? We may begin by noting that for Calvin there is still something lovable about humans after the fall. This just what we could expect from the earlier point I made that Calvin believes humans stand in relative independence from God. As we have seen, Calvin stresses that, 'However much we may be sinners by our own fault, we nevertheless remain his creatures. However much we have brought death upon ourselves. Yet he has created us unto life' (*Inst.* II.16.3). There is, in other words, something about our creatureliness, our being created in God's image that makes us proper objects of God's love despite our sinfulness in a way that plants and non-human beings can never be. Helm argues that the way to understand Calvin's position is that God loves

---

[35] Helm, *John Calvin's Ideas*, demonstrates (*contra* Peterson) that Calvin invokes accommodation precisely *not* to negate God's wrath, but to stress its reality. Accommodated expressions are merely those which are not qualified by other expressions.

us from eternity both by virtue of our creatureliness and in the light of our prospective reconciliation in Christ.[36]

But there is still a question lingering: Who receives the benefits of atonement? The human race? Does Christ atone for all humans, simply by virtue of their being human? What we have established so far is that Calvin's logic of the matter entails that there is a being a beginning in time for God's eternal love of us. God's eternal love is particularist at least in its implementation, even if ultimately it can be understood to be universalist in its application (which Calvin does not think it can). Calvin believes that God loves each human when they are born because they are made in his image and therefore potentially may be reconciled with him. All the same, it is still true that we remain in very real sense objects of God's wrath and are not yet reconciled to God. Thus, according to Calvin, it is also true that God's eternal love of humans in Christ begins at some point after birth at which it is true *for us* that God has reconciled us. There is a real transition to be made *in us* when we are reconciled to God – a transition from regarding God as our enemy and wrathful judge to regarding him as our savior – even if there is no transition to be made in God. Thus for Calvin reconciliation or atonement is applied to individuals – not the human race as a whole. Calvin upholds the New Testament distinction between the reprobate and the elect, according to which the reprobate are those who do not receive the benefits of Christ's atonement.[37] It is only the elect who actually benefit from the atonement.[38] From within time the transition to reconciliation is conditional (though from eternity is dependent only upon God's free grace in Jesus Christ), and only those individuals who meet those conditions in time receive the benefits of Christ's atonement and are reconciled to God.

Note that I am merely drawing the relatively uncontroversial conclusion that Calvin does not believe that Christ's atonement applies to those who are not elect. To say it differently, Calvin believes that Christ's atonement actually saves only a particular group of humanity called 'the elect'. I do not intend or think it necessary at this point to enter the perennial debate among scholars over whether or not Calvin taught the so-called doctrine of limited atonement, which says that Christ's atonement was *intended* only for the elect. The poles of the debate may be

---

[36] Helm, *John Calvin's Ideas*.

[37] *Inst*. III.2.7, 10. As Colin Brown argues, *Karl Barth and the Christian Message* (North Wells: Inter-Varsity Press, 1967), 135, the New Testament quite clearly and consistently portrays the death of Christ as conditionally effecting salvation only for those who appropriate it by faith. Even those place where Christ's atonement is spoken of in universal terms (e.g., in the first half of John 3:16), the context is qualified so that only those who respond in faith experience God's all-embracing love concretely. See such passages in the New Testament such as: Mt. 11: 27ff.; Jn 2:16-21,36; 5:24,40; 10:13ff.; Acts 2:38; 16:30ff.; Rom. 1:16; 3:25; 4:3; 5:1; 8:1ff.; 9:30ff; 2 Cor. 5:17-21; Gal. 2:26; 3:6; Eph. 2:1-10; Heb. 4:3ff.; 1 Pet. 2:10; 4:17ff.; and 1 Jn 1:9.

[38] *Inst*. III.2.7, 10. Paul Helm, *Calvin and the Calvinists* (Edinburgh: Banner of Truth, 1982), 16-18, demonstrates sufficiently, to my mind, that Calvin's *Institutes* teaches that only the elect are saved.

represented R.T. Kendall, who argues in his book, *Calvin and English Calvinism*,[39] that Calvin taught an *unlimited* atonement, that Christ's atonement was intended for the whole world and not for the elect only, and Paul Helm, who argues in his book, *Calvin and the Calvinists*, that Calvin taught a *limited* atonement intended for the elect only.[40] Calvin makes statements in his writings that provide fuel for both sides of the debate. The distinction itself is somewhat anachronistic, though, as there was no real controversy over limited atonement during (or prior to) Calvin's life and he was therefore not compelled to reach a definitive conclusion on it. Richard Muller observes, that 'the term "limited atonement" is not accurately descriptive of the themes of sixteenth- [sic] or even seventeenth-century theology.'[41] The situation may well be that Calvin never settled in his own mind exactly which is the best way of characterizing the extent of the atonement. This does not mean that one cannot or should not attempt to deem which position is the most consistent with Calvin's theology, but I do not find it especially helpful to try to reconstruct Calvin's personal position on the matter. Perhaps the strongest claim of this sort we may make is that Calvin apparently was familiar with and gave his limited acceptance to the scholastic formulation, 'Christ's death was sufficient for all but efficient for only those who believe.'[42] I will say, however, that the concept of limited atonement seems to fit more easily into Calvin's logic of atonement as I have developed it here, because it entails an atonement that is particular in both its implementation (one at a time) and its application (for the elect only).

The question of the extent of the atonement aside, Calvin explains the transition involved in reconciliation as the result of two important and conditions. These 'conditions' are not human works, though, as Calvin makes clear in *Institutes* III.11 (especially sections 2 and 11). They remain the products of God's activity in a person's life. The first condition of the transition is faith – which Calvin defines as 'a firm and certain knowledge of God's benevolence toward us, founded upon the truth of the freely given promise of Christ, both revealed to our minds and sealed upon our hearts through the Holy Spirit' (*Inst.* III.2.7). Faith is *transactional*[43] for Calvin for in some significant way it effects genuine change in our status.[44] It is a

---

[39] R.T. Kendall's book, *Calvin and English Calvinism* (Carlisle: Paternoster, 1997).

[40] For an excellent overview of the debate and the literature surrounding it, see G. Michael Thomas, 'Calvin and English Calvinism: A Review Article', *Scottish Bulletin of Evangelical Theology* 16 (Autumn, 1998): 111-27.

[41] Muller, *The Unaccommodated Calvin*, 6.

[42] For this claim, see Muller, *The Unaccommodated Calvin*, 55; and Roger Nicole, 'John Calvin's View of the Extent of the Atonement', *Westminster Theological Journal* (1985), 197. Cf. Helm, *Calvin and the Calvinists*, 39.

[43] Helm uses this apt term in *John Calvin's Ideas*.

[44] In *Inst.* III.14.17 Calvin employs Aristotle's and St Thomas Aquinas' four-fold causal distinction (efficient, material, formal, and final) that was standard in scholastic theology to describe the establishment of our salvation and describes faith as 'the formal or instrumental cause.' For more on Calvin's view of causation see Helm's discussion of Calvin and atonement in his *John Calvin's Ideas*.

necessary condition for an individual in time to be reconciled to God. By faith we realize and grasp hold of the righteousness of Christ and appropriate his atoning work.[45] The 'firm and certain knowledge' that comes by faith creates the conditions for us to be reconciled to God by providing us with the necessary knowledge – of God and of ourselves – to remove the ignorance that keeps us separated from God.[46] Faith causes a change in us when we exercise it and we are thereby restored to a right relation with God.

The second condition for the transition to reconciliation is the indwelling of the Holy Spirit.[47] The significance of the Holy Spirit's role in the atonement in Calvin's thought, especially with regard to our receiving the benefits of Christ, is not always properly appreciated. The Holy Spirit plays a significant and indispensable role in our reconciliation. In the first place, as we saw, the Holy Spirit bestows the gift of faith, by which we apprehend God's love of us in Christ. But the Holy Spirit furthermore effects or completes the reconciliation between the Father and believers begun by Jesus sacrificial death. Calvin goes so far as to say that Christ's atonement is ineffective without the further action of the Holy Spirit. Therefore we see that corresponding to Calvin's Christ-centered view of election is a trinitarian concept of atonement. In other words, Calvin sees the atonement as the result of the action of the Trinity – not just Christ (Cf. *Inst.* III.14.21). The focal member of the Trinity in the atonement is Jesus Christ, the Son of God, so that 'perfect salvation consists in the person of Christ' (*Inst.* III.1.1) but the Father is involved in sending and exalting the Son, as well as in accepting Christ's atonement and imputing Christ's righteousness to his people by adopting them as his sons. The Holy Spirit, in turn, is essential in mediating the reconciliation of Christ to us by uniting us to Christ so that we may be reconciled to God and receive the benefits of his life, death and resurrection. Calvin writes that,

> as long as Christ remains outside of us, and we are separated form him all that he has suffered and done for the salvation of the human race is useless and of no value for us. Therefore, to share with us what he has received from the *Father* he had to become ours and to dwell with us. . . . the *Holy Spirit* is the bond by which *Christ* effectually unites us to himself (*Inst.* III.1.1, my italics).

Calvin continues on to say that the Holy Spirit 'is called the "spirit of adoption" because he is the witness to us of the free benevolence of God with which the Father has embraced us in his only-begotten Son to become a Father to us' (*Inst.* III.1.3).

---

[45] *Inst.* III.11.7 declares faith to be 'the only instrument for receiving righteousness'.

[46] Note that for Calvin it is not ignorance that separates us from God, but *sin*. It is rather that ignorance *keeps* us separated from God. To say it differently, for Calvin sin separates us from God and produces an ignorance of God and ourselves which perpetuates that separation (and only in this limited way is the cause of our separation).

[47] Cf. Calvin's comments in *Inst.* III.1.1: 'It is true that we receive such communion [with Christ] through faith...we are inevitably led to go further and to enquire into the mysterious working of the Spirit through which we it happens that we come to enjoy the presence of Christ and all His benefits.'

Thus, for Calvin God – as Father, Son and Holy Spirit – acts in, with, and as Christ the Mediator to procure our salvation for us. Calvin's doctrine of atonement, then, is firmly grounded in a trinitarian theology. Together the combined coming of the Holy Spirit and the response of faith in an individual *effect* the reconciliation of that individual with the Father by securing the benefits of Christ's incarnational obedience (in his life, death, and resurrection) in time.

The Calvinist Barth?

The relationship of Barth's theology to Calvin's is complex. There is a sense in which Barth's *Dogmatics* may be viewed as a programmatic attempt to supply a systematic account of all of reality by re-working a key insight of Calvin's *Institutes* that links human knowledge of God through his revelation in Jesus Christ to human redemption.[48] Commentators widely agree that Calvin played a major role in the development of Barth's theology. Barth's lectures on Calvin in Göttingen in 1924-25[49] give evidence that Calvin's theology was a key a component of Barth's theological reconstruction, if you will, after his famous break with liberalism.[50] Barth, however, regularly disagrees with Calvin and often appropriates Calvin's categories in a manner that suits Barth's own program, with little regard to how those categories were employed by Calvin.[51] As I conclude this chapter I turn to some of the important challenges to Calvin's teaching on atonement presented by Barth's theology.

---

[48] The systematic and comprehensive of Barth's theological program has led some commentators to refer to Barth's theology in *Dogmatics* as a 'Christological metaphysics.' For this claim see Robert W. Jenson, *Alpha and Omega: A Study in the Theology of Karl Barth* (Thomas Nelson, 1963); and Fergus Kerr, 'Karl Barth's Christological Metaphysics', in Kerr's *Immortal Longings: Versions of Transcending Humanity* (London: SPCK, 1997), 23-45.

[49] These lectures are available in English as Karl Barth, *The Theology of John Calvin* (trans. G.W. Bromiley; Grand Rapids: Eerdmans, 1995).

[50] For the claim that these lectures constituted the theological platform for Barth's *Göttingen Dogmatics*, see S.W. Chung, 'An Ambivalent Disciple: Barth's Use of Calvin in the Göttingen Dogmatics', *European Journal of Theology* 8 (1999), 61-78, esp. 62-63. See also Bruce McCormack, *Karl Barth's Critically Realistic Dialectical Theology: Its Genesis and Development 1909–1936* (Oxford: Oxford University Press, 1995), 304-307.

[51] Chung, 'An Ambivalent Disciple'; and Gabriel Vahanian, 'Introduction', in Karl Barth, *The Faith of the Church: A Commentary on the Apostle's Creed According to Calvin's Catechism* (ed. J.-L. Leuba, trans. G. Vahanian; London: Fontana Books, 1958), 7. Cf. McCormack's statement, *Karl Barth's Critically Realistic Dialectical Theology*, 217, that 'Barth displayed a marked tendency throughout his life to use borrowed categories in a way that was entirely peculiar to himself (and which often contradicted the intentions of those who originally coined them).'

Barth for/against Calvin

Like Calvin, Barth does not offer us anything like the classical theories of atonement. I noted above that Calvin assumes a very high view of the role of Scripture in the theological task, and is therefore committed to understanding the atonement through the lens of the biblical witness. Francis Watson says of Barth that, 'From beginning to end, Barth's *Dogmatics* is nothing other than a sustained meditation on the texts of Holy Scripture, in all the richness and diversity with which these texts elaborate their single theme.'[52] Calvin and Barth, then, each are deriving their doctrines of atonement from Scripture. Furthermore, Barth shares Calvin's conviction that the center of the Scriptures is God's revelation of Jesus Christ.[53] Thus Barth and Calvin each derive their theologies of atonement from the revelation of God in Jesus Christ as presented in Holy Scripture. Barth's doctrine of atonement bears some further resemblances to the basic structure of Calvin's: he locates the atoning work of Christ in the whole of Christ's obedience – including all of his life, death, and resurrection; he also emphasizes the sacrificial and substitutionary nature of Christ's death on the cross to absorb God's wrath; and he emphasizes the trinitarian nature of God's action in Jesus Christ. But in spite of all it would be a grave mistake to represent Calvin's and Barth's theologies of atonement as doctrinally identical.

Christ, Election, and Atonement

Barth is deeply concerned that Calvin's doctrine of atonement entails a fracturing of the Trinity in a way that isolates Jesus from the Father and Holy Spirit.[54] Barth

---

[52] Francis Watson, 'The Bible', in J Webster (ed), *The Cambridge Companion to Karl Barth* (Cambridge: Cambridge University Press, 2000), 57. Watson, p. 58, points out a passage in the *Dogmatics* (*CD* I/1, 283-84) in which Barth stipulates that the decisive characteristic of a good systematic theologian is an 'indemonstrable and unassuming attention to the sign of Holy Scripture around which the Church gathers and continually becomes the Church. By this attention, and by nothing else, the theologian becomes a theologian.'

[53] See Barth *CD* IV/3, 38-164, esp. his clear statements on p. 39: 'We speak of Jesus Christ attested in Scripture; of the One to who the history of Israel attested in the Old Testament moves until it attains its goal and end in the history attested in the New Testament, which is still the history of Israel but also the origin and beginning of that of His community... The Subject of this central history which controls and determines the whole is Jesus Christ. And He lives. This is where we must begin.' See also See Barth *CD* I/1, the whole volume, but especially 119-20; and throughout the *Dogmatics* Barth makes statements such as *CD* IV/1, 366: 'For the texts of the Bible are all in some way or other oriented and determined and characterized by the substance of the Bible, in the Old Testament by God's covenant or grace with His people, and in the New by the appearance and person and work of Jesus Christ Himself as the fulfillment of the covenant proclaimed there.'

[54] For this reason Bruce McCormack, 'Grace and Being: The Role of God's Gracious Election in Karl Barth's Theological Ontology', in Webster (ed.), *Cambridge Companion*

follows Calvin in situating his doctrine of atonement in the incarnation of Jesus Christ, although Barth does not see Calvin as following this insight through consistently or thoroughly enough.[55] At the heart of Barth's doctrine of atonement, and indeed his theology, as well as his major criticism of Calvin, is his objection to the traditional Reformed doctrine of election that is derived from Calvin's *Institutes*. Barth describes election as 'sum of the Gospel,' whereas for Calvin election becomes (eventually) the 'dreadful' decree that some are reprobate.[56] Barth's position stems from his refusal to say anything of God (or humanity) outside of Christ. Calvin's attempt to locate God's election in Christ outside of time in eternity means that he is unable to give any doctrinal content to reprobation, and in the end must speak of God's 'hidden decrees' and 'secret will' to explain why some humans are damned.[57] Barth will have none of this. He thinks it compromises the gospel message as Gospel – that is, the Good News to humanity. Barth, in fact, believes that election is 'the best news of all' (*CD* II/2, 3). Calvin's doctrine of election, Barth contends, is not good news for humanity, but only for the elect.

To understand this properly let us visit Barth's reinterpretation of Calvin's touchstone thesis (thesis 1) – that the atonement is centered on the person and work of Jesus Christ.

Calvin's mistake, Barth thinks, is in his methodology. Calvin makes the two-natures theology of Christ as revealed in the incarnation the center of his doctrine of atonement, which provides the theological context for understanding both God and atonement as mysteriously determined in eternity. Barth, on the other hand, begins his theology of atonement with the *actual person* of Jesus Christ in the incarnation – what is sometimes called Barth's *actualism*. Barth argues that the fact, 'that Jesus Christ lives also tells us, however, that *His existence is act*; that it is being in spontaneous actualization [sic]' (*CD* IV/3, 40; my italics). Barth refuses to discuss Jesus Christ – and indeed the being of God in any way – abstractly, as if Christ (or God) were merely a doctrine. Barth believes that the incarnation is the starting point for all theology for it constitutes the fullness of God's revelation to us, but Barth insists that the incarnation is *concrete* history.[58] The incarnation is not an event that

---

to Karl Barth, 95-101, argues that Barth is adamantly opposed to anything like the *extra Calvinisticum* as it entails 'a God who could be known and whose divine essence could be defined on some other basis than in and from the perception of his presence and activity as incarnate Word.' *CD* IV/1, 181.

[55] For Barth's discussion of the incarnation in atonement see especially the section, 'The Way of the Son into the Far Country', *CD* IV/1, 157-210.

[56] See *CD* II/2, 13; and *Inst.* III.23.7.

[57] See especially *Inst.* III.23.4.

[58] Cf. Bruce McCormack's statement, in 'The Sum of the Gospel: The Doctrine of Election in the Theologies of Alexander Schweizer and Karl Barth', in David Willis and Michael Wilker (eds), *Toward the Future of Reformed Theology: Tasks, Topics, Traditions* (Grand Rapids, MI: Eerdmans, 1999), 488: 'Barth proposed to work in an *a posteriori* fashion, beginning not with a general concept of God or a general concept of human being but with a most highly concrete reality, Jesus Christ.'

statically reveals an inner essence of God that existed prior to the incarnation; rather it is the act in which God quite literally is who he is. In this act of incarnation we have God choosing his own being: 'his existence is act.' In other words, in the incarnation God is choosing to be the God who incarnates and redeems us in this way, and who is (exists) *only* in this way. The incarnation of Jesus is 'the beginning of God,' and in this act we have revealed that God elects in his free grace to include all things (humans and creation) in himself (*CD* II/2, 94). What is established, for Barth, in the incarnation is the absolute priority of 'the divine election of grace,' in which Christ 'is God's Word, God's decree, and God's beginning,' and by which Christ comprehends everything 'absolutely within Himself,' including 'all other words, decrees, and beginnings' (*CD* II/2, 95). With this move Barth reverses Calvin's method. Instead of situating election (along with the atonement) in the theological context of the pre-existent God-man, Jesus Christ, Barth fashions his understanding of Christ's two natures and the atonement in the light of God's election of the incarnate Jesus Christ.[59]

The incarnation is thus the *ending* point of all theology as well as the starting point, for there is nothing more to say about God than is revealed in the incarnational act. Barth's actualism, then, refers to Barth's claim that God's being consists in his revealing actions in Jesus Christ and Barth's corresponding insistence that we refrain from speaking of God outside of these actions. For Barth, Jesus Christ is the Word of God, and the *only* Word of God. God does not speak outside of Jesus and does not exist outside Jesus. Scripture is therefore subordinate to Jesus, the Word made flesh, but Scripture is also the indispensable means through which Christ (the Word) is mediated to us. Therefore, because it enables us to hear the Word in the flesh now, Scripture is also the Word of God.[60] Barth thus focuses his doctrine of atonement on the unfolding and dynamic revelation of God in Christ as witnessed to in Scripture.

In an important sense Barth agrees, then, with the touchstone thesis (1) of Calvin's grammar of atonement – that the atonement is centered on the person and work of Christ – but he does so in a way that completely transforms the doctrine of atonement. Barth agrees with Calvin that the saving significance of Christ's incarnation is only properly understood by understanding Christ as fully God and fully human, but Barth's actualism alters his understanding of Christ's two

---

[59] See McCormack's assertion, in 'The Sum of the Gospel', 491, that, 'That the doctrine of election is the sum of the gospel means ultimately for Barth that it is a doctrine which shapes both the form and the content of all other doctrines.' See also Colin E. Gunton, in 'Salvation', in Webster (ed), *Cambridge Companion to Barth*, 156, who describes Barth as making the 'dogmatic decision' to give 'election the priority over creation and eschatology' based on Barth's statements in *CD* II/2, 91, 168, and 89: 'It is because of this that we put the doctrine of election...at the very beginning, and indeed before the beginning, of what we have to say concerning God's dealings with his creation.'

[60] Watson, 'The Bible', 60-62. For Barth's view on the relationship between Christ and the Word of God see especially, Barth *CD* I/1, 88-124; and *CD* I/2, 457-740.

natures.[61] In *Dogmatics* IV Barth tells the story of the incarnation in terms of 'The Way of the Son into the Far Country' (as Christ's 'humiliation') and 'The Homecoming of the Son of Man' (as Christ's exaltation) which culminates in Christ's death on the cross.[62] As Barth develops it, Christ as human ('the Son of Man') is dually the human who is faithful to the covenant with God, yet made sinful humanity for us. As 'the Son of God' Christ is both the omnipotent God who is able to conquer sin and the God who is always 'for us' in election. The cross of Christ, for Barth, 'is the fulfillment of the incarnation of the Word and therefore the humiliation of God and the exaltation of the Son of Man' (*CD* IV/2, 140-41). In Jesus Christ, the incarnate Word of God, we have revealed the truth that God in Jesus is always 'for us' because Christ is 'the Judge judged in our place' (*CD* IV/1, 211-282)

We now are able see why Barth celebrates election as he does: for him all humanity is elected in Jesus Christ. Christ is both the subject and the object of election. Jesus is both the one electing humans and the One who is elected. Stephen R. Holmes illuminatingly argues that the real difference between them is not that Calvin lacks a Christ-centered concept of *election* that is present in Barth, as is typically thought (and Barth apparently believed).[63] I have already shown above that this is false: Calvin does in fact present election as Christ-centered in the *Institutes*. It is rather that Barth, unlike Calvin, understands both election *and* reprobation of the human race as taking place in Christ.[64] God (in Jesus) not only elects to provide atonement, but God (in Jesus) also elects himself (in Jesus) for damnation. In saying 'Yes' to us in Jesus God also elects for himself (in Jesus) the 'No' of his punishment for sin.[65] In taking upon himself the form of a human being, Christ

---

[61] See especially *CD* II/2, 24-25. I do not have space to develop this point more, but Barth by no means has a traditional view of Christ's two natures. Yet neither does he stand outside the Christian orthodox confession of Christ's two natures. He in fact wants to assert them both – but understands them in a new way. Barth has what can be a confusing way of speaking so that he often appears to retract what he is in fact asserting. This is due to his 'dialectical' way of speaking and doing theology. For an explanation of this and a rounded defense of Barth's commitment to Christ's two natures, see George Hunsinger, 'Karl Barth's Christology: Its Basic Chalcedonian Character', in Webster (ed), *Cambridge Companion to Barth*, 127-42. For an extremely thorough treatment of both Barth's dialectical method and his christology see McCormack, *Karl Barth's Critically Realistic Dialectical Theology*, *passim*.

[62] Hunsinger, 'Barth's Christology', 137. See especially *CD* IV/1, 157-211, and IV/2, 20-153.

[63] See Holmes, *Listening to the Past*, 125ff.

[64] This is Holmes careful argument in, *Listening to the Past*, 125ff

[65] See *CD* II/2, 164: '[I]f we would know what rejection is as determined in God's eternal counsel, the rejection of which we cannot but speak even in our doctrine of predestination, then we must look…to what God elected for Himself in His Son…by this same decree God decided that the risk which He allowed to threaten the creature and the plight into which He allowed it to plunge itself should be His own risk and His own plight.' See also *CD* II/2, 340-409, 'The Elect and the Rejected'.

took upon himself the ubiquitous nature of humanity, and not that of an individual human being *per se*.[66] This leads Colin Gunton to observe that Barth has a 'marked tendency...to see Jesus Christ as a kind of platonic form of humanity.'[67] Christ is, to say it differently, a sort of pattern or prototype of human nature for Barth. Thus, when God elects Jesus to pay the punishment for human sin, all of humanity is elected in him. In an important sense Christ is every person in a way that Adam could never be. Barth views Christ alone as the true root of humanity, not Adam. Christ 'is the first and true Adam of which the other is the type' (*CD* IV/1, 513).[68] All humans possess (to the degree that they are human) the redeemed nature of Jesus just as much as the fallen nature of Adam. Barth understands the atonement as the good news that each human being is elected in Christ because both elected and rejected individuals must be seen in Jesus Christ.[69]

Understanding election and reprobation together in Christ has several major consequences for Barth's doctrine of atonement. First, the status of humanity is not fallen in Adam, as for Calvin; rather humanity's state is redeemed in Christ. Fergus Kerr observes that for Barth the resurrection of Jesus transforms the whole human situation.[70] Thus, secondly, Barth does not agree with Calvin's particularism in atonement.[71] He tends to see Jesus as redeeming human nature first, and then individuals, as those who participate in this nature. Despite his insistence that, 'It is individuals who are chosen, not the totality of men,' Barth is referring to participation in *the Church* (or Israel), the community of those who have faith. These individuals, in turn, 'compose the race elected in Jesus Christ, and by means of the community.'[72] Undoubtedly Barth includes Calvin in the 'older Protestantism,' which 'steered the whole doctrine of atonement...into the cul-de-sac of the individual experience of grace' (*CD* IV/1, 150). While he is careful to maintain that 'the subjective apprehension of atonement by the individual man is

---

[66] Barth uses the theological construction 'anhypostasis-enhypostasis' to refer to Christ's human nature in order to protect the freedom and transcendence of God. See *CD* IV/2, 49ff and 91ff. Roughly what this distinction means is that Christ's human nature does not have an essence in itself (anhypostasis) and is dependent on its union with Christ's divine nature for its essence (enhypostasis). In short, for Barth, 'Jesus Christ is...a real man only as the Son of God, so that there can be no question of a peculiar and autonomous existence of His humanity' *CD* IV/2. 49.

[67] Gunton, 'Salvation', 155.

[68] See *CD* IV/1, 507-13.

[69] Holmes, *Listening to the Past*, 133.

[70] Kerr, 'Barth's Christological Metaphysics', 40. Cf. *CD* IV/2, 381-82: 'In this man God has elected humanity as such, and therefore all men, into covenant with Himself... Therefore the revelation of His exaltation as it has taken place in His resurrection is the revelation of theirs too.'

[71] See *CD* IV/1, 149-154, and especially 'Faith and its Object', 740-756.

[72] *CD* II/2, 313. For Barth, the community of the elect exists in the Old Testament as Israel, God's 'chosen people,' and in the New Testament as the church.

absolutely indispensable,' Barth very clearly understands the atonement to have first a universal application in that it applies to our human nature.[73]

Third, Barth makes the atonement utterly free from any temporal conditions whatsoever in a way that Calvin does not. For Calvin, faith and the indwelling of the Holy Spirit in the lives of individuals (the elect) is necessary for those persons to experience God's eternal love in time. Barth, however, understands the atonement as a reality for every person established by death of Christ and proclaimed in his resurrection. Faith does not accomplish a transition in us for Barth, as it does according to Calvin. It does not appropriate Christ's atonement in time, but instead faith for Barth brings about the recognition and acknowledgement of our simultaneous sinful-but-justified status before God.[74] Faith therefore is that which enables us to participate in the Church, through the Holy Spirit, as those who recognize and receive God's salvation in Jesus.

Insofar as there is a temporal implementation of the atonement for Barth, it occurs through the community of elect, the Church (*CD* II/2, 313ff; *CD* IV/1, 150-54). Barth does not have anything like a point in time in which God begins to love each person who is elect, as Calvin does. In Christ all human nature is redeemed and this includes all human beings. The closest thing to Calvin's concept of conversion for Barth would be one's entry into the Church, 'which in this particularity is ordained to the ministry of reconciliation and the witness of the grace of God to the rest of the world' (*CD* IV/1, 150). The proper way to understand the relationship between atonement and individuals is in reference to an individual's place in the Church. The Church, however, does not condition the actual atonement of the individual, only her recognition of it. Barth's point could be restated as saying that without the Church we wouldn't know of Christ's atonement, and thus would not participate in the community of the elect. The Holy Spirit's role in atonement is likewise not a condition of its application in a human life. Rather the Holy Spirit awakens individuals to faith; he is the 'enlightening power' of Christ and summons together the community of the elect (i.e., the Church).[75]

Calvin or Barth?

So where does this leave us? How should a Reformed thinker respond to Barth's criticisms of Calvin and his adjustments to the doctrine of atonement? Despite the value and immense richness of Barth's theological proposal, I want to close with a caution against a wholesale adoption of Barth's theological proposal regarding atonement. There is a critical departure from Calvin that, to my mind, impairs the

---

[73] The quote is from *CD* IV/1, 150; and then Barth immediately states, 'Our theme is the reconciliation of the world with God in Jesus Christ, and only in the greater context the reconciliation of the individual man.'

[74] *CD* IV/1, 616, 629-30. See Helm, *John Calvin's Ideas* for a thorough discussion of the different roles of faith in atonement in Calvin's and Barth's theologies.

[75] *CD* IV/1, 152-53. See esp. 'The Holy Spirit and Christ Faith', *CD* IV/1, 740-80.

potency of the gospel and seriously departs from the Reformed trajectory in theology.

Barth has done us an invaluable service by highlighting both the dynamic nature of Christ's revelatory role as the Word, and the deep connections between all revelation and Jesus, but he makes too much of this connection, especially as he goes on to use this as a basis of criticizing the traditional concept of election (stemming from Calvin) – and then by extension the traditional concepts of God and humanity as well. I want to suggest that insofar as it entails a rejection of Calvin's the particularist elements of atonement in Calvin's atonement, Barth's doctrine of atonement needs to be reconsidered. My argument is that, first of all, this shift cannot be justified; and secondly, it leaves some significant theological questions looming, which, as far as I can see, cannot be resolved.

The key to Barth's disagreement with Calvin on atonement is the particular methodological move that he makes with regard to the supremacy of Christ. The Barthian move I am referring to consists in the attempt to understand both election and reprobation in Jesus, and the placement of individual election in the more universal contexts of the community of elect (Church and Israel) and the human race. Barth interprets the supremacy of Christ in such a way that Scripture, God, or humanity (at large) cannot be discussed without direct reference to Christ.

But why should we follow Barth in this? First note that Barth seems to refuse to acknowledge a distinction between a strong and a weak sense of the proposition:

(C) 'Christ is the supreme Word of God and there is no knowledge of God outside of him.'

One may, as Barth does, understand (C) to entail the strong thesis that there is no knowledge of God, humanity, or the created order except by the direct mediation and person of Jesus Christ. In other words, this strong view of (C) understands the supremacy of Christ to entail the absolute and complete dependence (ontological, epistemological, and moral) of humanity and the created order on specifically the second person of the Trinity, the Son. In this case, there can be no strict separation from Christ for humanity in any sense (ontological, epistemological, or moral). But there is a weaker sense of (C), with which Calvin would agree, that understands the supremacy of Christ to entail simply that the person and mediation of Christ is the ground or basis of all knowledge of God, humanity, and creation. On this weaker view of (C), it is part of our likeness to Christ that makes humans genuine individuals with relative creaturely independence from Christ – creatures with relative autonomy, with responsibility, and the ability to (however imperfectly) image God.

Why, then, does Barth opt for the strong sense of (C)? Barth believes, as we have seen, that by placing election in Christ his theology avoids Calvin's putative error of separating Christ off from the Trinity. Calvin, however, does no such thing: for Calvin election takes place in Christ. Stephen Holmes therefore argues that the superiority of Barth's theology of atonement over Calvin's is in its ability to 'offer a long and richly theological account of God's "No" as it is pronounced in Jesus

Christ.'[76] In other words, it is Barth's account of reprobation that is superior to Calvin's because it makes more and consistent sense of our estrangement from God – it gives doctrinal content to reprobation, if you will, whereas Calvin's does not. This also has three desirable consequences for Holmes: first, it allows election to be 'the best news of all' for Barth; second, all cogent accounts of human being must contain explicit references to Jesus Christ and the Church; and third, any account of final human destiny must happen in the connection with Jesus Christ.[77] I will focus on the claim to give doctrinal content to reprobation rather than responding to the last three consequences of Barth's doctrine, because it is not at all clear to me from Scripture that (as in the first consequence) it is *election* that is supposed to be the best of all news, as Barth would have it, while consequences two and three could equally be said of Calvin's position.

What of the claim, then, that Barth's account of election and reprobation in Christ is superior to Calvin's because it offers us much more by way of an explanation of reprobation? Is this reason to follow Barth's crucial methodological shift? My answer is, of course, no. Why do we need more of an account of reprobation than Calvin provides? What if all there is to reprobation is doctrinal contentlessness? Perhaps Barth is wrong to try to give doctrinal content to reprobation. Perhaps reprobation is that which must be passed over in silence. For Calvin, "reprobation" is the theological category that signifies (not unlike Barth's own contention)[78] absurdity to the human mind: God is somehow glorified by beings who refuse to glorify him. It cannot be discussed, much less given doctrinal content, because it is the most irrational thing in the universe. And here we must heed what is a constant theme in Calvin: the theologian can only say as much about God as the Scriptures – particularly about reprobation. There is a rich tradition extending from St. Augustine, which says that sin is precisely a "no-thing." Perhaps this is why Calvin has so little to say about reprobation and its doctrinal content. The Scriptures simply point to God's election and human responsibility for sin. On this reading, then, it is a grave error for Barth to try and give doctrinal content to reprobation by understanding it in Christ. Calvin refers reprobation to God's mysterious silence precisely because it is *outside of Christ and cannot be brought into Christ*. Thus, Calvin professes the traditional doctrine of hell, which asserts the eternal banishment from Christ of the reprobate.

So, I do not find anything compelling us to follow Barth in his strong understanding of the supremacy of Christ. In addition to this, Barth's doctrine of atonement has completely removed the particularist facets of Calvin's theology of atonement – and this creates three unresolved questions for Barth's doctrine of atonement.

---

[76] Holmes, *Listening to the Past*, 134.
[77] Holmes, *Listening to the Past*, 134-35.
[78] For an explanation of Barth's concept of sin as 'the impossible possibility', see Wolf Krötke, 'The Humanity of the Person in Karl Barth's Anthropology', in Webster (ed), *Cambridge Companion to Barth*, 164-65.

First, the most serious question for Barth concerns whether his theology of Christ leaves us with a 'Christ' who can ground individual salvation. On Barth's view Jesus, the Son of Man, does not have an individual human nature. It is little wonder that Barth goes on to assert that salvation is not primarily understood in individual terms. But it is (even on Barth's account) we human individuals who must be saved. In what sense does Christ become like us, if it is not as an individual human being? Ultimately this radically changes the Reformation concept of *sola fide*, which refers to the application of the atonement to individuals who exercise faith.

Second, for all of Barth's efforts otherwise, it appears that his insistence that Christ is elected to receive the punishment for human sin ends up separating Jesus from the Trinity. The Holy Spirit's role in the atonement is all but invisible in Barth's theology. The Holy Spirit is involved in bringing faith and forming the community of the elect (the Church) but neither of these is a condition of atonement in any sense for Barth. There is little discussion of the roles of the other members of the Trinity in the atonement. One is left wondering how the atonement is a trinitarian action for Barth.

Third, Barth leaves a large question looming over the traditional doctrine of perdition. How is it that anyone is reprobate for Barth? Scripture clearly divides the human race into two categories – elect and reprobate – and the reprobate are those destined for a Christ-less eternity. There is a fundamental tension in Barth's theology of atonement over the fate of those outside the Church. On the one hand, Barth refused to draw the conclusion that all are saved in Christ, yet the way he develops his doctrine of election seems to entail just that.[79] The Scriptures depict Christ as the universal criterion for judgment, not the universal object of judgment, as he implies.[80] It seems doubtful whether Barth can satisfactorily deal with those passages in Scripture that teach of the eternal perdition for those who do not have faith.

To sum up, I see no reason to follow Barth in his central innovation on the atonement – his radical (strong) view of Christ's supremacy that entails that Jesus is redeemer of human nature. Reprobation is not explained this way and it takes us away from the traditional Reformed insight drawn from the Scriptures that salvation comes by faith through the indwelling of the individual human being.

Conclusion

I have sought to portray Calvin's theology of atonement in such a way that the qualities that make it irreplaceable as a staple of Reformed theology are obvious. Calvin's doctrine of atonement is able to unite the biblical metaphors of atonement in the person and ministry of Christ by explaining atonement in terms of Christ's three offices. At the same time, this account is located within the mainstream of

---

[79] Barth once made the enigmatic declaration recorded in, Eberhard Jüngel, *Karl Barth: A Theological Legacy* (trans. Garret E. Paul; Philadelphia: Westminster Press, 1986), 44-45: 'I do not teach it [universal salvation], but I also do teach it!' Dr Oliver D. Crisp brought this reference to my attention.

[80] Brown, *Karl Barth*, 134.

Christian orthodox trinitarian theology. For Calvin, Christ is the author of election who elects himself to save human individuals through his incarnation as a man; but this is a trinitarian action, requiring the Father who sends the Son and adopts the elected humans, and the Holy Spirit who calls and indwells the elect. What Calvin's doctrine of atonement highlights is, on the one hand, God's eternal, sovereign and free choice to save humans in Jesus Christ, and on the other hand, Calvin's theology of atonement is particularist in its implementation and its application. For Calvin, God's eternal love in Christ of the elect begins them at a particular point in time when we by faith appropriate Christ's atonement and are indwelled by the Holy Spirit. The significance of this is that it account is that it preserves God's secrecy, it upholds the biblical categories of elect and reprobate, and it results in a portrait of Christ in which he genuinely becomes like each individual human being.

Barth's attempt to extend Calvin's insight regarding the christological character of revelation and all knowledge of God is illuminating at many points. However, insofar as he abandons particularism in atonement, Barth's modifications to the doctrine of atonement need to be realigned with Calvin. In the end, the problem for Barth is that his methodological choices make it so that he cannot describe human salvation in terms of individual conversion. The conclusion is that he radically alters the meaning of the Reformation dictum *sola fide* – salvation through faith alone – that leaves some unresolved questions for his theological program.

PART FOUR

SCRIPTURE

CHAPTER 6

Calvin on Scripture

Stephen R. Holmes

Introduction

There are two errors, endemic in theologians' appeals to John Calvin, that must be avoided if we are to get a right view of his teaching concerning Scripture. Both stem from a failure to comprehend Calvin's intellectual context, although in different ways. The first is to misunderstand the nature of the *Institutes*: they look, on the surface, so like a modern (even early modern) compendium or system of theology that it is easy to assume that this is what they are, and so to offer an account of Calvin's thought on this or that topic merely by reading the relevant chapters of this work.[1] The second is to look to Calvin for answers to the doctrinal questions that concern us, and so to project issues, and thought-worlds, on his text that are foreign to it.[2]

As Richard Muller has carefully demonstrated,[3] and indeed as Calvin himself makes clear in the introductory material,[4] the *Institutes* were never intended to be read alone, as a summary of Christian doctrine. They form one node of a complex set of writings, relating most directly to the commentaries and sermons, but also to the controversial material and even the various summaries of faith Calvin (and his colleagues in Geneva) produced. We might understand the core of Calvin's writing

---

[1] Even otherwise perceptive accounts of Calvin are damaged by this error: most obviously, perhaps, Marijn de Kroon, *The Honour of God and Human Salvation: Calvin's Theology according to his* Institutes (Edinburgh: T&T Clark, 2001).

[2] As I have noted elsewhere, and will develop later in this chapter, the (sterile) debate about whether Calvin's doctrine of Scripture is inerrantist or neo-orthodox is a classic example of this failing: he can at times sound like both Warfield and Barth, which demonstrates only that the conceptual distinctions developed to differentiate their positions were not ones Calvin had made. See my *Listening to the Past: The Place of Tradition in Theology* (Carlisle: Paternoster, 2002), 82-83.

[3] Richard A. Muller, *The Unaccommodated Calvin: Studies in the Foundation of a Theological Tradition* (Oxford: Oxford University Press, 2000), 21-38.

[4] Both the various versions of the introductory letter 'John Calvin to the Reader' and of the 'Subject Matter of the Present Work' indicate very clearly that the *Institutes* are intended to make the writing of commentaries easier, and so should be seen as subsidiary to that task.

task as the production of Biblical commentary;[5] this necessarily raised issues of controversy, debate or possible confusion. Rather than insert long excurses offering synoptic accounts of a variety of Biblical passages and examining the history of thought in order to deal with such issues, Calvin consigns them all to a separate work, the *Institutes*, which thus served as a companion to the reading of the commentaries, rather than as a stand-alone work. The commentaries then, are the primary vehicle for teaching and the best way of ascertaining Calvin's doctrine of Scripture is to note the way he actually deals with the Biblical text in commenting on it.

The *Institutes*, however, while they deal with specific points of contemporary controversy, are not Calvin's vehicle for carrying on the detail of specific disputes on particular issues. So the error of Pighius (say) is exposed and condemned in the *Institutes*,[6] but the point-by-point refutation of Pighius's various claims and counter-claims is reserved for specific occasional controversial works.[7] These inevitably make appeal to Biblical proof, and offer refutation of supposedly Biblical arguments made by Calvin's opponents, and so are also an important, but secondary and incidental, witness to Calvin's beliefs concerning Scripture.

But if the *Institutes* are not to be read as a summary statement of Christian doctrine, what is? The best answer, I suspect, is the various confessions of faith and catechisms that were produced to state and propagate the beliefs of the Genevan church. Whilst these are often anonymous, and sometimes seem to be the work of several hands, or of someone other than Calvin, they have a public status, presumably with Calvin's full approval, which makes them of primary importance. These symbols encapsulate the doctrines which were derived from the Biblical commentary and defended in the *Institutes* and controversial works.

Turning to the second error, it is both easy and tempting to assume that Calvin was writing to address the same issues and questions as face us. Without considerable historical awareness, we can easily assume that the problems and arguments that seem obvious to us will have seemed obvious to all people in all historical and cultural contexts. One of the great services of liberation theology, feminist theology, and the other contextual theologies which have arisen in recent decades has been to press this point home more forcefully than the study of history ever could. Calvin, after all, is not here to tell us that we are misrepresenting him; certain of the contextual theologians have told us this with such vigour and zeal that all but the most deaf have been forced to hear.

---

[5] Note '*writing* task'; any evaluation of Calvin's work more generally would have to stress preaching above all else.

[6] Throughout *Inst.* III.21-22.

[7] See *De libero Arbitrio* and *De aeterna Praedestinatione Dei*, the latter translated as *Concerning the Eternal Predestination of God* (trans. J.K.S. Reid; London: James Clarke, 1961).

Calvin's Fundamental Beliefs about Scripture

There is, of course, a sense in which we are dealing with the same questions; there is a context we share with Calvin. As Christian theologians, both part of the one body of Christ which spans all ages and nations,[8] the historical gaps between us can never become unbridgeable chasms;[9] how God has revealed himself in Scripture is a perennial question that mattered to Calvin, and that matters to us. The context and challenges we face, however, are different. For Calvin, the challenge was, in a world where the truth and wisdom of Scripture was largely acknowledged,[10] to construct that in such a way that the business of the Reform of the church could go forward; we live in a different world, and need to defend things Calvin was able to assume, and also no doubt we can assume things that Calvin was forced to defend.[11] The point must go even deeper than this, however: we approach the questions, inevitably, with different assumptions and beliefs to Calvin, and so arguments that he found compelling might seem strangely barren to us, distinctions that seem vital and obvious to us might be glaringly absent from Calvin. 'The past is a foreign country; they do things differently there,' as L.P. Hartley famously claimed in the opening words of The Go-Between; learning the language and thought-patterns of that foreign country is vital to understanding any figure from the past.

With all this in mind, what did Calvin believe about Scripture? In the Genevan Catechism of 1545,[12] the child, having stated very briefly the content of Christian faith, is quickly asked 'Where will this be apparent to us?' The answer offered is: 'In his Word, where he reveals his mercy to us in Christ, and testifies of his love towards us.'[13] This simple statement opens up much of what needs to be said about Calvin's view of the Bible.

The first point is that the Bible alone is the source of all adequate knowledge of God, and more particularly of all adequate response to God. Calvin repeatedly stresses

---

[8] Calvin was of course insistent that belonging to the universal church was of vital importance, the *piorum ominum mater* (*Inst.* IV.1 title; see also *Inst.* IV.1.4).

[9] I have argued this point at more length, with some reference to Calvin, in my *Listening to the Past*: see esp. ch. 2.

[10] There are exceptions, but Roman Catholicism, Lutheranism, and the mainstream of the Swiss Anabaptist movement all held to some form of a Scripture principle.

[11] Both Barth and Calvin suggest at times that the text of Scripture is in some way wrong (see later for substantiation of this claim with respect to Calvin). I often point out to students that Barth wrote at the height of the acceptance of Biblical criticism, and so his concessions concerning possible errors in Scripture must be read in the context of an academic world in which many such failures were simply assumed. Calvin, by contrast, can speak unselfconsciously of 'correcting' Paul (again, see later) precisely because his intellectual context would never allow such a claim to be taken as in any way casting doubt on the trustworthiness and authority of Holy Scripture.

[12] This Latin Catechism was a translation and edition of an earlier French work.

[13] Genevan Catechism, from J.K.S. Reid (ed.), *Calvin: Theological Treatises* (Library of Christian Classics, 22; London: SCM Press, 1954), 92

this in commenting on the Scriptures, to cite only two examples, one on an Old Testament text, one from the New Testament:

> [T]he Psalmist does not simply pronounce those happy who fear God, as in other places, but designates godliness by the study of the law, teaching us that God is only rightly served when had law is obeyed. It is not left to every man to frame a system of religion according to his own judgment, but the standard of godliness is to be taken from the Word of God. When David here speaks of the law, it ought not to be understood as if the other parts of Scripture should be excluded, but rather, since the whole of Scripture is nothing else than an exposition of the law, under it as the head is comprehended the whole body. The prophet, therefore, in commending the law, includes all the rest of the inspired writings.[14]

Again:

> ...we are taught by this passage, that if we wish to obtain the knowledge of Christ, we must seek it from the Scriptures; for they who imagine whatever they choose concerning Christ will ultimately have nothing instead of him but a shadowy phantom. First, then, we ought to believe that Christ cannot be properly known in any other way than from the Scriptures; and if it be so, it follows that we ought to read the Scriptures with the express design of finding Christ in them. Whoever shall turn aside from this object, though he may weary himself throughout his whole life in learning, will never attain the knowledge of the truth; for what wisdom can we have without the wisdom of God?[15]

Knowledge of Christ, and service of God, are alike only possible through reading and hearing the Scripture. Nothing is more fundamental to Calvin's account of the Bible than this. We cannot know God, and all his benefits showered upon us in Christ, we cannot adequately pray or worship or live before God, unless we follow the one rule of Holy Scripture and ignore all others. Such an assertion betrays an assumption, which perhaps deserves investigation, which investigation will open up many of the important questions concerning Scripture.

Calvin clearly assumes that there is a unity to Scripture, both in what it teaches and in what it commands. This assumption is hardly unusual in the Christian tradition, of course, but nor is it uncontested, and the particular ways in which Calvin expounds the unity of Scripture are perhaps more unusual. Calvin recognises the varying human voices in Scripture,[16] and indeed makes much of them, as one would expect given his humanist training,[17] but never lets this recognition of human

---

[14] Comm. Ps. 1:2, CTS edition; emphasis original.
[15] Comm. John 5:39, CTS edition; emphasis original.
[16] So, famously, in the *Inst.* I.8.2; *cf* I.8.11.
[17] 'Humanism' in this context refers to the Renaissance movement that sought a return to the study of classical texts, particularly the Greek and Latin classics, and through them sought a clarity of thought and of literary style that (it was felt) contemporary thought had lost. The most direct impact of humanism on the Reformation was no doubt the emphasis on reading original texts in original languages, which was a great impetus to

diversity come into conflict with a belief in the Divine authorship, and so essential unity, of the Bible. It is perhaps important to note that to hold these two things together was simply not a problem or an issue for Calvin; that moderns find it troublesome is our problem, not his.[18]

Does this mean that there are no contradictions in Scripture? The short answer for Calvin must be 'yes'. He notices, of course, the places where apparent contradictions occur, and always offers attempts at harmonization. In one or two cases he resorts to an assumption that the extant manuscripts must be corrupt (see, for instance, the commentary on Acts 7:14); more often he employs other strategies, which include suggestions that a lack of precision in numbers is not a problem in Scripture. Perhaps the most interesting of these is on I Cor. 10:8, where Paul says 'We must not indulge in sexual immorality as some of them did, and twenty-three thousand fell in a single day.' (NRSV) The record in Numbers has 24,000 dying (Num. 25:9). In commenting on both passages, Calvin merely notes that the probable exact number lay somewhere between 23,000 and 24,000; in the commentary on I Corinthians, however, he also notes that there is an apparent contradiction concerning why these people died: Numbers has it as punishment for idolatry, Corinthians as punishment for fornication. Calvin is far more concerned with this apparent contradiction, affecting as it does the teaching of the passage, than with even a fairly significant numerical disagreement. In every case of apparent discrepancy, however, Calvin seeks harmony, and so we may say that he does believe that Scripture does not contain contradictions, and seeks to demonstrate this point.

The Unity of Scripture: The Person and Work of Jesus Christ

Calvin's account of the unity of the Bible deserves a little more comment than his assumption of it. Two things must be said: first, the unity is a singleness of meaning, not a more complex unity of promise and fulfilment, or something similar. Second, the unity consists in the constant witness of Scripture to the person and work of Jesus Christ. (The first of these is at least hinted at in the first of the quotations above, and the second in the second.)

As is well known, Calvin believed that God has one people under one covenant. The people of Israel who worshipped in the temple stood under the same dispensation as the apostles and other New Testament believers in all important

---

the production and careful examination of new Biblical editions—most famously Erasmus's Greek New Testament. Calvin demonstrates repeatedly a distinctively humanist concern for literary style, intending in his commentaries to meet the standard he laid down in a letter of 1539 to Simon Grynaeus: 'the chief virtue of an interpreter consists in clarity combined with brevity,' and so on.

[18] I suspect, and indeed have elsewhere argued (in a forthcoming paper entitled 'Christology, Scripture, Divine Action and Hermeneutics') that this is an issue of theology as well as cultural context. In his accounts of human freedom and predestination, Calvin has a worked-out philosophical account of how divine and human agency can, without contradiction, co-exist.

respects. As Hesselink puts it, '[t]he covenant takes several forms: Noahic, Abrahamic, Mosaic, the new covenant, etc., but the basic covenant promise is one: "I will be your God, and you shall be my people"—and the substance of all the covenants is Jesus Christ.'[19] (This stands in some contrast, of course, to later Reformed ideas of a covenant of works being replaced by a covenant of grace.) To believe this, it is clearly necessary also to believe that the full revelation of Christ was available to Old Testament saints from the earliest days. Calvin makes this, perhaps surprising, claim several times in expounding different texts of Scripture. In commentating on Jer. 26:4-5, Calvin picks up on the phrase 'If you will not listen to me, to walk in my law that I have set before you, and to heed the words of my servants the prophets whom I send to you urgently' (NRSV), first making the point I have already noted, that true religion consists in obedience to the Bible, but then lighting upon the words 'law' and 'prophets' and asking whether there is anything contained in the prophets that was absent from the law. The answer he gives is that there is nothing of substance, the law (presumably meaning the Pentateuch) contains all that is necessary for salvation, but the prophets interpret and apply the law in particular contexts and situations, and so to make its demands clearer.[20]

The point is extended in dealing with I Tim. 3:17, which claims that 'all scripture is given...that the man of God may be perfect...' (KJV, which reflects better the sense Calvin finds in the words). Calvin notes that the 'scripture' referred to here is merely the Old Testament, and so asks if the Old Testament is capable of making Christians perfect, of what use is the New? Calvin's, perhaps remarkable, response is that the New Testament added nothing to the Old, in terms of substance, but merely made clear what was already contained therein.[21]

The full truth of Christ, it would seem, was already present in the 'Five Books of Moses' all that came afterwards is exposition and application. The Prophets teach how the law is to be lived in every human situation; the New Testament demonstrates that the event which the law predicted, the coming of the Christ, happened in Jesus of Nazareth, and further explains the teaching of the law about that event. Calvin certainly does not mean by this to denigrate or demote in importance

---

[19] I. John Hesselink, 'Calvin's Theology', in D.M. McKim (ed.), *The Cambridge Companion to John Calvin* (Cambridge: Cambridge University Press, 2004), 74-92; quotation from pp. 85-86.

[20] 'But these two things well agree together: the Law alone was to be attended to, and also the prophets, for they were its interpreters. For God sent not his prophets to correct the Law, to change anything in it, to add or to take away; as it was an unalterable decree, not to add to it nor to diminish from it. What then was the benefit of sending the prophets? even to make more manifest the Law, and to apply it to the circumstances of the people. As then the prophets devised no new doctrine, but were faithful interpreters of the Law...' (CTS translation).

[21] 'so far as relates to the substance, nothing has been added; for the writings of the apostles [*i.e.* the NT] contain nothing else than a simple and natural explanation of the Law and the Prophets, together with a manifestation of the things expressed in them.' (CTS translation). The same point is made in the Commentary on I Peter 1:10-11.

the prophetic writings or (particularly) the New Testament – the clearest statement is the most important, not the earliest – but he wants to claim a complete uniformity in the teachings of Scripture. The Old Testament is not composed of shadows or types that need something more for their fulfilment; it is itself the Word of God, inspired and useful in teaching and training in righteousness.

There is, then, one constant message running through every book, indeed every sentence, of Scripture, regardless of the date or provenance of the writing. And, to move on to the second point, that message is simply the person and work of Jesus Christ. In 1534, very soon after his conversion, Calvin wrote a preface to Olivétan's French translation of the New Testament; in 1543 he edited this writing slightly, and it thereafter was reprinted in several contexts. One of the 1543 amendments was the insertion of a paragraph that included the following words:

> This is what we should in short seek in the whole of Scripture: truly to know Jesus Christ, and the infinite riches that are comprised in him and are offered to us by him from God the Father. If one were to sift thoroughly the Law and the Prophets, he would not find a single word which would not draw and bring us to him ... our minds ought to come to a halt at the point where we learn in Scripture to know Jesus Christ and him alone, so that we can be led by him to the Father who contains in himself all perfection.[22]

The position Calvin holds here could hardly be clearer; but how he holds it is more difficult. In particular, it stands in apparent contradiction to his (sometimes vitriolic) rejection of allegorical readings in favour of the 'plain sense' of Scripture.[23] The simple answer to this point is that Calvin believed the 'plain sense' of Scripture was Christological through-and-through. Again drawing on his humanist training, he tended to equate meaning with authorial intention (negotiating with some sophistication questions about the dual authorship of Scripture, and so the possibilities of divergent divine and human intentions), but, since his account of salvation history painted Moses and David as believers in Christ, had no difficulty in asserting that the authorial intention behind Leviticus or the Psalms[24] was Christological. Moses knew Christ and wrote to reveal Christ; we do violence to the historical reality of the text if we do not read it as a text that is fundamentally about Jesus and his benefits.

---

[22] Translation from J. Haroutunian (ed.) *Calvin's Commentaries* (Library of Christian Classics, 23) (London: SCM Press, 1958), 70.

[23] See especially, perhaps, the commentary on II Cor. 3:6, where Origen's deployment of 'the letter kills, but the Spirit gives life' in defence of allegorical exegesis is strongly rejected.

[24] Calvin generally believed in traditional accounts of authorship of Biblical books, although see later on 2 Peter.

Factual Error in the Claims of the Bible?

This raises a question for the late-modern reader. We have come to equate assertions that the subject-matter of the Bible is Christ with some degree of acceptance of factual error in the claims of the Bible. There is, of course, no reason why these two things should have been associated in Calvin's mind, and no evidence that they were, but this is perhaps nonetheless an appropriate point to deal with the question of errors in Scripture. Two texts are perhaps helpful here: Calvin's comments on the authorship of II Peter, and his discussions of how Genesis 1 related to recent astronomical discoveries.

In the 'Argument' to his commentary on 2 Peter, Calvin cites a comment of Jerome's, that some think the style of the letter is so different to I Peter that it cannot be by the same author. This was no doubt a powerful argument in a humanist context, as questions of authorial style were carefully explored and regarded as significant. Calvin concedes the point concerning style ('there is that manifest difference that distinguishes different writers'), but goes on to note that the contents are 'worthy' of the apostle. He then argues that if the book is accepted as canonical, its claim to be by Peter must be accepted, not because to do otherwise would involve an acceptance of factual error in canonical Scripture, but because pseudonymous authorship would involve a base falsehood on the part of the writer ('a fiction unworthy of a minister of Christ'), which action is impossible to imagine.[25] Calvin thus proposes the book is written by a disciple of Peter, in his own words, at his (now aged and infirm) master's instruction. Nonetheless, he continues to allow that 'it is not quite evident as to the author'.

Calvin lived, of course, at the birth of modern astronomy. He rejected the Copernican system, as is well-known, but in commenting on Genesis 1 addresses another recent astronomical discovery. The invention and deployment of the telescope had proved that Saturn was a much larger body than the moon, but much further away. Does, then, the account of the making of 'two great lights', of which one was the moon, in Genesis 1:16 stand contradicted? Calvin's response offers praise for the science of astronomy, but insists that Moses was seeking to instruct all people, and so wrote of things as they appear to the eye, not as they in fact are.[26]

---

[25] It is not clear whether Calvin thinks that an inspired author should not be guilty of such mendacity per se, or whether he thinks that an author capable of writing such words could not have been so guilty.

[26] 'Moses wrote in a popular style things which without instruction, all ordinary persons, endued with common sense, are able to understand; but astronomers investigate with great labor whatever the sagacity of the human mind can comprehend. Nevertheless, this study is not to be reprobated, nor this science to be condemned, because some frantic persons are wont boldly to reject whatever is unknown to them. For astronomy is not only pleasant, but also very useful to be known: it cannot be denied that this art unfolds the admirable wisdom of God. Wherefore, as ingenious men are to be honored who have expended useful labor on this subject, so they who have leisure and capacity ought not to neglect this kind of exercise. Nor did Moses truly wish to withdraw us from this pursuit in omitting such things as are peculiar to the art; but because he was ordained a teacher as

Is this an admission of error into Scripture? I think the only adequate response is to say that the question did not greatly interest Calvin. He believed that Scripture was trustworthy, true, authoritative – and that it spoke luminously and centrally about Christ. He believed that the authors knew whereof they spoke, and so could be trusted. He refused to make any hard distinctions between authority in 'matters of faith and morals' and other issues. Where, however, the text of Scripture seemed to contradict the best scientific knowledge of his day, he tried to explain why that should have been permitted by God, without worrying that it should have been permitted.

Natural Theology and Accommodation

This, then, is Calvin's account of the unity of Scripture. What of other issues? I phrased my opening statements with some care, insisting that the Bible alone is the source of all adequate knowledge of God, and of all adequate response to God. The inclusion of the word 'adequate' was an acknowledgement that Calvin does not believe that God is not known apart from the Bible, nor does he believe that the Bible offers us exhaustive knowledge of God. These two issues, of natural theology and accommodation, are both important in expounding account of Calvin on Scripture.

Calvin believes in natural theology.[27] He finds it clearly taught in Rom. 1, and echoes that passage, to assert that God has given clear testimony to himself in the created order. The revelation is abundantly clear, but sinful human beings work so hard at not seeing it that eventually we are blinded to it.[28] He also believes that all human beings have, given by God (as part of their being human) an inchoate awareness of God's existence and majesty.[29] Nonetheless, all this knowledge is empty, confused, fleeting – until brought into order by the Scriptures. Calvin famously compares the Bible to a pair of spectacles, enabling someone with weak eyes to make sense of the blurred words of a book. Just so, although the 'heavens declare the glory of God', we see nothing but a blur until we are given to see by

---

well of the unlearned and rude as of the learned, he could not otherwise fulfill his office than by descending to this grosser method of instruction. Had he spoken of things generally unknown, the uneducated might have pleaded in excuse that such subjects were beyond their capacity. Lastly since the Spirit of God here opens a common school for all, it is not surprising that he should chiefly choose those subjects which would be intelligible to all. If the astronomer inquires respecting the actual dimensions of the stars, he will find the moon to be less than Saturn; but this is something abstruse, for to the sight it appears differently. Moses, therefore, rather adapts his discourse to common usage.' (CTS translation).

[27] For an excellent discussion of the various issues raised in this area, see Paul Helm, *Calvin's Ideas* (Oxford: Oxford University Press, 2004), 209-45.

[28] See, variously, the commentaries on Acts 14, Acts 17, Rom. 1, Ps. 19, etc.

[29] The famous *sensus divinitatis*; see *Inst.* 1.3.1 for the basic statement.

Scripture. So there is knowledge of God apart from Scripture on Calvin's account, but no adequate knowledge of God.

Second, then, with Scripture there is adequate knowledge of God, but not complete knowledge. Calvin speaks famously of God 'accommodating' himself to our weakness, speaking in language we can understand, as a nurse 'lisps' or 'prattles' to a child, instead of speaking as an adult.[30] David Wright rejects any suggestion that this should be understood merely as a question of rhetoric or form,[31] arguing instead that it reflects a pattern that runs through Calvin's understanding of the being and act of God.[32] In *Inst.* 2.6.4, Calvin approvingly cites Irenaeus' claim that the 'immeasurable' Father is 'measured' in the Son, and uses the language of accommodation to describe the same process. Human minds cannot know God in himself,[33] but in the Incarnation God has given himself to be known.[34]

So too, then, in the Bible, God has given himself to be known. But true knowledge, adult speech, would be beyond us, and so God prattles and lisps through the mouths of the Biblical authors, speaking a simple truth, which is truth nonetheless, and which we can understand. Here we come face to face with what has been perceived as the central difficulty with Calvin's theology: we do not see the whole will of God, or the whole being of God.[35] There is that which remains hidden. How do we know that what God has spoken in Scripture is trustworthy and true? How do we know that in the infinite reserve that God has not revealed, that God could not reveal, at least not without changing the capacities of our minds, there is not a correction, an exception, that will so change the meaning of the accommodated revelation we have as to render it worthless or false? How, in short, can we trust the Bible?

Precisely because of his doctrine of accommodation, Calvin's answer to this question does not, indeed cannot, rely on any account of inspiration. Calvin believed, of course, that the Bible was inspired. I have no quibble at all with the resounding assertion of T.H.L. Parker: 'For Calvin the Bible, the whole Bible and every nook and cranny of the Bible, is the Word of God as completely as if God himself had

---

[30] 'Prattles' is David Wright's translation of *balbutio* (see 'Calvin's Accommodating God', in W.H. Neusner and B.G. Armstrong (eds), *Calvinus Sincerioris Religionis Vindex* (Kirksville: Sixteenth Century Journal Publishers, 1997), 3-20; p. 4); 'lisps' is the more common one in the translations.

[31] The example already cited of Calvin's comments on the moon and Saturn in Gen. 1:16 is perhaps adequate to make this point, although Wright makes it convincingly and at length. Wright, 'Calvin's Accommodating God', 7-17.

[32] Wright, 'Calvin's Accommodating God', 16-19.

[33] This is, I think, for Calvin both an aspect of createdness – *finitum non capax infiniti* – and of sinfulness.

[34] This links, as Wright 'Calvin's Accommodating God', points out, to questions of the hiddenness of God and the possibility of a double will in God, and so to questions of predestination. Such questions are well beyond the scope of this paper, however.

[35] The point is endlessly made. For what is perhaps the most rhetorically powerful presentation, however, see the repeated comments by Barth in *CD* II/2 when discussing Calvin's doctrine of election.

spoken the actual words.'[36] The words which God speaks, however, are not 'the truth, the whole truth and nothing but the truth', they are accommodated to the perceptions of the people. In matters of science, God spoke as things appeared, not as they actually are. In matters of morality, even, Calvin believes accommodation is at work: repeatedly in his commentary on the Mosaic law, he suggests that this or that was only permitted by God because the people were 'hard of heart',[37] but that the perfection of God lay elsewhere.[38] Even in speaking of his own attitude and action, God accommodates his language, so repeatedly when the Scripture speaks of God 'repenting', Calvin glosses it as an accommodation which should not be read as implying any change of attitude in God.[39]

If we ask how Calvin knows these phrases are to be read as accommodations and not at face value, the answers are various. In the case of God 'repenting', Calvin simply cites other Scriptures. The ethical questions in the law largely work similarly, drawing on the example of Jesus interpreting the commands about divorce against the backdrop of the institution of marriage in Genesis, but Calvin also seems to make reference to a 'natural law' at times,[40] and other arguments, particularly concerning slavery, are theological rather than straightforwardly exegetical.[41] The references to 'natural law' should not have too much read into them, I suspect, but the sense that Calvin believes he knows of standards by which the laws of Moses may be judged is inescapable. In the case of Gen. 1:16, it is recent scientific discoveries ('astronomers prove by conclusive reasons...') that lead Calvin to believe that this text is an example of accommodation.

The question that presses, of course, is how we can know that any given text is not an accommodation? (Did, for instance, God accommodate his revelation to a widespread homophobia, and so should we now discount texts condemning homosexual practice?) Calvin has introduced an exegetical practice whereby certain texts must be read against themselves, sometimes without the support of any other scriptural authority. How, on this account, can we trust any text? It seems that the Bible is inspired, it is the very words God has spoken, but that is – astonishingly,

---

[36] T.H.L. Parker, *Calvin's Old Testament Commentaries* (Edinburgh: T&T Clark, 1986), 66. For the same point in Calvin see, e.g., his commentary on 2 Tim. 3:16.

[37] The phrase, of course, picks up Jesus' own comments about God's permission of divorce in Mt. 19:8, which text presumably suggested this exegetical procedure to Calvin.

[38] See, e.g., comments on Deut. 24 (divorce); Ex. 21:7-11 (selling children into slavery, which Calvin describes as 'an act of barbarity'); Num. 35:19 (where the provision for the 'avenger of blood' 'seems to savour somewhat of barbarism' according to Calvin), *etc.*

[39] So on Gen. 6:6; Ps. 106:45; Jer. 26:19; Amos 7:3; Jon. 3:10, etc.

[40] On Ex. 21:1, concerning the retention in slavery of a wife and children when a husband is set free, Calvin says 'nothing could be more unnatural'. There are several other examples.

[41] On Lev. 25:42, Calvin suggests the limitations on the holding of Hebrew slaves are because God claims ownership of the Israelites, having redeemed them from Egypt, and therefore no Israelite should properly be owned by any other.

but apparently necessarily, on Calvin's telling – not enough reason for us to trust the Bible. Is there a way of avoiding this conclusion?

In the *Institutes* Calvin addresses head on the question of why the Bible should be believed (*Inst.* 1.7 *passim*). Several 'external testimonies' are adduced (in *Inst.* I.8), concerning the style and excellence of the Scriptural text, but Calvin appears to believe that these are all inadequate; the only adequate ground for belief is the testimony of the Holy Spirit.[42] In these passages the Spirit appears to testify to two separate things. On the one hand, 'the inward testimony of the Spirit' leads to 'the Word [finding] acceptance in men's hearts' (*Inst.* I.7.4); on the other, the Spirit merely bears testimony to the fact that 'Scripture is from God' (*Inst.* 1.7.5). The latter of these adds nothing to my previous argument: because of the doctrine of accommodation, the claim that Scripture is from God appears not to be enough. The former offers a possible answer, but one that I suppose Calvin would have rejected. We might claim that the Spirit illumines the readers of Scripture just as he illumined the writers of Scripture, so that the truth of God there communicated may be heard. The truth of Scripture is not evident to all, and its authority does not rest on any demonstrable argument, but only on the mysterious secret workings of the Holy Spirit in the human heart.

Such an argument appears coherent, but it surely concedes too much to notions of 'inner illumination' for Calvin to have any interest in it. In commenting on 1 Jn 4:1, he inveighs against 'fanatics' who claim the right of private judgement. Against these he sets the public discernment of the church, which again might offer a way through the problem, but he immediately draws back because, of course, any account of the authority of the Scripture which places a right of judgement in the hands of the Church would be a straightforward surrender to Rome. How, then, can Calvin claim the Bible is trustworthy and true?

I suspect that the best answer lies in a more careful account of the doctrine of accommodation. I expounded the problems with the doctrine on the basis of Calvin's deployment of it in his commentaries. If we look at the more formal statements of what the doctrine means, Christology is to the fore (as I have already indicated). Perhaps we do better to judge accommodation by asking how God is revealed (and concealed) in Christ. Calvin plays the metaphor of veiling and unveiling in various ways in his different comments on Christ, sometimes stressing the hiddenness of the glory,[43] sometimes stressing the visibility of the invisible God in him.[44] The dogmatic theme at play is the famous *extra calvinisticum*, the teaching that the divine Son continues to fill the universe even whilst incarnate as a human being.

Calvin repeatedly tells us that we must trust that God is as he is in Christ. There is no proof of this available to us: we cannot look behind Christ to see God unincarnate and then compare the two. God's life extends far beyond the incarnate

---

[42] '...the testimony of the Spirit is more excellent than all reason. For as God alone is a fit witness of himself in his Word, so also the Word will not find acceptance in men's hearts before it is sealed by the inward testimony of the Spirit.' *Inst.* 1.7.4.

[43] So, for instance, the commentary on Phil. 2:5-11.

[44] So, for instance, the commentary on 1 Pet. 1:21.

One, it is true, but, Calvin will insist at his most careful, there is nothing of God that is not incarnate in Christ.⁴⁵ The suspicion of a 'hidden God' in Calvin's theology comes always from suggestions that this is not in fact true, that there are places where he suggests that God is other than he is in Christ.⁴⁶ This takes us back to the potential problems with the doctrine of accommodation: there, it appeared that God could potentially say one thing and mean something completely different, and so the Scriptures appeared untrustworthy; if God can show himself as one thing in Christ and yet in fact be something completely different, then the fears concerning accommodation appear entirely justified. There is not space here for a full account of Calvin's Christology;⁴⁷ scholarly debate has long wrestled with a suspicion of Nestorianism, that Calvin overly separates the two natures.⁴⁸ If this is true, then it seems likely that all these problems will indeed follow. Let me then state a first conclusion in the conditional mood: if Calvin does in fact teach that God can be other than he is in Christ, then, on Calvin's telling, the Bible cannot be trustworthy.

If there is a Christological account of accommodation, derivable from Calvin, that avoids these problems such that God is luminously visible in Christ, then an account of Biblical accommodation that does not render the Bible untrustworthy is at least possible. The question remaining is whether the various examples of accommodation Calvin offers are consonant with such an account. It seems to me that they might be, although there is perhaps a need for a fairly clearly-stated set of hermeneutical principles derived from the basic idea of accommodation. Testing Scripture against Scripture, as Calvin does in discussing God's apparent 'repentance', is clearly going to be a permissible move; it seems to me that Calvin's arguments as to why God might have misrepresented certain scientific matters are also strong.⁴⁹ The moral arguments might be more difficult: while Calvin is relying on theology or other Scriptural references, they are defensible, but if he does rely on natural law, the argument is surely inadequate in his own terms.

Calvin believed strongly and unquestionably that the Bible is the Word of God, and the only rule for Christian faith and practice. His account of this, however, was sophisticated, relying on a notion of accommodation, derived from Christology, which shaped his exegetical practices in significant ways. If there are difficulties in particular exegetical moves, these should not blind us to the overall coherence. At

---

⁴⁵ This is clear in the statement of the *extra* in the *Institutes*.

⁴⁶ For a discussion of one such place, see my comments on reprobation in *Listening to the Past*, 124-25 and 129-30.

⁴⁷ A recent, and very worthwhile, treatment is Stephen Edmondson, *Calvin's Christology* (Cambridge: Cambridge University Press, 2004).

⁴⁸ For my own comments on this, see my 'Reformed Varieties of the *Communicatio Idiomatum*', in Stephen R. Holmes and Murray A. Rae (eds), *The Person of Christ* (London: T&T Clark, 2005), 70-86.

⁴⁹ Note, though, that Calvin does not simply accept that the Bible might be wrong on scientific matters, but offers arguments as to why the particular discrepancy may have been allowed.

root, however, the account relies on a trust and confidence that in Scripture, and indeed in Jesus, God has revealed himself accurately. Such confidence is the gift of the Spirit, according to Calvin; the history of theology in the past two centuries, at least, might lead us to conclude that it is a gift the Spirit has sometimes been pleased in large measure to withhold.

CHAPTER 7

Calvin, Barth, and Theological Interpretation

Craig G. Bartholomew

Introduction

Thomas Oden structures his book *Requiem* around the metaphor of 'the feast.' In his preface to Oden's book which he heads 'An Invitation to the Feast', Richard John Neuhaus says,

> More and more 'young fogeys' like Oden are discovering the truth that is 'ever ancient, ever new' (Augustine). It is called the catholic faith, and it is a feast to which he invites us. It is a movable feast, still developing under the guidance of the Spirit. Oden is like cinema's 'Auntie Mame,' who observed that life is a banquet and most poor slobs are starving to death. Origen, Irenaeus, Cyril of Alexandria, Thomas Aquinas, Teresa of Avila, Martin Luther, John Calvin, John Wesley – the names fall trippingly from Oden's tongue like a gourmet surveying a most spectacular table. Here are arguments you can sink your teeth into, conceptual flights of intoxicating complexity, and truths to die for. Far from the table, over there, way over there, is American theological education, where prodigal academics feed starving students on the dry husks of their clever unbelief.[1]

One need only reflect on Calvin's commentaries and sermons, for example, to realise just how absolutely central is the Bible to this feast of the catholic faith. And yet one can so easily replace 'American theological education' with 'academic biblical interpretation' in the above quote, such is the barren wilderness of so much that goes under the name of biblical studies nowadays. Even in our days of wild pluralism and tolerance of a great diversity of readings of the Bible, this does not necessarily mean that interpretation of the Bible as Christian Scripture is welcome.[2] Theological interpretation is fine in seminaries but not in the academy.

---

[1] Richard John Neuhaus, 'An Invitation to the Feast', in Thomas C. Oden, *Requiem: a Lament in Three Movements* (Nashville: Abington Press, 1995), 10.

[2] An Old Testament scholar like Phillip Davies can still argue that the interpretation of the Bible as canonical Scripture is inappropriate to the academy where the 'discourse of the academy should dominate'. See Craig Bartholomew, '"Warranted" Biblical Interpretation: Alvin Plantinga's 'Two (or More) Types of Scripture Scholarship', in C. Bartholomew, C.S. Evans, M. Healy, and M. Rae (eds), *'Behind' the Text: History and*

And in our seminaries, where one is more likely to find a concern with the Bible as Scripture, good academic work in the service of profound interpretation of the Bible as Scripture is rare. There has been an (understandable) tendency for orthodox scholars to fight the battle for Scripture where opponents have attacked. Thus a huge amount of Christian energy has been devoted to historical issues during the twentieth century. Far less, alas, to interpretation of the Bible as God's address.

Happily there are signs of a renaissance of interest in such work, which goes under the rubric of *theological interpretation*. A good aspect of postmodernism is that it has created room for Christian scholars to bring specifically Christian interests to bear on their biblical work. The current renaissance in theological interpretation is in its early days but it holds real potential for a recovery of hard academic work on the Bible as Scripture. The minority renewal I refer to is a broad church including such scholars as Stephen Fowl, Tom Wright, Brevard Childs, Christopher Seitz, Walter Brueggemann, Walter Moberley, John Webster, Francis Watson, Kevin Vanhoozer, Francis Martin, the Scripture and Hermeneutics Seminar, etc.

I learnt from the Canadian aesthetician, Calvin Seerveld, that practicing Christian scholarship today will often mean going back in history in your discipline until you find a healthy tradition, which you can then transfuse into the present.[3] Theological interpretation has few healthy, contemporary examples whether we look to theology or biblical studies. Childs, who is himself the great exception to this rule in biblical studies, notes, for example, that although 'scripture functions towards sanctification' there has been little attention during the reign of historical criticism to reading the Bible as a whole for ethics. Theological interpretation is thus in urgent need of Seerveld's strategy, and my plea in this chapter, is that Calvin and Barth are fecund sources for such a bloodline. Indeed, although one concern of this book is to examine the differences between Calvin and Barth, the major concern of this chapter will be to flag up their common ground with respect to theological interpretation. This is not to say that there are no differences between the two in this area – and my tendency would be to side with Calvin where there are. But I do hold that what Calvin and Barth have in common is more important than the differences.

Biblical Interpretation (Scripture and Hermeneutics Series, 4; Grand Rapids: Zondervan, 2004), 58-76.

[3] See Calvin Seerveld, *Rainbows for the Fallen World* (Toronto: Tuppence Press, 1980), 197, where he encourages Christian artists to 'distill a fruitful Christian art historical tradition in your own blood and pioneer its contribution in our day'. Note also Seerveld's, pp. 182-191, encouraging and vital comments about Christian work as a minority culture. Gordon Wenham's use of Ernst Wilhelm's Hengstenberg's *Dissertations on the Genuineness of the Pentateuch*, vol 1, trans. by J.C. Ryland (Edinburgh: T & T Clark, 1847) in Pentateuchal criticism is a good example of this. See G. Wenham, 'The Date of Deuteronomy: Linch-Pin of Old Testament Criticism. Part I', *Themelios* 10.3 (1985), 15-20.

Common Ground

Within Evangelical circles two tendencies have militated against taking Barth seriously as an exegete. Firstly there has been a tendency to see Barth as heterodox and thus an enemy of orthodoxy. Cornelius Van Til's philosophical and theological critique of Barth exemplifies this trend. Secondly, biblical scholars tend to see Barth as a theologian and not as an important exegete.[4]

However, exegesis is utterly central to the *Church Dogmatics*. What Barth says of Calvin's *Institutes* is true of the *Church Dogmatics*; it is a web of exegesis![5] The *Registerband* of the *Church Dogmatics* identifies some 15000 biblical references and 2000 plus pieces of detailed exegetical discussion of biblical texts. Thus, when he is dealing with the doctrine of creation, Barth has about a 100-page discussion of Genesis 1 and 2, a discussion which includes detailed exegetical considerations on par with the most rigorous commentary. Let me mention two examples from his exegesis to underline this point. Hasel, Wenham, Stek and others have rightly pointed out that the creation stories in Genesis are *inter alia* a polemic against worldviews present in the Ancient Near East.[6] This poignant insight, which is crucial for a theological understanding of Genesis, is already well developed in Barth's work on Genesis 1 and 2. Secondly, recent years have witnessed considerable debate about animal rights and Scripture. In the context of the creation of the beasts on the same day as humankind in Genesis 1, Barth has a wonderful discussion of animals and their connection with humankind, in which he ranges throughout Scripture, drawing in verses like Jonah 4:11.

The truth is that the *Church Dogmatics* and Barth's other works are an exegetical resource that has been sadly neglected by biblical scholars. But what of the claim that Barth is an enemy of theological orthodoxy – might this not support keeping him at arm's length? As we will note below, there are some important doctrinal differences between Calvin and Barth, and these should not be ignored or underplayed.[7] However, attention to these differences must be preceded by an understanding that Barth's theologically conservative reaction to the liberalism of his day, and his recovery of the Bible as Scripture, involved at its core a reappropriation of the Reformed tradition and of Calvin in particular.

---

[4] An example of this is exposition of Genesis. The best commentary on Genesis is in my opinion that of Gordon Wenham. See Gordon J. Wenham, *Genesis 1–15* (Word Biblical Commenatry, 1; Carlisle: Paternoster, 1986) and Wenham, *Genesis 16–50* (Word Biblical Commenatry, 2; Carlisle: Paternoster, 1995). However, Wenham only has a single reference to Barth in his volume on Genesis 1–15. There is no engagement with Barth's creative discussion of Genesis 1 and 2, for example. In this respect Wenham is no exception. See for example, Claus Westermann, *Genesis 1–11* (Minneapolis: Fortress Press, 1994), 74-278.

[5] K. Barth, *The Theology of John Calvin* (Grand Rapids: Eerdmans, 1995), 393.

[6] See, for example, Wenham's commentary on *Genesis*.

[7] Helpful works on Barth from a Reformed perspective are Klaus Runia, *Karl Barth's Doctrine of Holy Scripture* (Grand Rapids: Eerdmans, 1962), and G.C. Berkouwer, *The Triumph of Grace in the Theology of Karl Barth* (Grand Rapids: Eerdmans, 1956).

Barth's recovery of the Reformed tradition was so damaging to liberalism because he had been one of them. However, as a young pastor he found that liberalism was bankrupt when it came to addressing his congregation in the European context in the aftermath of World War I. Berkouwer says of Barth and Thurneysen,

> But ultimately and most importantly, it was the Bible which saved them from utter despair. 'We read the Bible anew, with far fewer presuppositions than before.' They heard again the message concerning the forgiveness of sins and the proclamation of the kingdom which is not of men but which comes from God Himself. 'From this meeting and confrontation with the Bible in the midst of the need of the time Karl Barth's *Römerbrief* was born.' They found again actual answers to the problems with which the times confronted them. They did not find an answer that remained distant from the reality in which they found themselves, but they discovered a *message* of God that was close as life to them.[8]

It was Calvin in particular that Barth drew upon as he sought to recover the Bible as the Word of God and as he sought to develop a truly biblical theology.[9] In his lectures on Calvin published in English as *The Theology of John Calvin*, Barth notes the unique contribution of Calvin as an expositor of Scripture to the Reformation – 'Scripture did not play quite the same part in Reformed Protestantism as in Lutheranism. Its dignity here was one of principle as it never was in Lutheranism, no matter how highly the latter regarded it.'[10] The big issue for Reformed Protestantism was 'how to give God, the true God, the glory, how to do it here and now',[11] and against the backdrop of mediaeval Catholicism its answer was to look to the Bible as the final norm in faith and life.

God is known through Scripture; hence the vital importance of exposition. 'The relation to the Bible is a living one. The spring does not flow of itself. It has to be tapped. Its waters have to be drawn. The answer is not already there; we have to ask what it is.'[12] Here as elsewhere Barth acknowledges the need to take the writtenness of Scripture seriously: 'We must study it, for it is here or nowhere that we shall find its divinity' (*CD* I/2, 463). This makes historical study of Scripture imperative although such study must never be only historical. Exegesis must aim finally at opening up the mind of Scripture: 'The Word ought to be exposed in the words.'[13] The work of the Spirit is fundamental to this process because 'God is not just the theme but also the Lord of biblical truth.'[14] Such a process demands hard, objective study of Scripture. Barth invokes the metaphor of listening for this activity:

---

[8] Berkouwer, *Triumph of Grace*, 44-45.

[9] See Barth, *The Theology of John Calvin*, 393, for the importance of Calvin for Barth's study of Romans, and the preface to the 1921 edition of his *Romans*.

[10] Barth, *The Theology of John Calvin*, 386.

[11] Barth, *The Theology of John Calvin*, 387.

[12] Barth, *The Theology of John Calvin*, 388.

[13] K. Barth, *Romans* (trans. E.C. Hoskyns; New York: Oxford University Press, 6th edn, 1968), 8.

[14] Barth, *The Theology of John Calvin*, 389.

'Listening, even if on the premise of secret identity with the one who speaks, is the task of the exegete.'[15]

Barth identifies three characteristics of Calvin's exegesis which he finds exemplary. Firstly there is the extraordinary *objectivity of his exegesis*. Of course Calvin does engage in eisegesis – 'if we read nothing into the Bible we will also read nothing out of it'![16] – but his exegesis is always characterised by a concern to stay close to the text and to do justice to what is actually there.[17] The example Barth gives of Calvin's eisegesis is that Calvin assumes the unity of the message of the Bible when he reads it – though Scripture is polyphonous, the diverse voices are all seeking to say the same thing.[18]

Secondly there is the *uniformity* of Calvin's exegesis. By this Barth refers to Calvin's concern to attend to individual books in their literary totality and to the whole of Scripture: 'If in principle it is seen to be right to listen to the Bible, then we should listen to the whole Bible.'[19] In his commentary work, for example, he is always concerned to expound the whole of a book and not just the parts that have been influential.[20] Calvin's premise of the verbal inspiration of the Bible did not prevent him from examining critically the trustworthiness of the Bible but it did give 'him a consistent zeal to track down the content of the whole Bible, a zeal incidentally that would also stand historical investigation of the Bible in good stead.'[21]

The third characteristic of Calvin's exegesis is its *relevance*. By relevance Barth is not thinking of application to the cultural and historical context but the sense that this is God's Word addressing us. Calvin is at pains to attend to the particularity of texts but at the same time he is busy with a living dialogue across the centuries. When Calvin expounds Paul, for example, 'We believe Calvin the more readily because he is not deliberately trying to make us believe but simply setting out what

---

[15] Barth, *The Theology of John Calvin*, 389.

[16] Barth, *The Theology of John Calvin*, 390.

[17] Here, as elsewhere, we see Barth's concern for a determinate text and interpretation, *contra* the suggestion of Graham Ward that Barth's theology fits well with the sort of postmodern philosophy of language of Derrida! G. Ward, *Barth, Derrida, and the Language of Theology* (Cambridge: Cambridge University Press, 1995). See Barth, *The Theology of John Calvin*, 390, on Calvin's dislike for 'the pleasurable playing about with every possible interpretation of the text'. See Barth, *Romans*, 10-11, for Barth's reply to the accusation of his bringing a system to Scripture. Barth says, 'Paul knows of God what most of us do not know; and his Epistles enable us to know what he knew.' Barth, *Romans*, 11. Barth is like Gadamer in his expectation that a false assumption will be exposed by the text.

[18] 'It is in its relation to the practical goal of systematics, though without prejudice to its own significance, that the importance of Calvin's exegesis finally lies.' Barth, *The Theology of John Calvin*, 393.

[19] Barth, *The Theology of John Calvin*, 391.

[20] Barth, *The Theology of John Calvin*, 391 Barth notes here that verbal inspiration is in the background here.

[21] Barth, *The Theology of John Calvin*, 391.

he finds in Paul, yet not, of course, without being able or even trying to hide the fact that he himself believes it. This quiet kinship between the apostle and the exegete speaks for itself.'[22]

In the Preface to the second edition of his Romans commentary Barth defends himself against the accusation that he is an enemy of historical criticism. He denies this but insists that historical criticism must be in the service of genuine understanding and interpretation:

> By genuine understanding and interpretation I mean that creative energy which Luther exercised with intuitive certainty in his exegesis; which underlies the systematic interpretation of Calvin... For example, place the work of Jülicher side by side with that of Calvin: how energetically Calvin, having first established what stands in the text, sets himself to re-think the whole material and to wrestle with it, till the walls which separate the sixteenth century from the first become transparent! Paul speaks, and the man of the sixteenth century hears... If a man persuades himself that Calvin's method can be dismissed with the old fashioned motto, 'The Compulsion of Inspiration,' he betrays himself as one who has never worked upon the interpretation of Scripture.[23]

The result is that Calvin's exegesis is very useful for the preacher.[24]

Of course there are differences between Calvin and Barth. Calvin wrote far more commentaries than Barth and less theology. But just as Calvin's commentaries are concerned with the theology of the text, so Barth's dogmatics takes the above characteristics of Calvin's exegesis with the utmost seriousness. It should thus be clear why Calvin and Barth represent the sort of historical bloodline that urgently needs transfusing into the present. If the Bible is to be recovered for the church as God's Word then Calvin and Barth, in my opinion, represent the type of biblical interpretation that we need to appropriate for our day. This will not mean simple repetition of Calvin and/or Barth – whether we agree with Barth's reading of Calvin or not, Barth's work alerts us to the way in which a tradition has to be developed and appropriated afresh in a new historical context. Nevertheless, Calvin and Barth's exegesis pulsate with concerns that biblical interpretation must recover if it is to assist the church in hearing God's address. These are emphases such as:

- A deep commitment to the Bible as God's Word. Both Calvin and Barth recognise that if we wish to glorify God here and now we must listen to Scripture for His address.
- A refusal to separate biblical study from Christian faith and theology.

---

[22] Barth, *The Theology of John Calvin*, 392.

[23] Barth, *Romans*, 7.

[24] Barth notes that, 'Whenever I have myself consulted Calvin's commentaries for my own use, I have found pleasure in his distinctive combination of historical and pneumatic exegesis even when I have permitted myself to go my own way.' Barth, *The Theology of John Calvin*, 392-93.

- A commitment to rigorous scholarship, both historical and theological, in the service of exegesis, but always in the service of listening to the whole of the Bible – *tota Scriptura* – as the word of God.

In what follows we will explore these issues in more detail with a focus on their relevance for today. These issues are also the ones in which the major differences between Calvin and Barth emerge and we will conclude by examining them.

The Bible as the Word of God

Early on in the *Institutes* Calvin discusses the Word of God as Holy Scripture (*Inst.* 1.VI), and Barth is clear that 'We believe in and with the Church that Holy Scripture as the original and legitimate witness of divine revelation is itself the Word of God' (*CD* 1/2, 502) Calvin is more open to God's revelation through creation, but both are clear that Scripture is the sole means by which we get to know God truly.[25] As Barth notes, 'We are tied to these texts. And we can only ask about revelation when we surrender to the expectation and recollection attested in these texts' (*CD* 1/2, 492).

Thus for both Calvin and Barth, if we wish to glorify God then we must listen to Scripture attentively and live under its authority. The health and well-being of the church depends on such an attitude to Scripture:

> But the Church has become increasingly strong and self-conscious and bold, and produced heroes and geniuses and benefactors, and been able to establish comfort and hope for all people, not only within but without its walls, and gained genuine respect for itself, even in the world, when it has had a humble mind, and been prepared to live not above or alongside, but *under the Word*... Death usually reigns in the church when it is thought that this acknowledgement [of the priority of the Bible] should not be made (*CD* 1/2, 502; italics mine).

For both Calvin and Barth we arrive at a view of Scripture as God's Word through the testimony of the Spirit to the church and in our own lives. There is a place for apologetics, but rational argument by itself cannot bring one to see Scripture for what it is, namely God's Word. And it is Scripture which calls forth the church and not the church which creates the canon. In this respect Barth, like Calvin, remains firmly Protestant.[26]

Calvin and Barth's massive attention to Scripture stems entirely from this perspective on the Bible: God is sovereign and he addresses us through his written Word. All their exegetical labours are thus aimed at hearing his address. In this sense their hermeneutic is overwhelmingly one of trust and not suspicion. It is hard to overestimate how far so much academic biblical interpretation has moved from this

---

[25] See *Inst.* 1.VI. 2,3,4.
[26] On these issues see *Inst.* 1.VII.

perspective today. Some time ago I attended a gathering of practical theologians in the UK to examine the role of the Bible in practical theology. One of the observers who was asked to keep notes and reflect on the process at the end, observed that he thought there was a consensus among us that we no longer wanted the Bible over us but saw it as a dialogue partner.[27] A courageous professor interjected that no, there was still some of us who see the Bible as over us. Such experiences alert one to the state of the academy and the extent to which, even in our postmodern times, the legacy of Calvin and Barth is marginal in biblical interpretation.

However, even in circles where the authority of Scripture is taken with the utmost seriousness, academic interpretation of the Bible has often failed to have as its goal hearing God's address.[28] Barth is at pains to defend historical criticism, but always insists that it must serve the large goal of listening to Scripture to hear God speak. The problem for Barth is that so much historical criticism stops way short of this goal. Sadly this has also been true of much orthodox biblical scholarship. Perhaps because of the fierceness of the battle, much Evangelical biblical scholarship has tended to cover the same ground as their liberal opponents but in a conservative fashion. Neither approach has had as its goal to *listening* to Scripture. Somehow this goal is regarded as an optional extra that does not really fit in the academy – it is application which is the (non-academic) work of pastors and preachers![29]

The result is that so much work on the Bible fails to help us hear God's address. As Childs notes, we need a hermeneutic in which 'The final task of exegesis is to seek to hear the Word of God, which means that the witness of Moses and Jeremiah, of Paul and John, must become a vehicle for another Word. The exegete must come to wrestle with the kerygmatic substance which brought into being the witness.'[30] It is encouraging that we are starting to see new types of commentaries emerging which make this their goal.[31] As we work and pray for such a recovery, Calvin and

---

[27] For an example of this sort of approach see Fretheim's contribution to Terence Fretheim and Karl Froehlich, *The Bible as Word of God in a Postmodern Age* (Augsburg: Fortress Press), Part II, 79-120. In this situation the following comment Barth makes in *CD* I/2 remains as relevant in our postmodern context as then: 'That God is in heaven and man on the earth, that God rules and man must obey, that the Word of God makes a total claim upon men – we have had to learn anew to accustom ourselves again to these simple truths, in contradiction to a theological liberalism which would have nothing to do with them.' *CD* I/2, 663.

[28] See Eugene H. Peterson, *Working the Angles: The Shape of Pastoral Integrity* (Grand Rapids: Eerdmans, 1990), chapter 4, for an important discussion of how the contemporary church has lost a capacity to listen.

[29] See Brevard Childs, 'Interpretation in Faith: The Theological Responsibility of an Old Testament Commentary', *Interpretation* 18 (1964), 432-49, for some of the problems with this kind of 'bridge approach' to application.

[30] Childs, 'Interpretation in Faith', 443.

[31] For example, see *The Two Horizons New Testament Commentary Series* edited by Joel B. Green and Max Turner, published by Eerdmans. See also *The Two Horizons Old Testament Commentary Series* edited by Craig Bartholomew and Gordon McConville, also published by Eerdmans.

Barth stand as exemplars of such an approach, and the challenge is how to appropriate their work in our day.

Biblical Interpretation and Theology

There are different levels of faith and/or theology. There is the level of believing faith, which expresses a real 'faith' in Jesus Christ. Then there are the more reflective levels with a stronger propositional and analytical content, ranging from the Apostles Creed to the confessions to systematic theology. Calvin and Barth know nothing of the chasm that has appeared between biblical interpretation and theology in the contemporary academy. All these levels of faith are deeply bound up with biblical exegesis in Calvin and Barth.

Both Calvin and Barth recognise that it is only in faith that one sees Scripture for what it is, namely the Word of God. It is as part of the church that one reads the Bible as Scripture, and as Barth says, 'The door of the Bible texts can be opened only from within' (*CD* 1/2, 533). This is what Barth means when, as described above, he refers to his exegesis as eisegesis. One comes to Scripture expecting to hear from God, giving the text the benefit of the doubt. In this sense both Calvin and Barth's exegesis is *thick* interpretation[32] in that it is informed by faith and interprets for God's address. Calvin explains in his 1536 Preface to the *Institutes* that he wrote them to prepare candidates for reading Scripture. Theology thereby aids in the task of interpreting Scripture, in which Jesus Christ is found.[33] Both Calvin and Barth are nevertheless deeply concerned to do justice to the particularities of texts even as they bring their theological presuppositions to the Bible. 'The idea with which scriptural exegesis must begin is that of fidelity in all circumstances to the object reflected in the words of the prophets and apostles' (*CD* 1/2, 725). One of the great characteristics of Barth's *Church Dogmatics* is that even as his conceptual framework takes hold, he does more and not less exegesis. It is as though the doctrinal framework stimulates rather than – as in too many contemporary theologies – suppresses exegesis.

In this way a dialogue is set up between the beliefs that are brought to Scripture and between particular texts and the whole of Scripture. Barth and Calvin are clear that it is the whole of the Bible that is God's Word so that we need to read for *tota Scriptura*. Barth asserts this principle as follows: 'An exposition is trustworthy to the extent that it not only expounds the text in front of it, but implicitly at least expounds all other texts, to the extent that it at any rate clears the way for the exposition of all other texts' (*CD* 1/2, 485).

---

[32] The reference is of course to Clifford Geertz's categories of 'thick' and 'thin' description. See Clifford Geertz, *Thick Description: Toward a Theory of Interpretation of Cultures* (New York: Basic Books, 1973).

[33] Brevard Childs, *Biblical Theology of the Old and New Testaments* (London: SCM Press, 1992), 49.

A good example of the way in which a reading of a text makes the rest of Scripture resonate, as it were, is Barth's rich reading of Genesis 1:2.4-25.[34] Barth explores the creation of the animals on the same day as humankind and the consequent links between them. Writing long before the current emphasis on animal rights Barth notes that:

> Man's salvation and perdition, his joy and sorrow, will be reflected in the weal and woe of this animal environment and company. Not as an independent partner of the covenant, but as an attendant, the animal will participate with man (the independent partner) in the covenant, sharing both the promise and the curse which shadows the promise. Full of forebodings, but also full of confidence, it will wait with man for its fulfilment, breathing freely again when this has taken place provisionally and will take place definitively (*CD* 3/1, 178).

In the small print exegetical discussion that follows this section, what is remarkable is the way Barth ranges across Scripture, thereby demonstrating just how fertile an exegetical principle *analogia Scriptura* can be. Noting that this linking of animal and humankind is a familiar thought in both Testaments, as exemplified in Psalm 36:6 in which the YHWH is praised because he preserves both man and beast, Barth has a fascinating tour of passages ranging from Isaiah 43:20-31, to Hosea 2:18, Ezekiel 34, Jonah 4:11 and 3:8, Mark 1:13, etc.

Such fertile ranging across Scripture raises the issue of the role of *biblical theology* in Calvin and Barth's exegesis. For both Calvin and Barth both Old Testament and New Testament are indispensable parts of Scripture. As Barth asserts: 'The Old and the New Testament both have as their distinctive feature to attest in the one case the Messiah who is to come, and in the other the Messiah who has already come' (*CD* 1/2 481; Cf. *Inst.* II.VI. 2,3,4). Barth strongly opposes the Marcionite tendency to play down the Old Testament: 'The Old Testament is not an introduction to the real New Testament Bible, which we can dispense with or replace ... Whether we like it nor not, the Christ of the New Testament is the Christ of the Old Testament, the Christ of Israel' (*CD* 1/2, 488). And, 'If Christ has risen from the dead, then the understanding of the Old Testament as a witness to Christ is not a later interpretation, but an understanding of its original and only legitimate sense' (*CD* 1/2, 488, 489). Or, as Calvin asserts, 'the hope of the godly has ever reposed in Christ alone' (*Inst.* II.VI.3).

Once again Calvin and Barth are here in the minority in the academy nowadays, with the tendency to refer to the Old Testament as the Hebrew Bible or the First Testament, and the common understanding that the New Testament interpretation of the Old is an imposition of an alien view on that text. However, while not for a moment denying others the freedom to read the Old Testament as first testament or Hebrew Bible, Chris Seitz and others have pointed out that theological interpretation

---

[34] See *CD* 3/1, 176ff. I cannot repeat all the details of Barth's exegesis and the reader is strongly encouraged to read these pages in Barth for him/her self.

of the Bible does well to retain the name 'Old Testament.'[35] By the name 'Old Testament' the church deliberately followed the apostles in seeing Christ as the fulfilment of the Law and the Prophets and thereby asserting the Christological centre to the Bible. 'As a term for Christians, "Hebrew Bible" fails to comprehend this Christological center, and for the simply curious it fails to explain how Israel's mail has become a word of address for all creation.'[36]

As regards what we nowadays call biblical theology, Calvin would not have known it as a distinct discipline but his understanding of the two covenants as one and the same in substance and his consequent emphasis on the history of Israel 'draws him fully within the orbit of a Biblical Theology'.[37] Barth is more cautious when it comes to biblical theology. He is of course concerned to take the unity of Scripture seriously, but he resists any abstraction of a historical or conceptual system from the Bible: 'There can be no biblical theology in this sense, either of the Old or New Testament, or of the Bible as a whole... [A] biblical theology can never consist in more than a series of attempted approximations, a collection of individual exegeses.'[38]

Contemporary proponents of theological interpretation have recognised that we need to break down the iron curtain that separates biblical interpretation from theology. Once again Calvin and Barth are exemplary in this respect.

Critical Scholarship and Exegesis

In *Church Dogmatics* 1/2, under the theme of freedom under the Word, Barth outlines the process of scriptural interpretation in three phases:[39] observation, reflection and appropriation. Observation involves working at understanding the meaning of the biblical text as we have it. All the tools available such as source criticism, lexicography, grammar, syntax, etc. are fully utilised in this process of literary-historical investigation. Such work provides the base for attending to what is spoken by the authors of the Bible, and in this respect the readers must be open to allowing their world to be redescribed.[40]

---

[35] See Christopher Seitz, 'Old Testament or Hebrew Bible?' in Christopher Seitz, *Word Without End: The Old Testament as Abiding Theological Witness* (Grand Rapids: Erdmans, 1998), chapter 6.

[36] Seitz, 'Old Testament or Hebrew Bible?', 74.

[37] Childs, *Biblical Theology*, 49.

[38] *CD* 1/2 483. Find the references to Calvin's stepped approach of which Barth is critical.

[39] These are three distinguishable moments in exegesis but not necessarily sequential in time. See Barth, *CD* 1/2, 727.

[40] I use here the language associated with Paul Ricoeur. See, for example, Paul Ricoeur, *Time and Narrative*, Volume 1 (trans. Kathleen McLaughlin and David Pellauer; Chicago: University of Chicago Press, 1984), pp. 80–81. For Barth's description, see *CD* 1/2 724. Barth is concerned that the otherness of the text be confronted.

The second moment in exegesis is *reflection* on what Scripture says to us. The reader can never be free of him/her self in the act of reading so that such reflection always accompanies explanation. The text is always approached from a particular epistemology, from some philosophy or other (*CD* 1/2, 728). 'If we cannot and must not dispute this, if we are not to dispute the grace and finally the incarnation of the Word of God, we cannot basically contest the use of philosophy in scriptural exegesis. Where the question of legitimacy arises is in regard to the How of this use' (*CD* 1/2, 729, 730). In this respect Barth discusses in some detail the relation between what we bring to Scripture and exegesis. He asserts that:

- the reader must be conscious of what he/she is doing. Our philosophy stands always in contrast to that of Scripture.
- The framework we bring to Scripture must be provisional and subject to reform by Scripture. It must be controlled by the text.
- We need to be cautious of philosophy in biblical interpretation – it can claim 'no independent interest in itself' (*CD* 1/2, 731). Barth refers here to Tertullian's warnings about the dangers of philosophy.
- There is no essential reason for preferring one framework over another.

The third moment in exegesis is appropriation. What is declared to us in Scripture must become our own; 'Because the Word of God meets us in the form of the scriptural word, assimilation means the contemporaneity, homogeneity and indirect identification of the reader and hearer of Scripture with the witness of the revelation. Assimilation means assuming the witness into our responsibility' (*CD* 1/2, 736). Appropriation is not a third act in exegesis but part of one totality of interpretation.[41] That about which Scripture speaks 'wills not merely to master our thinking about it, but our thinking and life generally, and our whole existence' (*CD* 1/2, 737).

The twenty-two pages in which Barth discusses these three moments in exegesis are remarkably rich in terms of hermeneutical reflection and repay careful study. Suffice it here to take up a few key points in relation to biblical interpretation today.

The Role of Historical Criticism

Here as in many other places Barth defends the role of historical criticism as long as it is in the service of understanding what the text is speaking of. As Barth says elsewhere, 'we must not and cannot ignore the insights won under the perverted sign of the earlier source-investigation of the Bible. There cannot, therefore, be any question of sealing off or abandoning so-called "criticism"... All relevant, historical questions must be put to the biblical texts, considered as witnesses in accordance with their literary form' (*CD* 1/2, 494). Barth is however highly critical of modern

---

[41] See Barth's strong comments in this respect in *CD* 1/2, 736-40.

historicism which seeks to locate revelation in the facts behind the text; the literary shape of the Canon as we have received it, and its character as witness must be taken seriously and it must be read as such. In this way Barth does not seek to annul historical criticism but to redirect it 'on the basis of the recognition that the biblical texts must be investigated for their own sake to the extent that the revelation which they attest does not stand or occur, and is not to be sought, behind or above them but in them' (*CD* 1/2, 494).

The rise of historical criticism postdates Calvin, of course, and Barth thus differs from Calvin in his positive appropriation of historical criticism. In this respect Barth has taken flack from all sides, with liberals accusing him of not taking historical criticism seriously enough and Evangelicals accusing him of succumbing to liberalism in his exegesis. Looking back on these debates now, Barth anticipates later developments. In works such as George Eldon Ladd's *The New Testament and Criticism* (Grand Rapids: Eerdmans, 1966) and Carl Armerding's *The Old Testament and Criticism* (Grand Rapids: Eerdmans, 1983 as well as seminal volumes such as *New Testament Interpretation: Essays on Principles and Methods*, edited by Howard Marshall (Carlisle: Paternoster: 1979 [revised edition]), evangelicals made peace with the role of criticism in biblical interpretation. The extent to which this has been done sufficiently critically from a Christian perspective remains a moot point,[42] but certainly Barth's point that such critical work must serve to help us understand the witness of the text remains vitally important.[43]

The Role of Philosophy and General Hermeneutics in Biblical Interpretation

Barth's caution about philosophy 'in theology' is well known, and it is helpful to have him address the issue so directly in relation to exegesis as described above. Indeed, a legacy of Barth's in the contemporary renewal of theological interpretation is that many of its best proponents are deeply cautious of 'the hermeneutic detour.' There are major scholars like Anthony Thiselton whose two major volumes on hermeneutics bear ample witness to his belief that philosophical hermeneutics has a great deal to offer biblical (and theological) interpretation. But scholars such as Francis Watson and John Webster, and many of the Yale school, are far more reticent about the help that general hermeneutics can provide. Watson and Webster plead for a regional theological hermeneutic for biblical interpretation that stems from Christian doctrine and is used for theological interpretation.

Barth seems to me to be caught in a dilemma when it comes to philosophy and biblical interpretation. On the one hand it is unavoidable but on the other it is dangerous. It is not surprising that he invokes Tertullian with his question 'What

---

[42] See the essays in Bartholomew, et al. (eds.), *Behind the Text*.
[43] Barth's view of the relationship between criticism and the theme of the text is akin to Sternberg's insightful explication of the relationship between diachronic and synchronic reading of the Old Testament. See Meir Sternberg, *The Poetics of Biblical Narrative: Ideological Literature and the Drama of Reading* (Bloomington: Indiana University Press, 1985).

has Jerusalem to do with Athens?' in this discussion, for it is Tertullian's type of understanding of the philosophy-theology relationship that underlies Barth's position.[44] Surprisingly Barth does not even seem to think that one type of philosophical framework is better than another when coming to interpret Scripture.

The role of hermeneutics in theological interpretation is a large issue. Suffice it here to note, as Barth accepts, that philosophy and hermeneutics cannot be kept out of exegesis – their presence is simply an extension of the way things are in the creation. The danger of hermeneutics, as Barth, Webster and others point out is that alien ideologies start to control exegesis and it is right to guard against this. What Barth does not explore is whether what Plantinga calls 'positive Christian philosophy' might be particularly helpful in bringing philosophy captive to Christ, so that it might more readily help exegesis in comparison to more alien philosophies. Barth is open to ways in which a theological hermeneutic might provide insights for general hermeneutics[45] but fails, I think, to take sufficiently seriously the insights that hermeneutics might provide for exegesis.

One has to be careful when comparing Calvin with Barth in this respect because of the very different contexts in which they worked. But a case can be made that Calvin would be more open to philosophy and hermeneutics than Barth and some of his followers. Indeed it was Calvin's work on legal hermeneutics that had a major influence on his biblical exegesis,[46] and his doctrine of general revelation is more open to such insights than Barth's more Christocentric theology allows.[47]

Calvin, Barth, and Postmodern Interpretation

Graham Ward and others have suggested that there may be strong links between Barth and postmoderns such as Derrida.[48] This suggestion founders when one looks closely at Barth's understanding of exegesis and his actual exegesis. Barth is quite clear, for example, that

> In demanding a historical appreciation of the Bible, it must also require – and self-evidently of every reader of the Bible – that his understanding of it should be based on what is said in the Bible and therefore on God's revelation. It cannot, therefore, be conceded that side by side with this there is another legitimate understanding of the Bible, that, e.g., in its own way it is right and possible when we hear and expound the Bible not to go beyond the humanity as such which is expressed in it...

---

[44] See Craig Bartholomew, 'Uncharted Waters: Philosophy, Theology and the Crisis in Biblical Interpretation', in C. Bartholomew, C. Greene and K. Müller (ed), *Renewing Biblical Interpretation* (Grand Rapids: Zondervan, 2000), 1–39.

[45] For an example, see *CD* 1/2 465, 466, 471.

[46] See Thomas F. Torrance, *The Hermeneutics of John Calvin* (Monograph Supplements to the *Scottish Journal of Theology*; Edinburgh: T & T Clark, 1988).

[47] See Christoph Schwöbel, 'Theology', in John Webster (ed.), *The Cambridge Companion to Karl Barth* (Cambridge: Cambridge University Press, 2000), 17-36, especially 34-35.

[48] See Ward, *Barth, Derrida, and the Language of Theology*.

[I]t does not speak of itself, but of God's revelation, and no honest and unprejudiced reader of the Bible can ignore this historical definiteness of the word (*CD* 1/2, 468).

Here, as elsewhere, Barth adopts an approach to interpretation much like that of Childs' canonical hermeneutic, in which he argues for determinate interpretation which interprets for God's revelation, and like Childs Barth is not prepared to see this as one amongst a smorgasbord of hermeneutic possibilities. Barth and Calvin's emphasis on the literal sense of Scripture[49] is contrary to the postmodern tendency to play with texts and to tease out as many meanings as possible. Barth, very much in the spirit of Calvin is adamant that 'In exegesis, too – and especially in exegesis – there is only one truth' (*CD* 1/2, 470). Barth says of Calvin that he 'hated what he called on one occasion the pleasurable playing about with every possible interpretation of the text that we can hardly avoid when it comes to Revelation, and wherever he could he avoided leaving us with two or more meanings… Each passage has its own truth. Each is self-grounded. Each must be expounded in its own context.'[50]

Such an orientation to exegesis is poles apart from that of Derrida and other postmoderns. Utterly central to so much of Derrida's strange reading of texts involves setting them in play so that the context cannot constrain the infinite range of possible interpretations. To take just one example: Derrida's reading of the Tower of Babel narrative in which he has God pronouncing God's name Babel over the city would be utterly anathema to Calvin and Barth.[51] Although of course, Calvin and Barth do not engage directly with postmodern debates about language, their approaches to interpretation fit with Thiselton's notion of adjectival intentionality, Wolterstorff's notion of what the author actually said and Sternberg's embodied intentionality rather than with Derrida and co.[52]

---

[49] See Kathryn Greene-McCreight, *Ad Litteram: How Augustine, Calvin, and Barth Read the "Plain Sense" of Genesis 1–3* (Issues in Systematic Theology, 5; New York and Frankfurt: Peter Lang, 1999).

[50] Barth, *The Theology of John Calvin*, 390.

[51] See Craig Bartholomew, 'Babel and Derrida: Postmodernism, Language and Biblical Interpretation', *Tyndale Bulletin* 49.2 (1998), 305-28.

[52] See Anthony C. Thiselton, *New Horizons in Hermeneutics: The Theory and Practice of Transforming Biblical Reading* (Grand Rapids: Eerdmans, 1997); Nicholas Wolterstorff, *Divine Discourse: Philosophical Reflection on the Claim that God Speaks* (Cambridge: Cambridge University Press, 1995); Meir Sternberg, *The Poetics of Biblical Narrative: Ideological Literature and the Drama of Biblical Reading* (Bloomington: Indiana University Press, 1985).

Author Index

Aland, Kurt, 76
Aristotle, 133
Armour, Rollin S., 73
Asselt, Willem J. Van, 4, 18, 23
Athanasius, 6
Augustine, 5, 17, 38, 40, 41, 58, 60, 62, 63, 67, 86, 93, 97, 107, 143, 163, 177

Baillie, D.M., 31
Baker, Mark D., 125
Balke, W., 67, 86
Balthasar, Hans Urs von, 19, 96
Barth, Markus, 51, 54, 60
Bartholomew, Craig, 163, 170, 175, 176, 177
Battles, Ford Lewis, 127
Baylor, Michael G., 73
Beasley-Murray, G.R., 80, 87
Berangarius of Tours, 36
Berkhof, Louis, 6
Berkouwer, G.C., 165, 166
Beza, Theodore, 111
Bizer, Ernst, 16, 17, 18
Blocher, Henri, 125
Boersma, Hans, 5
Bradshaw, Paul, 86
Bromiley, Geoffrey, 14, 15, 57, 61, 66, 92, 135
Brown, Colin, 132, 144
Bruce, F.F., 84
Brunner, Emil, 81
Bucer, Martin, 58, 59, 111
Buckley, James, 45, 46
Bullinger, Heinrich, 9, 66
Bultmann, Rudolf, 12, 93, 100, 116
Busch, Eberhard, 11, 12, 15

Campenhausen, Hans von, 95
Childs, Brevard S., 95, 164, 170, 171, 173, 177
Chung, S.W., 135
Clark, R. Scott, 4, 5, 6, 29, 57, 58, 79, 80, 82, 85, 94, 118, 149, 159, 161, 164, 176
Cocceius, Johannes, 11, 17, 18, 20, 21
Colwell, J.E., 61, 76, 79
Cross, Anthony R., 61, 69, 80, 81, 82, 83, 85
Crossan, Dominic, 102, 103
Cullmann, Oscar, 76

Dekker, Eef, 4, 23
Dunn, James D.G., 80, 83

Edmondson, Stephen, 161
Elert, Werner, 4, 19
Estep, W.R., 85
Evans, William B., 69

Fape, M.O., 85
Farley, E., 67, 85
Fee, Gordon D., 80
Ferguson, E., 80, 85
Feuerbach, Ludwig, 13
Fiddes, Paul S., 83
Fisher, Edward, 5
Flannery, Austin, 36
Fowler, S.K., 80, 81
Franke, John R, 23
Frei, Hans, 113
Fretheim, Terence, 170
Froehlich, Karl, 170

Gäbler, U., 66
Garcia, Mark A, 69

Geertz, Clifford, 171
George, T., 11, 66, 67, 73, 87, 112, 139, 175
Gräbe, Petrus J, 78
Green, Joel B., 125, 170
Greene-McCreight, K., 177
Grislis, Egil, 59, 63
Gunton, Colin E., 19, 125, 138, 140

Harnack, Adolf von, 11, 12, 13, 14, 20
Haroutunian, J., 57, 155
Hart, Trevor, 29, 43, 125
Hartman, L., 80
Hartwell, Herbert, 58, 79, 80
Haymes, B., 84, 85
Helm, Paul, 127, 130, 131, 132, 133, 141, 157
Hengstenberg, E.W., 164
Heppe, Heinrich, 10, 14, 16, 17, 18, 19, 20, 21, 25
Heron, Alasdair, 36, 37, 54
Hesselink, John, 154
Hinson, E. Glenn, 62
Holmes, Stephen R., 122, 139, 140, 142, 143, 149, 161
Hunsinger, George, 11, 139
Hunt, John P.W., 84

Israel, Jonathan I, 11

Jenson, Robert W., 135
Jeremias, Joachim, 76
Jewett, P.K., 84
Johnson, Galen, 67
Jüngel, Eberhard, 144
Junius, Francis, 23

Kähler, Martin, 99
Kant, Immanuel, 12, 93
Kendall, R.T., 133
Kerr, Fergus, 135, 140
Kierkegaard, Soren, 14
Kolb, Robert, 4

Krötke, Wolf, 143
Kümmel, Werner G., 103

Langer, Susanne, 39
Liechty, Daniel, 73
Lillback, Peter, 59, 84
Lohse, Bernhard, 6
Lombard, Peter, 17
Luther, Martin, 4, 5, 6, 16, 58, 77, 95, 97, 98, 163, 168

MacDonald, Neil B., 23, 91, 101, 104
Marshall, I. Howard, 69, 175
McClendon, J.W., 81
McCormack, Bruce L., 11, 14, 15, 18, 19, 135, 136, 137, 138, 139
McDonnell, K., 80
McNeill, James T., 91
Melanchthon, Philip, 17
Mergal, Angela M., 73
Migliore, Daniel, 14, 21, 23, 26
Molnar, Paul D., 46
Montague, G.T., 80
Moody, Dale, 61
Mueller, J.T., 6
Müller, E.F. Karl, 5, 8, 10, 18
Muller, Richard A., 8, 10, 12, 20, 21, 23, 91, 118, 119, 133, 149

Neuhaus, Richard J., 163
Niesel, Wilhelm, 120, 122
Nietzsche, Friedrich, 14

Oberman, Heiko, 5
Oden, Thomas, 163
Old, H.O., 58, 64, 69
Overbeck, Franz, 14

Parker, T.H.L., 65, 76, 98, 107, 158, 159
Pelikan, Jaroslav, 83
Peterson, Robert A., 121, 123, 124, 127, 129, 130, 131, 170

Pinnock, Clark H., 82, 83
Plantinga, Alvin, 163, 176
Popkin, Richard, 10
Porter, Stanley E., 61, 69, 80, 82, 83, 85
Preus, Robert D., 20, 23

Ricoeur, Paul, 173
Riggs, J.W., 58
Ritschl, Albrecht, 13, 16, 20
Roy, K., 81
Rumscheidt, H., 11, 12
Runia, Klaas, 23, 165

Said, Edward, 3, 26
Saussure, Ferdinand de, 39
Schillebeeckx, Edward, 33, 34, 35, 36, 37, 45
Schleiermacher, Friedrich, 10, 13, 16, 17, 21, 91, 98
Schmid, Heinrich, 16, 19, 20
Schreiner, Susan, 21
Schweitzer, Albert, 17, 100, 101, 103, 105, 110
Schweizer, Alexander, 17, 137
Schwöbel, Christoph, 176
Seerveld, Calvin, 164
Seitz, Christopher R., 164, 172, 173
Smith, L.P., 12, 57
Sontag, Susan, 42
Soulen, Kendall, 96
Steinmetz, David C., 67
Stephens, W.P., 6, 66
Sternberg, Meir, 175, 177

Tertullian, 70, 78, 86, 174, 175, 176
Theissen, Gerd, 116

Thiselton, Anthony C., 177
Thomas Aquinas, 6, 35, 36, 38, 41, 107, 133, 163
Thomas, G. Michael, 133
Torrance, T.F., 22, 33, 61, 98, 106, 107, 123, 176
Trueman, Carl R, 3, 4
Turner, Max, 170
Turretin, Francis, 20

Vahanian, Gabriel, 135
Vanhoozer, Kevin J., 125, 164
Verbeek, Theo, 10

Wallace, R.S., 57, 58, 59, 69, 70, 82, 83
Ward, Graham, 167, 176
Warfield, B.B., 25, 26, 149
Watson, Francis, 94, 136, 138, 164
Webster, John, 138, 164, 176
Weiss, Johannes, 110
Wendel, Francois, 59, 68, 121
Wengert, Timothy J., 4
Wenham, Gordon, 164
Westermann, Claus, 165
Williams, N.P., 86
Williams, Rowan, 12, 30, 31, 67, 73
Willis, E.D., 6, 137
Wolterstorff, Nicholas, 177
Wright, D.F., 67, 85, 86, 87, 158
Wright, N.T., 93, 100, 102, 110, 115, 116, 117, 164
Wyneken, Karl H., 67

Zwingli, Huldrych 5, 6, 9, 15, 31, 58, 62, 65, 66, 82, 92

Paternoster Biblical Monographs

(All titles uniform with this volume)
Dates in bold are of projected publication

Joseph Abraham
Eve: Accused or Acquitted?
A Reconsideration of Feminist Readings of the Creation Narrative Texts in Genesis 1–3
Two contrary views dominate contemporary feminist biblical scholarship. One finds in the Bible an unequivocal equality between the sexes from the very creation of humanity, whilst the other sees the biblical text as irredeemably patriarchal and androcentric. Dr Abraham enters into dialogue with both camps as well as introducing his own method of approach. An invaluable tool for any one who is interested in this contemporary debate.
2002 / 0-85364-971-5 / xxiv + 272pp

Octavian D. Baban
Mimesis and Luke's on the Road Encounters in Luke-Acts
Luke's Theology of the Way and its Literary Representation
The book argues on theological and literary (mimetic) grounds that Luke's on-the-road encounters, especially those belonging to the post-Easter period, are part of his complex theology of the Way. Jesus' teaching and that of the apostles is presented by Luke as a challenging answer to the Hellenistic reader's thirst for adventure, good literature, and existential paradigms.
2005 */ 1-84227-253-5 / approx. 374pp*

Paul Barker
The Triumph of Grace in Deuteronomy
This book is a textual and theological analysis of the interaction between the sin and faithlessness of Israel and the grace of Yahweh in response, looking especially at Deuteronomy chapters 1–3, 8–10 and 29–30. The author argues that the grace of Yahweh is determinative for the ongoing relationship between Yahweh and Israel and that Deuteronomy anticipates and fully expects Israel to be faithless.
2004 / 1-84227-226-8 / xxii + 270pp

Jonathan F. Bayes
The Weakness of the Law
God's Law and the Christian in New Testament Perspective
A study of the four New Testament books which refer to the law as weak (Acts, Romans, Galatians, Hebrews) leads to a defence of the third use in the Reformed debate about the law in the life of the believer.
2000 / 0-85364-957-X / xii + 244pp

Mark Bonnington
The Antioch Episode of Galatians 2:11-14 in Historical and Cultural Context

The Galatians 2 'incident' in Antioch over table-fellowship suggests significant disagreement between the leading apostles. This book analyses the background to the disagreement by locating the incident within the dynamics of social interaction between Jews and Gentiles. It proposes a new way of understanding the relationship between the individuals and issues involved.

2005 / 1-84227-050-8 / approx. 350pp

David Bostock
A Portrayal of Trust
The Theme of Faith in the Hezekiah Narratives

This study provides detailed and sensitive readings of the Hezekiah narratives (2 Kings 18–20 and Isaiah 36–39) from a theological perspective. It concentrates on the theme of faith, using narrative criticism as its methodology. Attention is paid especially to setting, plot, point of view and characterization within the narratives. A largely positive portrayal of Hezekiah emerges that underlines the importance and relevance of scripture.

2005 / 1-84227-314-0 / approx. 300pp

Mark Bredin
Jesus, Revolutionary of Peace
A Non-violent Christology in the Book of Revelation

This book aims to demonstrate that the figure of Jesus in the Book of Revelation can best be understood as an active non-violent revolutionary.

2003 / 1-84227-153-9 / xviii + 262pp

Robinson Butarbutar
Paul and Conflict Resolution
An Exegetical Study of Paul's Apostolic Paradigm in 1 Corinthians 9

The author sees the apostolic paradigm in 1 Corinthians 9 as part of Paul's unified arguments in 1 Corinthians 8–10 in which he seeks to mediate in the dispute over the issue of food offered to idols. The book also sees its relevance for dispute-resolution today, taking the conflict within the author's church as an example.

2006 / 1-84227-315-9 / approx. 280pp

Daniel J-S Chae
Paul as Apostle to the Gentiles
His Apostolic Self-awareness and its Influence on the Soteriological Argument in Romans

Opposing 'the post-Holocaust interpretation of Romans', Daniel Chae competently demonstrates that Paul argues for the equality of Jew and Gentile in Romans. Chae's fresh exegetical interpretation is academically outstanding and spiritually encouraging.

1997 / 0-85364-829-8 / xiv + 378pp

Luke L. Cheung
The Genre, Composition and Hermeneutics of the Epistle of James

The present work examines the employment of the wisdom genre with a certain compositional structure and the interpretation of the law through the Jesus tradition of the double love command by the author of the Epistle of James to serve his purpose in promoting perfection and warning against doubleness among the eschatologically renewed people of God in the Diaspora.

2003 / 1-84227-062-1 / xvi + 372pp

Youngmo Cho
Spirit and Kingdom in the Writings of Luke and Paul

The relationship between Spirit and Kingdom is a relatively unexplored area in Lukan and Pauline studies. This book offers a fresh perspective of two biblical writers on the subject. It explores the difference between Luke's and Paul's understanding of the Spirit by examining the specific question of the relationship of the concept of the Spirit to the concept of the Kingdom of God in each writer.

2005 / 1-84227-316-7 / approx. 270pp

Andrew C. Clark
Parallel Lives
The Relation of Paul to the Apostles in the Lucan Perspective

This study of the Peter-Paul parallels in Acts argues that their purpose was to emphasize the themes of continuity in salvation history and the unity of the Jewish and Gentile missions. New light is shed on Luke's literary techniques, partly through a comparison with Plutarch.

2001 / 1-84227-035-4 / xviii + 386pp

Andrew D. Clarke
Secular and Christian Leadership in Corinth
A Socio-Historical and Exegetical Study of 1 Corinthians 1–6

This volume is an investigation into the leadership structures and dynamics of first-century Roman Corinth. These are compared with the practice of leadership in the Corinthian Christian community which are reflected in 1 Corinthians 1–6, and contrasted with Paul's own principles of Christian leadership.

2005 / 1-84227-229-2 / 200pp

Stephen Finamore
God, Order and Chaos
René Girard and the Apocalypse

Readers are often disturbed by the images of destruction in the book of Revelation and unsure why they are unleashed after the exaltation of Jesus. This book examines past approaches to these texts and uses René Girard's theories to revive some old ideas and propose some new ones.

2005 / 1-84227-197-0 / approx. 344pp

David G. Firth
Surrendering Retribution in the Psalms
Responses to Violence in the Individual Complaints

In *Surrendering Retribution in the Psalms*, David Firth examines the ways in which the book of Psalms inculcates a model response to violence through the repetition of standard patterns of prayer. Rather than seeking justification for retributive violence, Psalms encourages not only a surrender of the right of retribution to Yahweh, but also sets limits on the retribution that can be sought in imprecations. Arising initially from the author's experience in South Africa, the possibilities of this model to a particular context of violence is then briefly explored.

2005 / 1-84227-337-X / xviii + 154pp

Scott J. Hafemann
Suffering and Ministry in the Spirit
Paul's Defence of His Ministry in II Corinthians 2:14–3:3

Shedding new light on the way Paul defended his apostleship, the author offers a careful, detailed study of 2 Corinthians 2:14–3:3 linked with other key passages throughout 1 and 2 Corinthians. Demonstrating the unity and coherence of Paul's argument in this passage, the author shows that Paul's suffering served as the vehicle for revealing God's power and glory through the Spirit.

2000 / 0-85364-967-7 / xiv + 262pp

Scott J. Hafemann
Paul, Moses and the History of Israel
The Letter/Spirit Contrast and the Argument from Scripture in 2 Corinthians 3
An exegetical study of the call of Moses, the second giving of the Law (Exodus 32–34), the new covenant, and the prophetic understanding of the history of Israel in 2 Corinthians 3. Hafemann's work demonstrates Paul's contextual use of the Old Testament and the essential unity between the Law and the Gospel within the context of the distinctive ministries of Moses and Paul.
2005 / 1-84227-317-5 / xii + 498pp

Douglas S. McComiskey
Lukan Theology in the Light of the Gospel's Literary Structure
Luke's Gospel was purposefully written with theology embedded in its patterned literary structure. A critical analysis of this cyclical structure provides new windows into Luke's interpretation of the individual pericopes comprising the Gospel and illuminates several of his theological interests.
2004 / 1-84227-148-2 / xviii + 388pp

Stephen Motyer
Your Father the Devil?
A New Approach to John and 'The Jews'
Who are 'the Jews' in John's Gospel? Defending John against the charge of antisemitism, Motyer argues that, far from demonising the Jews, the Gospel seeks to present Jesus as 'Good News for Jews' in a late first century setting.
1997 / 0-85364-832-8 / xiv + 260pp

Esther Ng
Reconstructing Christian Origins?
The Feminist Theology of Elizabeth Schüssler Fiorenza: An Evaluation
In a detailed evaluation, the author challenges Elizabeth Schüssler Fiorenza's reconstruction of early Christian origins and her underlying presuppositions. The author also presents her own views on women's roles both then and now.
2002 / 1-84227-055-9 / xxiv + 468pp

Robin Parry
Old Testament Story and Christian Ethics
The Rape of Dinah as a Case Study

What is the role of story in ethics and, more particularly, what is the role of Old Testament story in Christian ethics? This book, drawing on the work of contemporary philosophers, argues that narrative is crucial in the ethical shaping of people and, drawing on the work of contemporary Old Testament scholars, that story plays a key role in Old Testament ethics. Parry then argues that when situated in canonical context Old Testament stories can be reappropriated by Christian readers in their own ethical formation. The shocking story of the rape of Dinah and the massacre of the Shechemites provides a fascinating case study for exploring the parameters within which Christian ethical appropriations of Old Testament stories can live.

2004 / 1-84227-210-1 / xx + 350pp

Ian Paul
Power to See the World Anew
The Value of Paul Ricoeur's Hermeneutic of Metaphor in Interpreting the Symbolism of Revelation 12 and 13

This book is a study of the hermeneutics of metaphor of Paul Ricoeur, one of the most important writers on hermeneutics and metaphor of the last century. It sets out the key points of his theory, important criticisms of his work, and how his approach, modified in the light of these criticisms, offers a methodological framework for reading apocalyptic texts.

2006 / 1-84227-056-7 / approx. 350pp

Robert L. Plummer
Paul's Understanding of the Church's Mission
Did the Apostle Paul Expect the Early Christian Communities to Evangelize?

This book engages in a careful study of Paul's letters to determine if the apostle expected the communities to which he wrote to engage in missionary activity. It helpfully summarizes the discussion on this debated issue, judiciously handling contested texts, and provides a way forward in addressing this critical question. While admitting that Paul rarely explicitly commands the communities he founded to evangelize, Plummer amasses significant incidental data to provide a convincing case that Paul did indeed expect his churches to engage in mission activity. Throughout the study, Plummer progressively builds a theological basis for the church's mission that is both distinctively Pauline and compelling.

2006 / 1-84227-333-7 / approx. 324pp

David Powys
'Hell': A Hard Look at a Hard Question
The Fate of the Unrighteous in New Testament Thought
This comprehensive treatment seeks to unlock the original meaning of terms and phrases long thought to support the traditional doctrine of hell. It concludes that there is an alternative—one which is more biblical, and which can positively revive the rationale for Christian mission.
1997 / 0-85364-831-X / xxii + 478pp

Sorin Sabou
Between Horror and Hope
Paul's Metaphorical Language of Death in Romans 6.1-11
This book argues that Paul's metaphorical language of death in Romans 6.1-11 conveys two aspects: horror and hope. The 'horror' aspect is conveyed by the 'crucifixion' language, and the 'hope' aspect by 'burial' language. The life of the Christian believer is understood, as relationship with sin is concerned ('death to sin'), between these two realities: horror and hope.
2005 / 1-84227-322-1 / approx. 224pp

Rosalind Selby
The Comical Doctrine
The Epistemology of New Testament Hermeneutics
This book argues that the gospel breaks through postmodernity's critique of truth and the referential possibilities of textuality with its gift of grace. With a rigorous, philosophical challenge to modernist and postmodernist assumptions, Selby offers an alternative epistemology to all who would still read with faith *and* with academic credibility.
2005 / 1-84227-212-8 / approx. 350pp

Kiwoong Son
Zion Symbolism in Hebrews
Hebrews 12.18-24 as a Hermeneutical Key to the Epistle
This book challenges the general tendency of understanding the Epistle to the Hebrews against a Hellenistic background and suggests that the Epistle should be understood in the light of the Jewish apocalyptic tradition. The author especially argues for the importance of the theological symbolism of Sinai and Zion (Heb. 12:18-24) as it provides the Epistle's theological background as well as the rhetorical basis of the superiority motif of Jesus throughout the Epistle.
2005 / 1-84227-368-X / approx. 280pp

Kevin Walton
Thou Traveller Unknown
The Presence and Absence of God in the Jacob Narrative

The author offers a fresh reading of the story of Jacob in the book of Genesis through the paradox of divine presence and absence. The work also seeks to make a contribution to Pentateuchal studies by bringing together a close reading of the final text with historical critical insights, doing justice to the text's historical depth, final form and canonical status.

2003 / 1-84227-059-1 / xvi + 238pp

George M. Wieland
The Significance of Salvation
A Study of Salvation Language in the Pastoral Epistles

The language and ideas of salvation pervade the three Pastoral Epistles. This study offers a close examination of their soteriological statements. In all three letters the idea of salvation is found to play a vital paraenetic role, but each also exhibits distinctive soteriological emphases. The results challenge common assumptions about the Pastoral Epistles as a corpus.

2005 / 1-84227-257-8 / approx. 324pp

Alistair Wilson
When Will These Things Happen?
A Study of Jesus as Judge in Matthew 21–25

This study seeks to allow Matthew's carefully constructed presentation of Jesus to be given full weight in the modern evaluation of Jesus' eschatology. Careful analysis of the text of Matthew 21–25 reveals Jesus to be standing firmly in the Jewish prophetic and wisdom traditions as he proclaims and enacts imminent judgement on the Jewish authorities then boldly claims the central role in the final and universal judgement.

2004 / 1-84227-146-6 / xxii + 272pp

Lindsay Wilson
Joseph Wise and Otherwise
The Intersection of Covenant and Wisdom in Genesis 37–50

This book offers a careful literary reading of Genesis 37–50 that argues that the Joseph story contains both strong covenant themes and many wisdom-like elements. The connections between the two helps to explore how covenant and wisdom might intersect in an integrated biblical theology.

2004 / 1-84227-140-7 / xvi + 340pp

Stephen I. Wright
The Voice of Jesus
Studies in the Interpretation of Six Gospel Parables
This literary study considers how the 'voice' of Jesus has been heard in different periods of parable interpretation, and how the categories of figure and trope may help us towards a sensitive reading of the parables today.
2000 / 0-85364-975-8 / xiv + 280pp

Paternoster
9 Holdom Avenue,
Bletchley,
Milton Keynes MK1 1QR,
United Kingdom
Web: www.authenticmedia.co.uk/paternoster

Paternoster Theological Monographs

(All titles uniform with this volume)
Dates in bold are of projected publication

Emil Bartos
Deification in Eastern Orthodox Theology
An Evaluation and Critique of the Theology of Dumitru Staniloae
Bartos studies a fundamental yet neglected aspect of Orthodox theology: deification. By examining the doctrines of anthropology, christology, soteriology and ecclesiology as they relate to deification, he provides an important contribution to contemporary dialogue between Eastern and Western theologians.
1999 / 0-85364-956-1 / xii + 370pp

Graham Buxton
The Trinity, Creation and Pastoral Ministry
Imaging the Perichoretic God
In this book the author proposes a three-way conversation between theology, science and pastoral ministry. His approach draws on a Trinitarian understanding of God as a relational being of love, whose life 'spills over' into all created reality, human and non-human. By locating human meaning and purpose within God's 'creation-community' this book offers the possibility of a transforming engagement between those in pastoral ministry and the scientific community.
2005 */ 1-84227-369-8 / approx. 380 pp*

Iain D. Campbell
Fixing the Indemnity
The Life and Work of George Adam Smith
When Old Testament scholar George Adam Smith (1856–1942) delivered the Lyman Beecher lectures at Yale University in 1899, he confidently declared that 'modern criticism has won its war against traditional theories. It only remains to fix the amount of the indemnity.' In this biography, Iain D. Campbell assesses Smith's critical approach to the Old Testament and evaluates its consequences, showing that Smith's life and work still raises questions about the relationship between biblical scholarship and evangelical faith.
2004 / 1-84227-228-4 / xx + 256pp

Tim Chester
Mission and the Coming of God
Eschatology, the Trinity and Mission in the Theology of Jürgen Moltmann
This book explores the theology and missiology of the influential contemporary theologian, Jürgen Moltmann. It highlights the important contribution Moltmann has made while offering a critique of his thought from an evangelical perspective. In so doing, it touches on pertinent issues for evangelical missiology. The conclusion takes Calvin as a starting point, proposing 'an eschatology of the cross' which offers a critique of the over-realised eschatologies in liberation theology and certain forms of evangelicalism.
2006 / 1-84227-320-5 / approx. 224pp

Sylvia Wilkey Collinson
Making Disciples
The Significance of Jesus' Educational Strategy for Today's Church
This study examines the biblical practice of discipling, formulates a definition, and makes comparisons with modern models of education. A recommendation is made for greater attention to its practice today.
2004 / 1-84227-116-4 / xiv + 278pp

Darrell Cosden
A Theology of Work
Work and the New Creation
Through dialogue with Moltmann, Pope John Paul II and others, this book develops a genitive 'theology of work', presenting a theological definition of work and a model for a theological ethics of work that shows work's nature, value and meaning now and eschatologically. Work is shown to be a transformative activity consisting of three dynamically inter-related dimensions: the instrumental, relational and ontological.
2005 / 1-84227-332-9 / xvi + 208pp

Stephen M. Dunning
The Crisis and the Quest
A Kierkegaardian Reading of Charles Williams
Employing Kierkegaardian categories and analysis, this study investigates both the central crisis in Charles Williams's authorship between hermetism and Christianity (Kierkegaard's Religions A and B), and the quest to resolve this crisis, a quest that ultimately presses the bounds of orthodoxy.
2000 / 0-85364-985-5 / xxiv + 254pp

Keith Ferdinando
The Triumph of Christ in African Perspective
A Study of Demonology and Redemption in the African Context
The book explores the implications of the gospel for traditional African fears of occult aggression. It analyses such traditional approaches to suffering and biblical responses to fears of demonic evil, concluding with an evaluation of African beliefs from the perspective of the gospel.

1999 / 0-85364-830-1 / xviii + 450pp

Andrew Goddard
Living the Word, Resisting the World
The Life and Thought of Jacques Ellul
This work offers a definitive study of both the life and thought of the French Reformed thinker Jacques Ellul (1912-1994). It will prove an indispensable resource for those interested in this influential theologian and sociologist and for Christian ethics and political thought generally.

2002 / 1-84227-053-2 / xxiv + 378pp

David Hilborn
The Words of our Lips
Language-Use in Free Church Worship
Studies of liturgical language have tended to focus on the written canons of Roman Catholic and Anglican communities. By contrast, David Hilborn analyses the more extemporary approach of English Nonconformity. Drawing on recent developments in linguistic pragmatics, he explores similarities and differences between 'fixed' and 'free' worship, and argues for the interdependence of each.

2006 / 0-85364-977-4 / approx. 350pp

Roger Hitching
The Church and Deaf People
A Study of Identity, Communication and Relationships with Special Reference to the Ecclesiology of Jürgen Moltmann
In *The Church and Deaf People* Roger Hitching sensitively examines the history and present experience of deaf people and finds similarities between aspects of sign language and Moltmann's theological method that 'open up' new ways of understanding theological concepts.

2003 / 1-84227-222-5 / xxii + 236pp

John G. Kelly
One God, One People
The Differentiated Unity of the People of God in the Theology of Jürgen Moltmann
The author expounds and critiques Moltmann's doctrine of God and highlights the systematic connections between it and Moltmann's influential discussion of Israel. He then proposes a fresh approach to Jewish–Christian relations building on Moltmann's work using insights from Habermas and Rawls.
2005 / 0-85346-969-3 / approx. 350pp

Mark F.W. Lovatt
Confronting the Will-to-Power
A Reconsideration of the Theology of Reinhold Niebuhr
Confronting the Will-to-Power is an analysis of the theology of Reinhold Niebuhr, arguing that his work is an attempt to identify, and provide a practical theological answer to, the existence and nature of human evil.
2001 / 1-84227-054-0 / xviii + 216pp

Neil B. MacDonald
Karl Barth and the Strange New World within the Bible
Barth, Wittgenstein, and the Metadilemmas of the Enlightenment
Barth's discovery of the strange new world within the Bible is examined in the context of Kant, Hume, Overbeck, and, most importantly, Wittgenstein. MacDonald covers some fundamental issues in theology today: epistemology, the final form of the text and biblical truth-claims.
2000 / 0-85364-970-7 / xxvi + 374pp

Keith A. Mascord
Alvin Plantinga and Christian Apologetics
This book draws together the contributions of the philosopher Alvin Plantinga to the major contemporary challenges to Christian belief, highlighting in particular his ground-breaking work in epistemology and the problem of evil. Plantinga's theory that both theistic and Christian belief is warrantedly basic is explored and critiqued, and an assessment offered as to the significance of his work for apologetic theory and practice.
2005 / 1-84227-256-X / approx. 304pp

Gillian McCulloch
The Deconstruction of Dualism in Theology
With Reference to Ecofeminist Theology and New Age Spirituality
This book challenges eco-theological anti-dualism in Christian theology, arguing that dualism has a twofold function in Christian religious discourse. Firstly, it enables us to express the discontinuities and divisions that are part of the process of reality. Secondly, dualistic language allows us to express the mysteries of divine transcendence/immanence and the survival of the soul without collapsing into monism and materialism, both of which are problematic for Christian epistemology.
2002 / 1-84227-044-3 / xii + 282pp

Leslie McCurdy
Attributes and Atonement
The Holy Love of God in the Theology of P.T. Forsyth
Attributes and Atonement is an intriguing full-length study of P.T. Forsyth's doctrine of the cross as it relates particularly to God's holy love. It includes an unparalleled bibliography of both primary and secondary material relating to Forsyth.
1999 / 0-85364-833-6 / xiv + 328pp

Nozomu Miyahira
Towards a Theology of the Concord of God
A Japanese Perspective on the Trinity
This book introduces a new Japanese theology and a unique Trinitarian formula based on the Japanese intellectual climate: three betweennesses and one concord. It also presents a new interpretation of the Trinity, a co-subordinationism, which is in line with orthodox Trinitarianism; each single person of the Trinity is eternally and equally subordinate (or serviceable) to the other persons, so that they retain the mutual dynamic equality.
2000 / 0-85364-863-8 / xiv + 256pp

Eddy José Muskus
The Origins and Early Development of Liberation Theology in Latin America
With Particular Reference to Gustavo Gutiérrez
This work challenges the fundamental premise of Liberation Theology, 'opting for the poor', and its claim that Christ is found in them. It also argues that Liberation Theology emerged as a direct result of the failure of the Roman Catholic Church in Latin America.
2002 / 0-85364-974-X / xiv + 296pp

Jim Purves
The Triune God and the Charismatic Movement
A Critical Appraisal from a Scottish Perspective

All emotion and no theology? Or a fundamental challenge to reappraise and realign our trinitarian theology in the light of Christian experience? This study of charismatic renewal as it found expression within Scotland at the end of the twentieth century evaluates the use of Patristic, Reformed and contemporary models of the Trinity in explaining the workings of the Holy Spirit.

2004 / 1-84227-321-3 / xxiv + 246pp

Anna Robbins
Methods in the Madness
Diversity in Twentieth-Century Christian Social Ethics

The author compares the ethical methods of Walter Rauschenbusch, Reinhold Niebuhr and others. She argues that unless Christians are clear about the ways that theology and philosophy are expressed practically they may lose the ability to discuss social ethics across contexts, let alone reach effective agreements.

2004 / 1-84227-211-X / xx + 294pp

Ed Rybarczyk
Beyond Salvation
Eastern Orthodoxy and Classical Pentecostalism on Becoming Like Christ

At first glance eastern Orthodoxy and classical Pentecostalism seem quite distinct. This ground-breaking study shows they share much in common, especially as it concerns the experiential elements of following Christ. Both traditions assert that authentic Christianity transcends the wooden categories of modernism.

2004 / 1-84227-144-X / xii + 356pp

Signe Sandsmark
Is World View Neutral Education Possible and Desirable?
A Christian Response to Liberal Arguments
(Published jointly with The Stapleford Centre)

This book discusses reasons for belief in world view neutrality, and argues that 'neutral' education will have a hidden, but strong world view influence. It discusses the place for Christian education in the common school.

2000 / 0-85364-973-1 / xiv + 182pp

Hazel Sherman
Reading Zechariah
The Allegorical Tradition of Biblical Interpretation through the Commentary of Didymus the Blind and Theodore of Mopsuestia
A close reading of the commentary on Zechariah by Didymus the Blind alongside that of Theodore of Mopsuestia suggests that popular categorising of Antiochene and Alexandrian biblical exegesis as 'historical' or 'allegorical' is inadequate and misleading.
2005 / 1-84227-213-6 / approx. 280pp

Andrew Sloane
On Being a Christian in the Academy
Nicholas Wolterstorff and the Practice of Christian Scholarship
An exposition and critical appraisal of Nicholas Wolterstorff's epistemology in the light of the philosophy of science, and an application of his thought to the practice of Christian scholarship.
2003 / 1-84227-058-3 / xvi + 274pp

Damon W.K. So
Jesus' Revelation of His Father
A Narrative-Conceptual Study of the Trinity with Special Reference to Karl Barth
This book explores the trinitarian dynamics in the context of Jesus' revelation of his Father in his earthly ministry with references to key passages in Matthew's Gospel. It develops from the exegeses of these passages a non-linear concept of revelation which links Jesus' communion with his Father to his revelatory words and actions through a nuanced understanding of the Holy Spirit, with references to K. Barth, G.W.H. Lampe, J.D.G. Dunn and E. Irving.
2005 / 1-84227-323-X / approx. 380pp

Daniel Strange
The Possibility of Salvation Among the Unevangelised
An Analysis of Inclusivism in Recent Evangelical Theology
For evangelical theologians the 'fate of the unevangelised' impinges upon fundamental tenets of evangelical identity. The position known as 'inclusivism', defined by the belief that the unevangelised can be ontologically saved by Christ whilst being epistemologically unaware of him, has been defended most vigorously by the Canadian evangelical Clark H. Pinnock. Through a detailed analysis and critique of Pinnock's work, this book examines a cluster of issues surrounding the unevangelised and its implications for christology, soteriology and the doctrine of revelation.
2002 / 1-84227-047-8 / xviii + 362pp

Scott Swain
God According to the Gospel
Biblical Narrative and the Identity of God in the Theology of Robert W. Jenson
Robert W. Jenson is one of the leading voices in contemporary Trinitarian theology. His boldest contribution in this area concerns his use of biblical narrative both to ground and explicate the Christian doctrine of God. *God According to the Gospel* critically examines Jenson's proposal and suggests an alternative way of reading the biblical portrayal of the triune God.
2006 / 1-84227-258-6 / approx. 180pp

Justyn Terry
The Justifying Judgement of God
A Reassessment of the Place of Judgement in the Saving Work of Christ
The argument of this book is that judgement, understood as the whole process of bringing justice, is the primary metaphor of atonement, with others, such as victory, redemption and sacrifice, subordinate to it. Judgement also provides the proper context for understanding penal substitution and the call to repentance, baptism, eucharist and holiness.
2005 / 1-84227-370-1 / approx. 274 pp

Graham Tomlin
The Power of the Cross
Theology and the Death of Christ in Paul, Luther and Pascal
This book explores the theology of the cross in St Paul, Luther and Pascal. It offers new perspectives on the theology of each, and some implications for the nature of power, apologetics, theology and church life in a postmodern context.
1999 / 0-85364-984-7 / xiv + 344pp

Adonis Vidu
Postliberal Theological Method
A Critical Study
The postliberal theology of Hans Frei, George Lindbeck, Ronald Thiemann, John Milbank and others is one of the more influential contemporary options. This book focuses on several aspects pertaining to its theological method, specifically its understanding of background, hermeneutics, epistemic justification, ontology, the nature of doctrine and, finally, Christological method.
2005 / 1-84227-395-7 / approx. 324pp

Graham J. Watts
Revelation and the Spirit
A Comparative Study of the Relationship between the Doctrine of Revelation and Pneumatology in the Theology of Eberhard Jüngel and of Wolfhart Pannenberg

The relationship between revelation and pneumatology is relatively unexplored. This approach offers a fresh angle on two important twentieth century theologians and raises pneumatological questions which are theologically crucial and relevant to mission in a postmodern culture.

2005 / 1-84227-104-0 / xxii + 232pp

Nigel G. Wright
Disavowing Constantine
Mission, Church and the Social Order in the Theologies of John Howard Yoder and Jürgen Moltmann

This book is a timely restatement of a radical theology of church and state in the Anabaptist and Baptist tradition. Dr Wright constructs his argument in dialogue and debate with Yoder and Moltmann, major contributors to a free church perspective.

2000 / 0-85364-978-2 / xvi + 252pp

Paternoster
9 Holdom Avenue,
Bletchley,
Milton Keynes MK1 1QR,
United Kingdom
Web: www.authenticmedia.co.uk/paternoster

www.ingramcontent.com/pod-product-compliance
Lightning Source LLC
Chambersburg PA
CBHW060608230426
43670CB00011B/2023